Eastern Seeds, Western Soil

Eastern Seeds, Western Soil

Three Gurus in America

Polly Trout

San Diego State University

Mayfield Publishing Company
Mountain View, California
London • Toronto

Library of Congress Cataloging-in-Publication Data
Trout, Polly.
    Eastern seeds, western soil : three gurus in America / Polly Trout.
      p. cm.
    Includes bibliographical references.
    ISBN 0-7674-2577-4
    1. Gurus—Biography.   2. Paramananda, Swami.   3. Yogananda,
Swami.   4. Krishnamurti, J. (Jiddu), 1895–   . 5. Hinduism—
United States.   I. Title.
BL1171.T76 2000
294.5'092'254—dc21
[B]
                         00-064733

Manufactured in the United States of America
10   9   8   7   6   5   4   3   2

Mayfield Publishing Company
1280 Villa Street
Mountain View, CA 94041

Sponsoring editor, Kenneth King; signing representative, Heather Strat-
ton; production editor, Julianna Scott Fein; manuscript editor, Margaret
Moore; design manager and text and cover designer, Violeta Díaz; art
editor, Rennie Evans; manufacturing manager, Randy Hurst. The text
was set in 10.5/14 New Baskerville by TBH Typecast, Inc., and printed
on acid-free 45# Highland Plus by Malloy Lithographing, Inc.

For Noah

Preface

This book examines the lives and teachings of three spiritual leaders born in India who came to the United States in the first half of the twentieth century and made important contributions to the American religious counterculture. Paramananda, Yogananda, and Krishnamurti helped disseminate Hindu ideas into American popular culture. They also contributed to the modern phenomenon of the search for universal religion—a spiritual worldview in which the world's religions are unraveled in a search for relevant wisdom and recombined into a pluralistic tapestry.

In telling this story I have two goals. First, I wish to sharpen our understanding of the lives and teachings of these three men by placing them in historical context and applying interpretive strategies drawn from psychology and the social sciences. Second, I want to encourage readers to reflect on what these historical figures can teach us about living a fulfilling spiritual life in the modern world. I hope readers find this book to be entertaining and accessible, but at the same time scholarly and educational. The book is designed to complement the curriculum of a wide range of classes within Religious Studies, such as Introduction to Religion, Religion in America, Psychology of Religion, Hinduism, Mysticism, Asian Religions in America, Religion and Culture in Modern Society, and New Religious Movements. The following features should enhance the effectiveness of this text in the classroom.

I demonstrate the interdisciplinary methodology of Religious Studies. By drawing on the social sciences, psychology, history, and hermeneutics, a concrete example of how the multidisciplinary approach can produce a more nuanced and sophisticated understanding of religious material is provided.

Chapter 2 gives an overview of the basic tenets and practices of Hinduism. Paramananda, Yogananda, and Krishnamurti were deeply influenced by Modern Hinduism and the historical trajectory that produced it. I review the basics of Hinduism and sketch the cultural background of the religious teachers in such a way that their creative innovations can be better understood.

Chapter 3 surveys the growth of the religious counterculture in the United States. When these teachers came from India to the United States in the first half of the twentieth century, they were welcomed by American sympathizers and seekers. The reactions and motivations of their American followers make more sense when viewed in historical perspective as the outcome of a long period of religious change and modernization.

Chapters 4–6 summarize the biographies and messages of Paramananda, Yogananda, and Krishnamurti. Although the three men shared important interests, each has a fascinating story of his own. The life and beliefs of each are presented in a succinct and clear manner.

After chapters featuring each teacher, I compare and contrast their views along several dimensions. Once the students are familiar with the basic messages of Paramananda, Yogananda, and Krishnamurti, they will be ready to tackle key themes with more depth. I focus on two clusters of interpretive issues: the way the three teachers struggled with issues of power and authority in the American cultural context and their quest for a universal religion that would speak to the specific challenges to traditional religion posed by social modernization.

I balance the social scientific approach with the phenomenological approach. Finally, the text illustrates a perennial debate within Religious Studies: When is it appropriate to take a secular, critical stance in the interpretation of religion, and when is it more appropriate to emphasize respect for and acceptance of beliefs that challenge the scientific worldview? I offer critical theories as interpretive strategies, but I remind the reader throughout that these are only theories. In the final analysis, each reader must decide for him- or herself where to draw the line.

My scholarship has been informed by the trend within American religious history, pioneered by Sidney Ahlstrom, of understanding the religious narrative as one of diversity and competition rather than homogeneity. Within this broader movement, some scholars have worked specifically on Buddhist contributions to American religious history; their work has been invaluable to me. I have particularly relied on the interpretive models of Thomas Tweed, Stephen Prothero, and Richard Seager.

ACKNOWLEDGMENTS

This project began as a doctoral dissertation at Boston University's Division of Religious and Theological Studies, where I was privileged to have Peter L. Berger as a thesis adviser. I am also indebted to M. David Eckel, Stephen Prothero, John Berthrong, Richard W. Fox, and Stephen Kalberg. The Division's administrative assistant, Mary Ann Lesh, benevolently kept my paperwork in order despite my disorganized attempts to thwart her. The Division's Tuesday Night Pub crew was more instrumental than they realized in helping me make it through graduate school; thank you all for letting me take it out on you. So to speak.

I completed this project while lecturing in the Religious Studies Department of San Diego State University. I would like to thank the faculty and staff for their support, especially Irving Alan

Sparks, Linda Holler, Rebecca Moore, Risa Kohn, Willard Johnson, Pat Boni, Elaine Rother, and Marge Thompson.

I would also like to thank Ramdas Lamb, University of Hawaii, for reviewing my manuscript.

Reverend Mother Sudha Puri Devi of the Vedanta Centre of Cohasset and Ananda Ashrama of La Crescenta inspired me, both by her spiritual presence and her kind encouragement for my project.

Eric Lyon, Maria Silkey, Graham Robertson, Jane Cormuss, Corrie Rosasharn, and Sue Johnson helped proofread the manuscript.

Beloved friends and family, without whom I would not have carried this project to completion, include Noah Gervais, Tina Larson, Eric Lyon, Barbara Moss, Joanna Pauw, Corrie Rosasharn, Maria Silkey, Kathy Taddy, and Nick Taddy.

I would also like to thank the staff at Mayfield Publishing Company, especially Ken King.

I am most grateful, however, to the memories of the gurus themselves. I have listened carefully to their messages for many years now, and although I have not always agreed with them, they have taught me important lessons about how to live honestly, joyfully, and lovingly.

Contents

CHAPTER 1

Introduction

In 1893, a young missionary from Calcutta shivered miserably on the deck of a steamer, eyeing the fur coats of his fellow travelers with envy as they regarded his tropical robe with a mixture of disdain and fascination. His name was **Swami** Vivekananda, and he was headed for the New World. He had no money, no connections, and no invitation. He believed that his divine calling was to spread the universal truths embedded within Hinduism to the West, and that he would do so on a podium at the World's Parliament of Religions. Against great odds, it worked: A few months later he catapulted from obscurity to instant fame, the darling of the American press as his rhetoric rang out triumphantly in Chicago.

Perhaps his success was the result of his own chutzpah; perhaps it was an inevitable outcome of that dense tapestry of cause and accident we call history. Either way, the forces that propelled Vivekananda across the Pacific have left a faint trace over American culture. Today, as I leaf through the *American Heritage College Dictionary,* the vocabulary of his conquest shimmers in the halflight of imagination. Karma. Reincarnation. Dharma. Brahman. Atman. Yoga. All, now, a part of our language—a part of "American heritage." I want to tell you part of the story of how Americans came to embrace the language of Hinduism as a part of the vocabulary we use to construct our world.

Vivekananda's journey represents the beginning of a new era in which Hindu religious teachers and their American disciples embarked on a quest for the Holy Grail of modern religion: a universal teaching that could lead each and every person, regardless of their point of origin, to spiritual perfection. They believed that they could accomplish this by creating a *science* of religion. Through reason and experiment, they believed they could cull what was good and true out of all the world's religious traditions, leaving superstition behind. This is the story of the women and men who made that journey, of what they learned, and of the limits of their success. The search for universal religion led them to believe that at its best religion is as individual and personal as a love affair. The **gurus** (authoritative spiritual teachers with Asian Indian philosophical leanings) had hoped to transcend the confining grid of cultural assumptions, but their disciples hijacked their vision to help build a worldview that was unmistakably American.

In the decades that followed Vivekananda's passage, a handful of Indian religious teachers journeyed to the United States and joined this new religious counterculture. I compare three representatives from this movement: Swami Paramananda of the Ramakrishna-Vedanta Society, **Paramahansa** Yogananda of the Self-Realization Fellowship, and Jiddu Krishnamurti.

The individual lives of these teachers and their students cannot be fully appreciated unless they are viewed within their social and historical contexts. To that end, I argue that early American Hindu movements can be viewed as a case study in religious modernization, and that thinking about them in this way helps us both to better understand the movements themselves and to better understand what it is like to live a reflectively religious life in the modern world.

To focus my discussion of such a broad theme, I look in particular at the relationships between these teachers and their students. What goals did they have in common? Where do their

needs and dreams differ? Did cultural assumptions bind them
or separate them? What role did gender play in the way male
gurus influenced female disciples? What does it mean to have or
be a "guru," and how has this role influenced the development
of the American religious counterculture? When the lives of
these people are examined in light of these questions, two
patterns emerge. First, the students, regardless of their rhetoric
of obedience, were active players in this drama, shaping the
teachings to meet their particular needs. Second, while the
rational quest for universal truth brought the gurus and disciples together, what kept them together in the end was the
redemptive miracle of face-to-face love, the healing encounter
between self and other that transcends reason and renders the
quest for **universalism** meaningless. These patterns of interpersonal relationships have something to teach us about why religion remains a vital force in American society, and how the idea
of the religious quest is continuously modified to meet the spiritual and psychological demands of individuals living in modern
society.

In order to provide a deeper understanding of the religious
worldviews of these historical figures, I use methods from psychology and the social sciences. The academic study of religion
is a multidisciplinary field, and religion scholars use many
different interpretive strategies. Some scholars practice the phenomenological approach. This means that they report thought-
fully and carefully on the beliefs of others, but do not think that
it is appropriate to pass judgment on whether these beliefs are
true. A scholar using this method, for example, would faithfully
report on the belief that a miracle had occurred and leave it at
that. Another approach used by scholars in religious studies is
the social scientific approach, also called the critical or skeptical
approach. These scholars seek natural explanations for religious
phenomena. When these scholars study the report of a miracle,
they ask whether the event can be conclusively documented. If
not, they ask if it is possible to explain the belief in the miracle
in a scientific way, without reference to supernatural events.

In this book, I offer critical theories concerning some aspects of religion and the teachings of the gurus I study. They are *only* theories; there is no way to scientifically prove or disprove the truth of religious beliefs. However, by looking at them from a variety of perspectives and considering in turn both phenomenological and social scientific interpretations, we have an opportunity to deepen our appreciation for the complexity and mystery of the human condition. In the end, each reader must decide for himself or herself whether the supernatural events reported by these gurus are literally true or can be better understood from a critical perspective.

THE HISTORY OF AMERICA'S
FASCINATION WITH HINDUISM

American fascination with Hindu ideas has a long history and can be divided into three periods. The first period lasted from the early nineteenth century to 1893.[1] During this time, English translations of Asian philosophical texts were increasingly available to American intellectuals and sparked a fair amount of interest. Salient ideas were plucked out of the Asian context and reworked by American thinkers, filtering in turn to their readers, who first came across ideas such as reincarnation and **karma** as embedded planks in non-Hindu worldviews. During this time, American interaction with Hinduism was entirely intellectual and textual; how actual Indians lived and thought was not considered relevant.

This situation changed in 1893, when the Chicago World's Fair hosted what was to become a watershed event in American religious history: the World's Parliament of Religions. The Parliament gathered speakers from the world's religious traditions to share their beliefs in a relatively tolerant setting. One of the speakers, the dynamic Swami Vivekananda, stayed on in America. He made an extensive lecture tour and set up the Ramakrishna-Vedanta Society, which for many decades would be the most successful disseminator of Hindu teachings in the United States. His success was enthusiastically followed by Indian nationalist newspapers and inspired other Hindu teachers to follow his example. From 1893 onward Americans interested in Hindu philosophy had the opportunity to study under actual Indian gurus rather than from texts alone. It is this second period of American Hinduism, lasting from 1893 to 1965, that is the scope of this book.

In the early 1920s, a series of bigoted immigration laws made it difficult for many ethnic groups, including those from Asia, to come to the United States. These laws were lifted in 1965, ushering in the third and contemporary period of the history of Hinduism in America. The subsequent explosion of Asian religious options in the United States is more familiar to the American public. It is often forgotten that this explosion was in part made possible by earlier pioneers, who for decades had been publishing, speaking, and organizing as a vital part of the American religious counterculture. The Asian flavor of the 1970s counterculture was the fruition of a long flirtation with Indian philosophy.[2]

The increase of Hindu religious options in the United States has coincided with a larger trend in American religion. Since the early nineteenth century, American religion has become increasingly diversified and privatized, especially among the intellectual elite. From the Transcendentalists onward, a distinct American subculture has been developing within which experimentation with religious ways of life beyond Christianity is commonplace. Within this movement Hindu ideas have jockeyed for position with a colorful menagerie of spiritual options: Spiritualism, Theosophy, New Thought, New Age, Neo-Shamanism—the list goes on and on, yet members of all these groups are in some sense co-travelers. Among them, individual choice based on reason and personal experience is more important to the participants than inherited dogma. Individuals often move from group to group within the counterculture, and over time creatively combine elements gathered from a variety of traditions into a uniquely personalized religious worldview.[3] American Hindu groups, from their inception, not only have participated in this counterculture, but also have intentionally helped shape and defend it. In fact, all three of the teachers discussed in this book—Paramananda,

Yogananda, and Krishnamurti—defined themselves primarily as internationalists who transcended local traditions rather than as Hindus.

The desire to transcend cultural assumptions and grasp absolute truth has been a part of the Hindu tradition since . ancient times. These men did not invent this attitude but, rather, rediscovered it and refashioned it to meet the spiritual needs of a new generation. They then brought it to the United States. Many of their Western disciples came to believe that this way of looking at religion—as an experimental quest for truth rather than an act of blind faith in received dogma—provided them with a new way of living a spiritual life that was in step with the challenges of the modern world.

THE RISE OF AMERICAN HINDUISM

I am getting ahead of the story. First, it is necessary to backtrack to India and the social forces that propelled these teachers toward America in the first place. In the nineteenth century, religious options in India were also shifting due to rapidly changing social conditions. Calcutta was the hub of a religious reform movement known as the Indian Renaissance. The Renaissance was driven by Indian intellectuals who had received Western educations and ingested many modern, Western values, but who retained an affection for their own traditions and an appreciation for the complexity and sophistication of Asian religious philosophies. They found Western science, democracy, and ethics enormously compelling, but a combination of cultural pride and keen observation of the failures of Western culture ruled out straightforward assimilation. Although the Renaissance affected a variety of cultural activities—literature, music, philosophy, politics, economics —I am concerned here only with the rise of Modern Hinduism, a reform movement that sought to purge traditional Hinduism of what was seen as superstition and social injustice while preserving its philosophical grandeur. During this time, a variety of religious teachers, influenced by Western education and national pride, set about to create a reformed, modernized version of Hinduism that could proudly dispute nasty colonial assumptions about Indian primitivism and decadence. The result was Modern Hinduism.

Modern Hinduism is the only form of Hinduism to impact American culture. Among Hindu immigrants to the United States, most are either secularized or influenced by Modern Hinduism (defined more fully in the next chapter). **Orthodox Hinduism** is not a missionary religion but, rather, a closed hereditary group. (I use the word *orthodox* throughout to mean "loyal to the specific religious traditions and rituals of one's ancestors." In the Hindu context, it implies acceptance of the traditional **caste system.**) According to Orthodox Hinduism, non-Indian people are barbarian untouchables; when they are ready for religious truth and purity, they will be reborn into one of the Hindu castes. It follows that the religious teachers who did reach out from the Hindu tradition toward the West were all from the liberal, reformist end of the spectrum. Their Western education and interest in modernizing Hinduism by combining its truths with the truths available in other cultures provided a natural bridge between Renaissance intellectuals and religious seekers in America and Europe. The social and historical background of Modern Hinduism is detailed in Chapter 2.

Chapter 3 provides a sketch of the Americans who attended lectures by Hindu gurus, sympathized with the speakers, and sometimes dedicated their lives to a guru and his message. Like the teachers themselves, American devotees were drawn primarily from an intellectual middle class in a large, pluralistic, and rapidly modernizing society. Both groups shared common concerns that were the product of changes outside the religious sphere. In a world where technological advances in media and travel made contact between different peoples increasingly common, both gurus and disciples were challenged to craft a religious faith that could accommodate a variety of competing, equally plausible, belief systems. Intellectuals felt driven to purge the religious sphere of premises about the physical world that were contradicted by modern scientific discoveries, and attempted to sort through religious beliefs and divide them into truths that should be kept and superstitions that should be abandoned.

Out of this social context arose an American subculture of radical religious experimentation, which I will call the *radical religious counterculture*. It stretches with historical continuities from the nineteenth century to the present day. Today, this subculture is sometimes equated with the New Age movement but also includes many radical religious individualists who reject the New Age label. They view the New Age as a highly commercialized subsection of the religious underground. America's contemporary radical religious left includes Wiccans, Engaged Buddhists, Simple Living advocates, "A Course in Miracles" students, and Rumi aficionados. When Modern Hinduism was first brought to the United States, it was absorbed by an earlier version of this same subculture as an additional alternative in an already diverse movement. How it became an alternative is the subject of this book.

PARAMANANDA, YOGANANDA, AND KRISHNAMURTI

After introducing the reader to the cultural and historical background that led to the joint religious collaboration of Indians and Americans, I illustrate the process by tracing the biographies, beliefs, and practices of three men who taught Hindu practices in the United States: Swami Paramananda (1884–1940), Paramahansa Yogananda (1893–1952), and Jiddu Krishnamurti (1895–1986).

Swami Paramananda was a disciple of Swami Vivekananda, founder of the Ramakrishna Math and Mission (American branches of this organization are often called Vedanta Societies).[4] In turn, Vivekananda was a devotee of the nineteenth-century Bengali mystic, Sri Ramakrishna. Sri Ramakrishna is one of the patron saints of Modern Hinduism; he believed that all religions pointed toward the same ultimate truth, and his electrifying personal charisma drove many secularized Renaissance intellectuals to reconsider the possibility that the spiritual life was indeed a source of truth and meaning.

A sunny and loving boy, Paramananda joined Vivekananda's monastic order as an adolescent and came to the United States as a missionary in 1906 at the age of twenty-two. He stayed in America, teaching, writing and shepherding his small but devoted flock until his death in 1940. His youthful good looks and gentle, playful charm made him a media favorite, although his distaste for modern advertising techniques hampered his public career. In his straightforward espousal of love over knowledge, Paramananda had more in common with the devotional Ramakrishna than the intellectual Vivekananda.

Paramananda founded two communities: the Ananda Ashrama in La Crescenta, California, and the Vedanta Centre in Cohasset, Massachusetts. Both are small but extant today. His closest devotees were almost exclusively middle- and upper-class unmarried women who found in his **ashrams** a meaning-charged, heroic way of life not offered to them elsewhere. Partly because these were the disciples who presented themselves, but largely because Paramananda followed Vivekananda's lead in insisting that gender was irrelevant in monastic life, the swami gave his female disciples much more power and voice than they would have enjoyed at any other Vedanta Center. At his death, his niece became heir to his spiritual authority but the society's parent organization in India, the Ramakrishna Math and Mission, refused to accept a female swami. Paramananda's followers defected rather than accept an externally imposed leader. Paramananda's life illustrates themes perennial to American religious radicalism: egalitarianism, women's rights, communalism, the primacy of love and relationship over dogma and intellect, and the centrality of charisma to religious authority.

Yogananda came to America in 1920 and was active here until his death in 1952. His early life parallels Paramananda's in some striking ways. Both were middle-class Bengalis from families who cooperated with the British; both received Western educations in India. They were both religiously precocious and dedicated themselves to a radical, reformist spiritual director early in life. At the behest of their respective gurus, each devoted his life to sharing the teachings of his master with the West.

What separated the two were the masters and the messages. Yogananda was a disciple of Swami Sri Yukteswar, who combined traditional yogic practices with the liberal, modern idea that yoga was good for everyone, regardless of their level of spiritual advancement. Traditionally, yoga was primarily the full-time job of world renouncers; Yukteswar taught that it should be streamlined for the householder, who had a limited amount of time to devote to spiritual exercises. Yogananda faithfully transmitted the message of his guru, continuing to offer laypeople a physical, structured program of yoga that emphasized devotional and magical themes. Yogananda's most widely read work, *Autobiography of a Yogi* (1946), became a minor countercultural classic and helped lay a foundation for the subsequent expansion of American interest in yoga and meditative practices during the 1960s. From its center in California, Yogananda's Self-Realization Fellowship developed a mail-order campaign of yogic instruction specifically designed to gradually introduce Hindu concepts and values to an uninformed American audience. Unlike Paramananda, Yogananda enthusiastically embraced self-promotion and excelled in modern advertising techniques.

If Paramananda can be said to represent the **bhakti** strand of Hinduism and its emphasis on devotional love, while Yogananda represents the **yogic** school of approach to the divine through ritualized control of the body, Krishnamurti best embodies the path of **jnana,** or wisdom gained through careful examination of the internal thought process. Born as an Indian **brahmin,** Krishnamurti was raised from the age of fourteen by the elite of the Theosophical Society to believe that he was destined to be the next "World Teacher"—a divine being inhabiting a human body in order to help humanity evolve spiritually, like Jesus or the Buddha. Krishnamurti shocked the international occult community in 1929 by declining this honor, instead going on to preach an extreme form of individualistic, experimental monism in which the concept of a messiah had no place. Dividing his time between the United States, Europe, and India, Krishnamurti had a long and distinguished career as a spiritual teacher, lecturer, and educator. A charismatic mystic, Krishnamurti encouraged his sympathizers to follow their own intuitive visions and distrust religious institutions and authorities.

In a sense, I am being mischievous in comparing Krishnamurti with Paramananda and Yogananda. Krishnamurti did not think of himself as a Hindu or a guru. Rhetoric aside, however, Krishnamurti functioned as a guru-like figure to many Americans, and his philosophy overlaps both with monistic traditions of India and the American project of constructing a therapeutic spirituality based on private experience. Although Krishnamurti taught a form of meditation and a monistic spiritual philosophy that was similar to advaita vedanta (a school of philosophy within Hinduism) and Zen Buddhism, his loyalty to Asian traditions was slight. I have included him here as a representative of the universalizing project in modern religion. Like Paramananda and Yogananda, Krishnamurti wished to transcend cultural and regional barriers and construct a science of religion, a spiritual technology based on reason and experimentation that could be relied on to produce enlightenment. In other words, Krishnamurti's message can be seen as a logical extension of ideas that were more tentatively present in the teachings of Paramananda and Yogananda.

It should be noted that working with **hagiographic** materials presents special problems to the historical researcher. In my biographical accounts I have relied almost exclusively on the loving and supportive descriptions of the gurus that have been given by their disciples and remain ensconced in the movement's official archives. An exception is an exposé of Krishnamurti's personal life, *Lives in the Shadow with J. Krishnamurti,* by Radha Rajagopal Sloss. Having this document makes it possible to examine the ethical dimension of Krishnamurti's life in a more intimate way than would otherwise be possible. I wish to emphasize, however, that it does not necessarily mean that Krishnamurti was not as "nice" as

Paramananda and Yogananda; perhaps our memories of the latter figures are simply less detailed. I do not mean to imply that their autobiographical writings or the writings of their followers are factually inaccurate. However, the interpretive lens of the devotee is strongly conditioned to see the guru in the most positive light possible. Even in the best of circumstances, accurate recall of the past is subjective. In short, the gurus I describe may well be partly fictional; we can never portray historical figures in all of their complexity and humanity. I have tried to recount how their disciples saw them and, when possible, I suggest alternative interpretations.

The stories of Paramananda, Yogananda, and Krishnamurti do more than illustrate the availability of Hindu religious options in America before 1965. They also draw attention to broader trends in American religion that can be conceptually linked to trends in modernization. The image of Indian gurus and their American disciples working together to fashion a creative, innovative spiritual path that was emotionally, intellectually, and practically satisfying is a suggestive metaphor for the American religious quest of the twentieth century. To focus my discussion of religious modernization, I concentrate on the creative adaptation of the guru-disciple relationship to its new, American social environment. The relationship between guru and disciple illustrates many recurring motifs in the struggle between authority and individuation, a conflict that lies at the heart of religious modernization.

THE EFFECT OF MODERNIZATION ON RELIGION

The time has come to define some terms. There are a variety of definitions for the words *modern, modernity,* and *modernization.* By modernization, I mean the changes in human life that have been driven forward by the scientific and industrial revolutions. These changes have been so enormous that they have produced a social world that is distinct from all of those which have gone before it in history; I call this social world *modernity.* Movements and cultural innovations that react to these changes and attempt to integrate them into a meaningful way of life can be called modern.

The word *modern* is sometimes used in other contexts to refer to a specific kind of cultural adaptation to the technological age that is favored by liberal, bourgeois intellectuals and which includes values such as secular humanism and privileging individual rights over collective norms. I do not use *modern* in this way, since competing worldviews, such as Christian Evangelicalism or Pentecostalism, can also be seen as functional adaptations to the peculiarities of the modern environment. That being said, I do focus on the liberal, democratic way of being modern—as did the gurus I present.

Modernization is a social phenomenon that has been gaining momentum and size since the Enlightenment, one initiated by a handful of scientists and intellectuals in Europe and that now affects the lives of almost everyone on earth. Modern science and technology have revolutionized the way people solve the most basic problems of life: shelter, food, warmth, reproduction, and locomotion. Changes in the material world cause responding changes in psychological worlds, in worldviews. Science and technology have made global travel and trade efficient and omnipresent, linking cultures and bombarding individuals of any particular culture with the lifestyles and worldviews of other cultures. Medical advances have extended life expectancy and, as a result, have changed the way people think about mortality and suffering. Reliable birth control changes the ethical dimensions of sexual behavior, for the root of ethics is avoiding harm and meeting one's responsibilities; and whether or not a sex act is likely to result in a child surely changes the level of responsibility involved, even within a monogamous marriage. These links between interior and exterior experience are usually complex, multicausal, and only half-understood. They are also dialectically related: Just as changes in the material world cause changes in worldview, changes in worldview affect choices, actions, and inventions that, in turn, change and shape the physical world in which we live. This side of the equation has become unusually apparent during the modern period, because science and technology—which spring from a certain way of looking at the world and our role in it—have physically altered our environment in much more obvious and alien ways than humanity previously imagined possible.

One area of life to be affected by modernization is religion. I use the word *religion* in a broad sense here, but not the broadest possible: I limit its application to worldviews that include references to a supernatural or spiritual dimension, in order to distinguish these worldviews from purely secular or materialistic ways of ordering life. I also limit *religion* to worldviews that include an ethical dimension in order to distinguish it from philosophy, used here informally to mean an explanation of how the world works that does not necessarily include a prescription for how to appropriately react to the world. My working definition for *religion,* then, is this: a system of beliefs and actions that renders life meaningful and understandable to its adherents, that includes (a) descriptions of supernatural or spiritual forces and (b) an ethical hierarchy of human goals.

The ways in which modernization has affected religion are open to debate, but some patterns are recognizable. Religion in modern life tends to be more individualized, freely chosen, creative, and diverse than in premodern periods. Science has weakened the authority of orthodox religions by contradicting literal interpretations of some scriptural passages. Massive immigration, travel, and communications between different cultures have presented each individual with a variety of plausible religious worldviews, rather than a single doctrine that can be assumed to be true.

By calling a religious movement modern, such as Modern Hinduism, I mean that the religion has been modified in order to answer the particular challenges of modern society. This does not mean that everything about it is new; often, a tradition will be reinterpreted and articulated in a new way while retaining strong similarities with the old ways. For example, vedanta philosophy is an ancient part of the Hindu tradition; part of making it modern was simply in dusting it off and making obvious the useful connections between vedanta and modern philosophy. Often, religious modernization is a matter of choosing what to emphasize and what to quietly let lapse. For example, some Hindu monastic traditions have a long history of modifying their language and customs as the monks move between cultures, in order to make the basic ideas more accessible. This practice is especially well suited to modern, pluralistic society, and so Modern Hindus tend to accentuate and expand the role of this older practice. Other Hindu monastics were quite rigid about retaining ritual practices unchanged through the generations. Because this attitude was less helpful in a modern, pluralistic context, Modern Hindus tend to repudiate it.

Although a small phenomenon in terms of numbers of participants, the spread of Hinduism in the United States before World War II illustrates several recurring motifs in the modernization of religious life: heroic religious individualism that promotes a mix-and-match approach to tradition; ambivalence concerning religious leadership, reflected in an obsession with charismatic leaders coupled with the devaluation of institutional authority; and the quest for a mystical state of consciousness that is compatible with the scientific worldview. Viewed as a whole, this sort of experimental, creative, synthetic approach can be seen as one of several viable and lively responses to the modernization of religious options. I use the stories of these characters to illustrate this trend in the history of American religion.

Indian gurus and their American disciples found a natural meeting ground in their shared sensitivity to changes wrought by the processes of modernization: secularization in the public sphere, religious pluralism, democratization, and the challenges to spiritual faith presented by science. By paying attention to how social conditions affected the spiritual experience of these people, I do not mean to imply that this is the whole story. I want to draw attention to how these individuals creatively responded to their world. Shared social context was not the only bond that drew these seekers together; indeed, many of the tenets of Hinduism touch deep, universal chords in the human psyche, and that bond alone could be enough to spark communion between individuals, regardless of the surrounding social context. However, their shared response to the modernizing social context provided an additional point of contact between the worldviews of the Indian gurus and the American converts and sympathizers. Shared experience heightened their sense of solidarity. For example, leading a religious life in modern society means paying attention to conflicts between institutionalized authority and personal freedom. The Indian gurus and American disciples of this story were forced by social circumstance to address anew this ancient conflict.

THE CHANGING RELATIONSHIP BETWEEN THE INDIVIDUAL AND SOCIETY

As traditional cultures are replaced by modern ones, tension inevitably arises over the proper relationship between the individual and society. Prizing personal autonomy over communal solidarity is not limited to the modern period, nor has it been valued by all modernizing movements. The totalitarian regime is no less modern than the democracy. However, the idea that all individuals have the right to create a style of life based on their own needs and preferences has grown in tandem with modernization since the Enlightenment. In the United States in particular, individualism is cherished as a shared cultural value; yet, even Americans struggle to find a working balance between the need for autonomy and the need for community.

In the United States, separation of church and state has removed legal and social constraints from religious affiliation. The individual is free to choose a particular religious lifestyle, or none at all. Far from removing anxiety concerning the proper relationship between the individual and the community in a religious setting, the absence of set norms concerning religion has often led to increased awareness of the moral and philosophical tensions of the individualist ethic, especially among the new religious movements examined here. Yogananda, Paramananda,

Krishnamurti, and their supporters often struggled to define the ideal self and the ideal relationship between self and other. These concerns may not have been so pressing for them in a different social context—for example, a traditional, homogenous society with standardized avenues of power that valued conformity over autonomy. American religious history, with its absence of a homogenous religious worldview and its cultural stress on the primacy of individual freedom, has often privileged the interior, personal spiritual vision at the expense of the communal. This has been especially true at the radical fringe (notwithstanding totalitarian cults like Heaven's Gate or the People's Temple), characterized by the pursuit of the personally relevant at the expense of the culturally sanctioned. The idea that each individual should have religious autonomy is not new and can be found in some ancient forms of Hinduism. However, in the modern context, interest in the question of how to properly balance external authority and internal freedom tends to be more universal and intense than it has been for preceding generations. Also, a greater percentage of modern religious seekers seem to favor personal freedom rather than obedience to outside authorities.

As will become evident in later chapters, each of the three teachers came to a different conclusion concerning how to best balance authority and freedom. Yogananda was the least enthusiastic about individual freedom and encouraged his followers to transcend their egos through obedience to his authority. Krishnamurti rejected all communal effort in a stark and heroic defense of individual freedom. He defined the spiritual path as a relationship between a lower and higher self mediated through increasing self-awareness. He did not place any value on communal responsibility; as a result, his life was oddly and sadly removed from meaningful and lasting relationships with beloved others. Paramananda tried to direct his followers toward a middle route in which individualism and communalism could be brought into harmony through the transforming power of spiritual love. This sort of compromise seems to work best when the community is small; in this respect, Paramananda was a forerunner of the "think globally, act locally" ethic of contemporary American liberal countercultures.

Having abandoned traditional patterns of religious authority, Hindu-American congregations still needed leadership. Individuals were given greater responsibility for their final allegiances, but their decisions were molded in an atmosphere that accorded tremendous authority and power to the guru. All three teachers displayed a classic trait of the charismatic religious leader: Their authority was generated not through external institutions but, rather, through the intense emotions the guru inspired in the disciple.

This shift in the source of religious authority from institution to personal charisma parallels the modern, Western shift in marriage from an emphasis on family loyalty to one of romantic love. In both instances, it is the personal relationship and the intensely experienced emotions generated by the relationship, rather than tradition or force, that provides the motivation to submit to the will of the other. In a pluralistic, democratic age, it is not surprising that religious leaders would become increasingly dependent on personality and emotion to attract and maintain the support of the religious consumer. The charismatic guru is a feature of traditional Hinduism; the role was invented long ago. It did, however, take on new dimensions in the American context. This issue is discussed in greater detail in Chapter 7.

The importance of personal charisma in maintaining the plausibility of the guru's teachings brings us to another pervasive characteristic of American radical religion in the modern era: a shift in focus from dogma and ritual to sentiment and personal enhancement. From the pietists through the Romantics and on through the (misleadingly labeled) New Age, there has been a substantial stream of Western spirituality in which the final, undeniable validation of a religious path is characterized by what it makes believers *feel,* as opposed to how it makes them think or act. Asian traditions that emphasized inner, subjective states of consciousness—**yoga,** meditation, **vedanta**—dovetailed with this trend. During the twentieth century, Americans increasingly came to view religion as a personal therapy, a route to psychological wholeness rather than existential salvation. This "triumph of the therapeutic" rendered the need for universal religious truth less and less pressing.

There may have always been a handful of people in every culture and age to whom the expression of personal religious perception was more important than the maintenance of social norms. Max Weber called them *religious virtuosi*—the kind of person to whom spirituality is as real and compelling an experience as any other, or even more so. Weber referred to himself as "religiously unmusical," meaning that just as the tone-deaf person cannot personally experience the passion and transcendence of music, he was left personally unmoved by the religious life. The religious virtuoso lives or dies for the infatuating power of a set of primary experiences, just as a musical virtuoso has the same relationship to a different stimulus. In neither case does the virtuoso feel as if she has chosen her art. Rather, the muse has chosen her.

EXPANDING RELIGIOUS OPTIONS

Twenty years ago, it was fashionable in sociology to posit that modernization would necessarily lead to secularization. This theory has been largely abandoned; it does not coincide with known facts. For example, the United States is one of the most modernized nations of the world, yet it is also overwhelmingly and vigorously religious. One reason for this situation may be that while a society in which religion is optional secularizes the sort of person who in a previous time would have conformed to a church in order to avoid censure, it also gives greater range and freedom to the virtuoso, the sort of person who would be driven to explore questions of meaning and transcendence regardless of the social situation.

"Religious virtuosi," said Weber seventy-five years ago in Germany, "are bound to be met with suspicion if instead of relying on the capacity of the institutionalized church to distribute grace they seek to attain grace by their own unaided power, treading their own pathway to God."[5] In the United States today, there is no institutionalized church, and thus no institutionalized sanctions against the unchurched seeker. Suspicions there may be, but Americans have available to them a large and politically protected subculture within which it is possible for individuals to "tread their own pathway to God" without fear of persecution. Secularization theorists did not adequately take into account the extent to which this freedom would be enthusiastically exercised.

Yogananda, Paramananda, Krishnamurti, and their students took this freedom and ran with it. They also contributed to it; their pioneering efforts enlivened an already existing subculture of independent religious seekers. All bearers of non-Christian religious traditions to America contributed to this outcome; the mere existence of competing religious worldviews teaches the religious seeker that personal experience and choice must have a bearing on shaping a religious path. The Indian gurus discussed here moved beyond implicit contribution to explicit sponsorship. Each had his own particular religious path and offered it as a viable option. They also reminded their audiences repeatedly that there was one goal, but many paths, and that each individual was responsible for actively charting a religious lifestyle that would accommodate personal experience and character.

The early history of Hinduism in America is primarily a story of how a group of radical religious leaders from India, who were themselves not exactly Hindu in an orthodox sense, had a profound impact on the spiritual quest of a group of Americans who could no longer fairly be classified as Christians but never really became Hindus either. Paramananda, Yogananda, and Krishnamurti wanted to reach beyond sectarian boundaries to discover a universal and scientific way of living a spiritual life, and in many ways their loyalty to this project was greater than their loyalty to their Hindu background. Their stories illustrate the tendency of religion in a modern society to become increasingly individualized, creative, and voluntary while becoming decreasingly institutional, dogmatic, and prescribed. Their stories speak to the endurance of religious ways of thinking, an endurance based on the resilience of tradition and the fertility of inspiration.

NOTES

1. For a book-length treatment of this period, see Jackson, *The Oriental Religions and American Thought.*
2. See Melton, "How New Is New?"
3. Tweed, "Inclusivism and the Spiritual Journey of Marie de Souza Canavarro."
4. The Vedanta Societies of the Ramakrishna Math and Mission are by far the best documented of the American Hindu movements. For a good overview and bibliography, see Jackson's *Vedanta for the West.*
5. Weber, *The Sociology of Religion,* 187.

CHAPTER 2

Indian Roots

Defining Hinduism was the bane of early British ethnographers, and the difficulties of the task continue to haunt scholars today. "Hinduism," wrote one early British Indologist, is "a general expression devoid of precision, embracing alike the most punctilious disciple of pure Vedantism, the Agnostic youth who is the product of Western education, and the semi-barbarous hillman, who eats without scruple anything that he can procure and is as ignorant of the Hindu theology as the stone which he worships in times of danger."[1] Bourdillon could have been more polite, but not more accurate. Philosophically, Hinduism ranges between devotional theism and absolute non-dualism; ethically, between nonviolence and human sacrifice; socially, between acceptance of a static hierarchy and anarchic revolt; emotionally, between aristocratic prudery and ecstatic possession.

The term *Hindu* was coined by the conquering medieval Muslims. It originally meant nothing more than "the religion of the infidels of the subcontinent that we don't know much about." This definition had not changed much by 1909, when W. Crooke's article on Hinduism in the *Encyclopedia of Religion and Ethics* described it as "that form of religion which prevails among the vast majority of the present population of the Indian Empire."

The term *Hinduism,* then, lumps together a diverse group of philosophies, practices, and religious worldviews native to India. It is better understood as a family of religions rather than a single religion. Unlike Europe with its comparatively homogenous Christian history, India has never had a unifying religious creed or institution. For some groups in some times and places, Orthodox Hinduism provided a baseline of proscribed ritual and social behavior. However, within Orthodoxy there was a diversity of philosophical and devotional options, and Orthodoxy was continuously challenged on the margins by the unorthodox practices of tribal cultures, the lower castes, and sects.

THE DIVERSITY OF HINDUISM

There are both intentional and accidental reasons for Hindu diversity. Orthodox Hinduism assumes a gradation of religious beliefs and practices that are appropriate for different status groups. In other words, fundamental metaphysical beliefs as well as ritual practices not only *do* vary but *ought* to vary according to one's social position and age. For example, study of the **Vedic** texts was the exclusive right of twice-born males; the formal, textual, and philosophical forms of Hinduism that are best known in the West today were not available to most Indians. As far as the orthodox brahmins were concerned, **sudras** (the fourth, lowest, and most populous social class in the orthodox caste system) could not utter Vedic **mantras** nor serve as gurus; their religious duties were limited to bowing to and serving the brahmins and devotion to personal deities such as **Krishna.**

Classical Indian philosophy is divided into six schools; only one greatly affects our story—**vedanta.** This school, based on the study and interpretation of the **Upanishads** (Hindu sacred texts) as perfected wisdom, is itself divided into three main branches. These are the monistic **advaita** of Shankara, the dualistic **dvaita** of Madhva, and the **vishishtadvaita**—qualified nondualism, or the

belief that the self and other are essentially the same but relation-
ally unique—of Ramanuja. Most Westerners today equate Hinduism with the advaitin concept that the Self and **God** are
identical and that the apparent differences between things are
merely an illusion masking their fundamental unity. In India, however, how to interpret the ambiguous, multivalent teachings of the
Upanishads has never ceased to be a subject of dispute. It can be
argued that Ramanuja's philosophically subtle vishishtadvaita best
characterizes modern Hinduism; this school teaches that God and
the individual are both unified and separate, depending on how
one's terms are defined. Ramanuja believed that the relationship
between God and the human being was analogous to the relationship between a person and his cells. The cells are separate entities
in a sense, but meaningless (and dead) apart from their relationship with the greater whole.

Some—but not all—Hindus think of the deities as symbols for
the formless Brahman; each spiritual person is viewed as a shard
of the all-embracing One. This belief is popular with modern
apologists like Radhakrishnan and Arvind Sharma. Within this
worldview, Hinduism is not truly polytheistic, since all individual
facets of creation, whether a god or a rock, are nothing but illusory manifestations of indivisible Being.

For most Indians, these philosophical subtleties have little or
nothing to do with religious life. Instead, village devotionalism
centers around rituals, song, dance, festivals, and the worship of
specific deities. In this mode, the deity—whether a **Puranic** deity,
a local icon, or a guru—is worshipped primarily in and of itself,
rather than as a symbol of **Brahman.** If pushed, the devotee might
agree that a common sacred core does indeed link the household
deity, the guru, and the deity presiding over the village temple.
However, the act of worship is subjectively experienced as an act
directed toward that particular being, not toward an abstract ultimate the icon merely points toward.

In the folk devotional traditions known as bhakti, the mood
is more theistic than polytheistic. Either **Shiva** or **Vishnu** (or, especially in Bengal, the Great Mother) is understood to be the

supreme spiritual person who creates, preserves, and destroys. Devotion is primarily rendered to that Divine Ruler; other "gods" are merely the spiritual servants of the highest power. Attention is paid to these lesser spiritual beings when appropriate, but the soul of the bhakta sings for "The Lord of the Heart," who is also the Lord of the universe. Among many worshippers of Krishna, for example, it is formally acknowledged that Krishna is one of many incarnations of Vishnu, but in practice the devotees focus their fervor and praise on Krishna in such a way that he is, for all practical purposes, identical with the supreme underlying power of the universe. This way of thinking is not unlike that of devotional Christians who always address their prayers to Jesus directly and do not trouble themselves with theoretical abstractions concerning the Trinity.

The diversity of the Hindu tradition is more intellectually problematic to the scholar than to the particular individuals who have lived within the system, because any given time, place, and caste would have had a comparatively standardized and coherent worldview. Hinduism has always been regionally specific, philosophically sprawling, and ritually and mythologically diversified. There were broad similarities that cut across some of the boundaries—the Vedas, the caste system, purity laws, Puranic deities, image worship, gurus—but these were not sufficient to unite Hindus into a religious coalition, any more (in fact, far less) than monotheism and the Hebrew Bible united Jews, Christians, and Muslims.

HINDUISM
IN THE NINETEENTH CENTURY

As the nineteenth century progressed, the amorphous nature of Hinduism became a sore spot for the British-educated Hindu elites. Nascent Indian nationalism groped for a religious basis of solidarity, while the adoption of modern skepticism discredited many of the rituals and myths that contributed to Hinduism's regional and fractured character. One challenge the modern reformers faced during the Hindu Renaissance was to create a basic creed that would unite Indians philosophically in the same way nationalism was attempting to unite them politically.

As David Kopf shows in *British Orientalism and the Bengal Renaissance,* during the late eighteenth and early nineteenth centuries the British empire was marked by a surprising degree of cooperation and cross-fertilization between British and Indian intellectuals. The principal setting for this was Calcutta, the capital of British India. Enlightenment enthusiasm for the equality and dignity of humankind drove a generation of British scholars and civil servants to study Indian languages and to both cherish and translate Indian literature. They were, to quote Kopf, "classicist rather than 'progressive' in their historical outlook, cosmopolitan rather than nationalist in their view of other cultures, and rationalist rather than romantic in their quest for those 'constant and universal principles' that express the unity of human nature."[2] The Orientalists were to have a long-lasting impact on the growth of modern Hinduism through these same Enlightenment ideals; the entire idea of an Indian Renaissance stems from the classicist obsessions with a golden age of literary, rational, philosophic religion only later sullied by ritual and superstition. This model was mapped from Europe onto India as Western scholars discovered classic Hindu scriptures that mirrored their own interest in abstract, universal religious philosophy as opposed to traditional religious ritual and dogma. This is not to say that the Orientalists met today's standards for ethical cross-cultural behavior. They did, however, behave more tolerantly than their Victorian heirs.

At the same time, Calcutta was developing an Indian middle class with a vigorous interest in British culture. Calcutta had begun as three villages near the swampy mouth of the Ganges, leased by the British East India Company as a trading post in 1690. Although the location was malarial, the rich material resources of the province and the riverine trade route turned the settlement into a boomtown. In 1772, Calcutta became the British capital in India. By the early nineteenth century, it had become the "City of

Palaces." Until the capital was moved to Delhi in 1911 in a bid to disrupt the nationalist movement, Calcutta was the center of Anglo-Indian power, culture, and wealth.

As British power grew, Indians began to migrate into their sphere in search of employment—first from Bengal, but, as the nineteenth century drew to a close, more often from further afield. Rural Bihari men, then as now, came in large numbers seeking employment, hoping to earn enough to send something back to their families. Parsi and Jain merchants came to make the best use of their traditional business skills. Most important for this story, the Hindus who had worked as middlemen, scribes, and landlords for the Moghul and regional princes came to offer their expertise as government servants to the new British overlords. As an immigrant culture, Calcutta was made up of individuals who had pressing reasons to leave the protective world of their birth-place and family, and who had the audacity to do something radi-cal to better their lives. There were, of course, many traditionalists in Calcutta, but from the start the community was weighted toward those who had already distanced themselves from ortho-dox routines. Weirdly, given India's antiquity, from a strictly socio-logical viewpoint Calcutta had more in common with Manhattan than Banaras.

For Hindus, the shift to the city provided both challenges to and escapes from their religious way of life. The religious authori-ties of their childhood—the guru, the father, and the community —were suddenly absent, as were the village shrines, deities, and holy places that had made up the geographic fabric of religious life. Although they congregated in different neighborhoods than the Christians, Muslims, and religious minorities, the Hindus still faced daily contact with individuals from unknown regions, castes, and sects who had puzzling ideas about what it meant to be Hindu. For some, the move provided an opportunity to establish a new identity with higher social standing; disgraces too well known in the village were forgotten and habits of higher castes were adopted. For the financially successful, the move could entirely change the daily life of the family.

By the mid-nineteenth century, the most successful of the Hindu émigrés had coalesced into a recognizable status group known as the **bhadralok.**[3] Like today's knowledge class, most of the bhadralok were rich in cultural capital but relatively poor in material wealth. Although technically bhadralok status was based on class rather than caste, the education-based membership qualifications and the urbanized system of etiquette made it nearly impossible for lower castes to remake themselves as bhadralok, but sufficient education and a job in the civil service, combined with the correct clothes and literary pursuits, did give entry to a few outsiders. This elite cadre of Bengali intelligentsia provided the original rank and file for the Indian Renaissance, Indian nationalism, and Modern Hinduism. As Westernization spread across the subcontinent these movements became more geographically diverse, but the Bengali literati of Calcutta remained a driving force well into the twentieth century, until more vigorous intellectual and political movements in Delhi, Bombay, and Madras eclipsed the entrenched **babus.**

Ironically, as Kopf traces, the mushrooming numbers of British-educated, English-speaking, Locke-quoting Hindu Indians collided with a growing distaste for all things foreign on the part of the British themselves. The early decades of the nineteenth century were characterized by Enlightenment-inspired cooperation and mutual esteem between white and brown scholars, but as the British replaced classicism and universalism with romanticism and nationalism, relations between the two groups became increasingly strained. The British government revoked its ban on Christian missions in India, and the Victorian crusade for missionary activity joined with snowballing imperialist snobbery to create increasingly racist attitudes. Social Darwinism exacerbated the growing trend toward racism, as did the fact that the now-established Indian colleges were churning out credentialed Hindus who wished to compete with Europeans for the same coveted civil service jobs. From an Indian point of view, the glass ceiling in the Indian Civil Service was so low it was tough on the knees.

MODERN HINDU MOVEMENTS

This, in very broad strokes indeed, was the social context that created modern Hinduism: a cosmopolitan, intellectual, knowledge-class Hindu elite trapped in a colonial nightmare where Western philosophical ideals (equality, democracy, progress) grated up against a racist economic straight jacket, Westernized sensibilities competing with cultural pride and patriotism, and a class of bureaucrats displaced from tradition but unable to find a home in modernity. Modern Hinduism was a creative series of solutions to these problems hammered out on Indian soil. When missionaries of the movement crossed over to America fifty years later, they would find a ready-made audience of displaced Americans struggling with many of the same themes.

In *India's Agony over Religion,* Gerald Larson summarizes the common points among modern Hindu movements as follows:

> (1) the use of English as a primary medium of discourse, (2) a reliance on modern methods of education in contrast to traditional methods, (3) a rejection of the ritual-based hierarchies of the traditional caste-system, (4) a self-confident assertion of the value and global importance of certain fundamental Hindu notions such as a broadly pluralistic notion of *dharma,* the practice of meditation of one kind or another, and the need for an exemplary spiritual guide or guru, and (5) the utilization of modern means of communication, including newspapers, pamphlets, tracts, film and public broadcasting of all kinds.[4]

To Larson's list of family resemblances among modern Hindu movements, the following can be added: a preference for text-based doctrines, with special emphasis on the Upanishads; a conscious sense of tension between rationality and mysticism; an affirmation of the reality of the world, based on a rejection of the advaitin doctrine of **maya;** and a tendency toward religious tolerance and universalism.

Larson additionally divides Modern Hinduism into two categories: the reformist/nationalist movements and the revisionist/internationalist movements. The first, prominent in the nine-

teenth century, "focused primarily on the reform and modernization of older Hindu practices and the political development of
India into a modern, secular nation-state." The second, which
overtook the first around the turn of the century and continues to
grow in importance to the present day, "focused largely on a kind
of reverse missionizing, that is, the export of a variety of . . . 'yoga-
oriented guru-disciple movements' to Western Europe and the
United States, especially after the achievement of the independence of India."[5]

The reformist/nationalist movements, typified by the Brahmo
Samaj (a modernizing Hindu movement of the nineteenth century), varied from radical extremism to moderate reformism, but
shared the following features:

> (1) a primary focus on developing among the people of India a
> self-confident national awareness that will provide a solid foun-
> dation for India as a modern nation-state; (2) the reform of
> outdated, parochial and superstitious Hindu practices; (3) the
> rejection or radical reform of the caste system; (4) female eman-
> cipation; (5) the improvement of social conditions for the poor;
> (6) economic progress for the entire nation; and (7) the devel-
> opment of techniques of communication and propaganda bor-
> rowed largely from Protestant Christian models.[6]

Revisionist and international movements, in contrast, share
these common features:

> (1) devotion to a deified guru or teacher; (2) total obedience
> to the will of the guru or teacher; (3) the practice of one or
> another type of yoga or disciplined meditation; (4) the claim
> that all religions are basically valid; (5) the claim that one's eth-
> nic identity has no bearing on the practice of the particular Neo-
> Hindu, so long as the devotee has been properly initiated; and
> (6) a tendency to deemphasize social work and secular political
> or ideological involvement of any kind.[7]

Although Larson's distinction is helpful, it should be noted
that these artificial categories do not always perfectly represent

the goals of individual reformers; Vivekananda, for example, combined characteristics of both trajectories in his work. Refracted through Larson's lens, the entire period examined here, 1893–1965, can be seen as a time of transition between the national and international modes of modern Hinduism, a transition from the Brahmo Samaj to Transcendental Meditation.

Larson's dichotomy emphasizes a common conflict within reform movements between rationalism and devotionalism. Modern religious trends, in an attempt to become more scientific, have been critical of the devotional approach; for example, liberal Protestantism combined the quietistic strain of the Puritans with the urbane, bourgeois complacency of the middle classes to produce a subdued devotional format that minimized emotional fervor. Early Hindu reformers were keen on making their worship as acceptable as possible to the British and were also themselves products of a British social ethic that favored emotional restraint and social propriety. Ironically, when the next generation of modern Hindus went West the following century, they would often confront Americans who were fed up with dry, reasoned religion and who were searching for a worldview that would speak to their hearts.

MODERN HINDU REFORM

The history of modern Hindu reform begins with the man eulogized as the Father of Modern India. Rammohun Roy (1772–1833), a deeply rational and reserved man, worked until his mid-forties as an administrator for the Bengal Civil Service. Frugality and business acumen allowed him to retire and spend his remaining two decades fighting for social and religious reform. A tireless self-taught man and a linguist, he was inspired not only by Hinduism but also by Islam and Unitarianism. He helped found a Unitarian Committee in Calcutta and corresponded with Unitarian leaders in America and Europe. Concluding that institutionalized Unitarianism was too narrowly and ethnocentrically Christian, he abandoned the Unitarians in 1829 and founded the Brahmo Sabha, later renamed the Brahmo

Samaj. Roy advocated a puritanical, universalistic theism stripped of ritual, idolatry, and superstition. However, most of his reformist zeal centered on social issues rather than theological debate. Roy promoted women's rights and opposed widow burning, child marriage, and **purdah.**

After Roy's untimely death in 1833, the mantle of religious reform passed to Devendranath Tagore (1817–1905), son of the wealthy Dwarkanath and father of the poet Rabindranath. At the age of eighteen, Devendranath was deeply shaken by a mystical experience; as he sat at night at the edge of the river, where he had come to be near his beloved grandmother during her last hours, "a strange sense of the unreality of all things suddenly entered my mind. I was as if no longer the same man. A strong aversion to wealth arose within me. The coarse bamboo-mat on which I sat seemed my fitting seat, carpets and costly spreadings seemed hateful, in my mind was awakened a joy unfelt before."[8]

Under Tagore's leadership, the Samaj was transformed between 1842 and 1863 from a small intellectual forum to an organized religious institution complete with a creed, membership rites, standard scripture, and missionaries. Although a monotheistic worshipper of a formless Creator, Devendranath relied almost entirely on the Upanishads for his religious inspiration, rather than drawing eclectically from world religions, as Roy had done before him and Sen would after. The Brahmo scripture, compiled by Devendranath, contained selections from the Upanishads, the **Mahabharata,** and the **Laws of Manu.** He culled prayers and hymns from a variety of Hindu sources and was not averse to editing them when monotheism was obscured, absent, or contradicted. These texts were viewed as inspirational but not infallible: "Reason and Conscience were to be the supreme authority, and the teachings of the scriptures were to be accepted only in so far as they harmonized with the light within us."[9]

The strict monotheism of the Brahmos, while certainly influenced by Western sources, has its own Indian roots. Polytheism, monism, and monotheism have vied for attention throughout the history of Hinduism, as the threefold division of vedanta suggests.

Additionally, devotional and monotheistic trends were particularly prevalent in Bengal. Bengal was colonized by Orthodox Hinduism late, and in some districts Sufi saints may have preceded Hinduism, directly coating the preexisting, tribal polytheism with a veneer of monotheistic doctrines. Before the colonial period, **Vaishnavism** was probably the most popular form of religion in Bengal; as the eighteenth century progressed, **Shaktism** catapulted into prominence as well. Both traditions focus devotional attention on a single deity to the exclusion of all others and, as a result, veer toward monotheism in practice, if not in theory. The Krishna Consciousness of Chaitanya is more purely monotheistic, and, although Shaktism has formal roots in both monism and the dual-divinity principle of classical **yoga,** folk worship of the Supreme Being as feminine was for all practical purposes equally monotheistic, with Shiva marginalized to the point where his only role was to suggest a link to Puranic orthodoxy. Therefore, the monotheistic strain in modern Hinduism cannot be read exclusively as a colonial response to Western hegemony, but, rather, should be seen as one of many indigenous religious options that was brought to the forefront and accentuated because of its congruence with British values.

In Bengal, the Brahmo insistence on austerity and emotional restraint was more of an import than monotheism. Bengali Hinduism was enthusiastic. The puritanical note in Brahmoism was the result of two powerful cultural magnets: Victorian social norms and the newly rediscovered ancient Indian philosophical texts. In their agonized identity search, the bhadralok wished to be both good Indians and good moderns; they accomplished this by scapegoating the folk religion of their day and region as a garish, primitive, shameless debasement of the classical age of Indian thought. As Stephen Prothero points out in *The White Buddhist,* this kind of primitivism can be seen as a "Protestant" strategy, reminiscent of early Protestantism's distaste for popish embellishments on the original, pure, textual doctrine.

Tagore shared Roy's rationalism, emotional restraint, iconoclasm, and leadership ability. He pushed the Brahmo Samajis to reject the notion of the infallibility of the scriptures, image worship, incarnational doctrines, and caste distinctions. Tagore's autobiography portrays a mystic with a profound sense of spiritual peace, but he often came off as a cold, imposing figure. He was a private man, more drawn to solitary contemplation than social action. When the youthful Vivekananda, then involved with the Samaj, went to visit Tagore in search of a spiritual answer to his angst-ridden confusion, he asked Tagore if he had seen God and was disappointed when Tagore evaded the question. Later, when he first met his future guru Ramakrishna, Vivekananda asked the same question. Unlike Tagore, Ramakrishna replied, "Yes, I have seen God. I see Him as I see you here, only more clearly. God can be seen. One can talk to him. But who cares for God? People shed torrents of tears for their wives, children, wealth, and property, but who weeps for the vision of God? If one cries sincerely for God, one can surely see Him."[10]

This exchange, and the "eureka" response Vivekananda had to it, illustrate the limitations of the Samaj's restrained approach and the abiding fascination of experiential religion. Despite this, and despite a series of bitter splits within the Samaj, the society remained the flagship of modern Hinduism throughout the nineteenth century. Roy, Tagore, and their Samaj were marked by the same rationalism, emotional restraint, and intellectualism that infused the Protestant ethic:

> Reviewing the Maharshi's autobiography in 1914, E. M. Forster remarked that Brahmoism was "not so much a creed as an attitude of mind, and would particularly appeal to a spiritual rebel." While this was true, Brahmoism could easily turn sectarian, puritanical and somewhat ridiculous: a mixture of Sunday school earnestness, Victorian prudishness and old-fashioned vicarage tea-party. The stereotype of a Brahmo among more orthodox Bengalis became, as it still is, the one-time behavior of the principal of the main Brahmo College in Calcutta. He was walking in the street when a man asked him the way to the Star Theater. "I don't know," he replied shortly and walked on. Then realizing he had told an untruth, he ran back to the man and said, "I know, but I won't tell you."[11]

Although influential on the intellectual development of the Renaissance, this approach never had mass appeal, any more than New England's Transcendentalism made any great impact when compared to evangelical revivalism during the same period in the United States. It was, perhaps, too "corpse-cold," as Emerson quipped of the Unitarian ministers in his youth—not only for the masses, but even for the religious virtuosi who were seeking safe passage to "the other side" in the most modern vessel available. As the preceding anecdote about Vivekananda shows, many found such a vessel in Sri Ramakrishna (1836–1886). For the cosmopolitan, educated, skeptical, and deeply confused Generation X of Young Bengal, this childlike devotee of Kali represented the polar opposite of Roy's rationalistic iconoclasm.

Ramakrishna should be remembered for both his intense personal charisma and his creative synthesis of various Hindu traditions into a coherent worldview. In person, he was both troubling and riveting. He fell into trances, acted in a childlike manner, and went through periods of extreme asceticism mixed with bouts of eccentric behavior. Other gurus in the Hindu tradition also act in unusual or unexpected ways; this is understood as the normal result of what happens when a person rejects the trivial concerns of everyday social life in order to completely concentrate on the transcendent life of the spirit. Ramakrishna's touch was electrifying; Vivekananda reports that on his second visit to his future Master, Ramakrishna touched him with his foot, at which point everything seemed to vanish and Vivekananda felt himself disappearing into a void. It was this sort of magnetism that sustained Vivekananda's devotion to Ramakrishna, rather than—or perhaps in spite of—Ramakrishna's message or example. Vivekananda had tormenting doubts concerning the philosophical justifications for many of Ramakrishna's statements but did not doubt Ramakrishna's enlightened status. For Ramakrishna, religion was not primarily a matter of philosophy or ethics but, rather, of the vivid experience of loving communion with the Divine. To quote Paramananda,

> Sri Ramakrishna's greatest contribution to the modern world of religious thought was to bring into it a note of definiteness. Our

present age of multiple theories and intellectual speculation had set the hearts of men adrift in regard to God and the ultimate realities. Here we find Sri Ramakrishna rising like a star of hope in the midst of chaos and confusion. His equipment and self-expression did not lie in erudition and intellectual cleverness, but in direct vision and perception. When we approach him, he does not try to confuse our minds with theological doctrines and metaphysical implications. Instead, he gives us this unique and convincing statement: "Yes, I have seen God and known Him. Furthermore, I can help you to see and know Him."[12]

In his simplified, wholehearted devotion, Ramakrishna studied a variety of traditions and consistently melded them together into a single, unified worldview. Vaishnavism, tantra, advaita vedanta, and Shaktism all appeared to him as different paths to the same goal. He also experimented with meditating on the personalities and scriptures of Christianity and Islam. His followers would later bill this as a universalist harmonizing of the world's religions, but it seems clear that Ramakrishna simply added new faces and myths to an already realized, and very Hindu, religious system. This process of melding different traditions into a larger picture of universal truth has long been an important feature of Hindu philosophy. Ramakrishna's practice of looking for the best features in each religion and combining them into a unified picture of the world drew on this philosophical tradition.

Ramakrishna's syncretic policy was carried even further by one of his protégés, Keshub Chunder Sen (1838–1884). Sen began his public career as a Brahmo, but left the organization because it would not renounce caste prejudices. In 1880, Sen attempted to start his own new religion, which he called the New Dispensation. Its precepts were not unlike the Samaj's: monotheistic, progressive, egalitarian, and promoting "harmony of knowledge and Holiness, Love and Work, Yoga and Asceticism in their highest development."[13] Sen was a brilliant scholar of religion, knowledgeable in all of the major faiths, but Christianity, Vaishnavism, and the Shaktism of Ramakrishna stood out in his mind. Although he was never a formal disciple of Ramakrishna, the saint strongly influenced the later stages of his career. Sen believed that devotion to the Supreme as Mother would unite Hindus and Christians as nothing else could. Unlike the Samaj, he did not shy away from emotional and ritual aspects of religion. He regularly organized **kirtans,** Vaishnava festivals of devotional song and dance. With "tears running down his handsome face" he sang of his love for the Lord.[14] The New Dispensation was meant to be the crowning, progressive synthesis of all religious traditions, a new religion for a new age. Unlike past dispensations, the individual would commune directly with God without any intermediary. It would be entirely inclusive, eschewing sexism and caste. It would be Christ's prophecy fulfilled. On his deathbed he is said to "have cried out 'Mother, Mother of Buddha,' and to have asked for a hymn about Christ's sufferings in Gethsemane."[15]

Despite his huge popularity during his life, Sen is rarely remembered today. He was too loyal to the British crown for Indian taste and not Christian enough for the British. However, his message foreshadows those of many later reformers, including Vivekananda, who knew Sen during his youth and would later follow his lead in moving from agnosticism through Brahmoism and Ramakrishna, to an eclectic synthesis of his own making. Paramananda and Yogananda, each in his own way, carried on Sen's quest for a universal religion that would satisfy both the mind and the heart.

SWAMI VIVEKANANDA
AND THE VEDANTA SOCIETY

If Sen was Ramakrishna's prodigal child, then Swami Vivekananda (1863–1902) played the dutiful son. He was born to bhadralok parents and typified the young Bengal's search for identity throughout his college years, flirting with Brahmoism, Freemasonry, and secularism before yielding, reluctantly, to Ramakrishna's charisma. Ramakrishna encouraged him to study advaita, perhaps realizing that his Westernized background was better suited to jnana than bhakti, but he also made certain that Vivekananda worshipped **Kali.** On his deathbed, Ramakrishna designated Vivekananda as his spiritual heir—the repository of his transferred charisma and authority—and left him in charge of his small band of disciples with instructions to "keep my boys together."

This was to prove to be a difficult task. In the years that followed Ramakrishna's death, his devotees did not always see eye-to-eye on the nature of their calling. Vivekananda, in particular, was impatient with the traditional approach of most of the brotherhood, who were content with the ritual worship of Kali and their departed guru. Vivekananda wandered restlessly during these years, returning to his early skepticism and bouts of depression. The extreme poverty in India that he faced during his travels as a wandering renunciant troubled him and made it difficult for him to justify a life of contemplation. Finally, he had a vision that made a future plan of action clear to him; sitting on a rock at Cape Comorin, recalling the horrible physical deprivations he had seen, he realized that the God he had vowed to serve was Everyman: "the only God in whom I believe, the sum total of all souls, and above all, my God the wicked, my God the afflicted, my God the poor of all races!"[16] Not long after this, he decided to go to America, ostensibly to trade the spiritual wealth of the East for the material wealth of the West, thus feeding both the Western soul and Indian belly. Perhaps his irritation with the ritualistic complacency of his brother monks, who he was supposed to be shepherding, contributed to his decision.

When Vivekananda came to Chicago to speak at the World's Parliament of Religions in 1893, he was a youthful monk from an obscure Bengali devotional order. When he returned triumphantly to India three years later, newspaper reports of his stirring speeches and enthusiastic response preceded him, and he found himself transformed into a national hero. Vivekananda had been a success at the Parliament, arguing forcefully for the unity of religions and the honor of Hinduism and of India, and against the ugliness of the missionary mentality. His handsome appearance, exotic dress, and eloquent command of the English language contributed greatly to his success. After the Parliament, Vivekananda traveled in the United States and Europe until 1897; he made another tour of the West in 1898–1900. After his second return to India, he entered a period of semiretirement, which ended with his death in 1902 at the age of thirty-nine.

Vivekananda's tour of the West was a turning point in his life, and it affected his message in ways that are now difficult to unravel, for much of our knowledge of him comes from hagiographic sources that reify his message rather than presenting it as an evolving process. Additionally, it is sometimes difficult to ascertain what Vivekananda thought at a particular time because he was a skilled diplomat and cultural translator. His speeches in India and in the West were not identical. Instead, he crafted each to best capture the hearts of his particular audience. His first trip to America, however, seems to have solidified two of his subsequent concerns: the importance of service and the importance of organization.

Vivekananda had suffered over the question of how much time and effort to devote to the service of humanity before coming to the United States. It was only after his journey to the West, however, that he made a concerted effort to organize the tattered remnant of Ramakrishna disciples primarily into a humanitarian organization, as opposed to a devotional movement. In 1897, the Ramakrishna monks formally organized themselves into the Ramakrishna Math (monastic order) and Mission, adopting a formal set of rules and administrative procedures.

If Vivekananda was impressed by the Western ideal of service on behalf of humanity, he was equally impressed by Western techniques of organization and administration, which he saw as efficient and rational use of time and energy that could maximize one's effect in the world. His arrival in the United States underlined the importance of organization to him. He had arrived in Chicago with no invitation or credentials, expecting to be able to speak; it was only through a fortuitous series of interventions that he was able to secure a spot on the roster after his arrival. "Nothing could have been more typical of the lack of organizedness of Hinduism itself than this going forth of its representative unannounced, and without formal credentials, to enter the strongly guarded door of the world's wealth and power," he later ruefully recalled.[17]

After the Parliament, Vivekananda toured the United States on a lecture circuit, visiting Iowa City, Des Moines, Memphis, Indianapolis, Minneapolis, Detroit, Buffalo, Hartford, Boston, Cambridge, New York City, Baltimore, and Washington D.C. He received surprisingly good press, although he was attacked publicly and vociferously by both Christian missionaries and Theosophists. But by March 1894, he had grown tired of the circus atmosphere of the lecture circuit. He wrote to a friend in Chicago that "I have become sad in my heart since I am here. I do not know why. I am wearied of lecturing and all that nonsense. This mixing with hundreds of human animals, male and female, has disturbed me. I will tell you what is to my taste. I cannot write—cannot speak—but I can think deep, and when I am heated can speak fire. But it should be to a select few—a very select few."[18] Vivekananda then left the organization that set up his lecture circuit and began dividing his time between permanent centers in Chicago, New York, and Boston. Today, the Vedanta Society is the oldest continuous Hindu organization in the United States, with centers in many major cities. The individual centers are administered by the international headquarters of the Ramakrishna Math and Mission, which sends monks from the order to head each center.

Vivekananda was both a charismatic speaker and shrewd politician; without these skills his movement would not have had the success that it did. Additionally, however, he did a brilliant job of synthesizing and articulating the modern Hindu message; perhaps no single person did more to standardize Modern Hinduism. For example, Vivekananda organized his Vedanta into a fourfold path, each of which he deemed suitable for different personality types: *bhakti yoga,* the path of devotion and love to God or guru; *jnana yoga,* the path of intellectual wisdom; *karma yoga,* the path of active service on the behalf of humanity; and *raja yoga,* the path of mystic perfection through the use of traditional techniques of bodily control. This framework emphasized the importance of personal freedom in the spiritual quest while reconciling seemingly contradictory strands of the Hindu tradition.

In its contemporary rendition, Vivekananda's neo-vedanta rests on the following fundamental principles:

1. Truth is one; sages call it variously. In other words, God is one; people worship Him in different forms.
2. Man, in his essential nature, is divine.
3. The goal of man is to realize this divinity.
4. The ways to realize this divinity are innumerable. They are called the Yogas. As Sri Ramakrishna declared, "As many faiths, so many paths."[19]

While it is unlikely that Ramakrishna would have disagreed with these statements, it should be kept in mind that Vivekananda reshaped Ramakrishna's message in many ways. Unable to accept Ramakrishna's indiscriminate joy in all religious forms, Vivekananda deftly reinterpreted his guru's message into a standard Victorian evolutionary hierarchy of progress. Vivekananda was particularly disdainful of anything that seemed superstitious or "primitive" and preferred a rationalized philosophy coupled with service to humanity viewed as worship of the divine within Everyman. Vivekananda de-emphasized the ecstatic and tantric elements in Ramakrishna and added his own emphasis on service, work in the world, national pride, administrative order, and reason. Vivekananda's Divine Mother, like Devendranath Tagore's Divine Father, was an abstract, dignified, disembodied spirit, more at home at a social club than an Indian village.

The Vedanta Society became the most enduring and successful of the international Hindu movements. Today, excessive bureaucracy, sexism, a jingoistic attitude toward full monastic participation by non-Indians, and the natural torpor of time and tradition has made the Societies in the United States less popular than they have been in the past with European Americans, although there is some evidence that Indian immigrants will continue to make them viable. They also face intense competition from other alternative religious groups. Before World War II, however, vedanta was by far the most popular Hindu group in the United States. The Belur Math provided a central administration, the most important function of which was to send a steady supply of eager young monks to the various centers and to field conflicts between the different monks, forcing them to work together in a more concerted manner than they would otherwise have done. Paramananda would become one of these monks.

To circle back to the problem of defining Hinduism, it should be noted that none of the three "Hindu" missionaries discussed here called themselves, their movements, or their American disciples, Hindu. Paramananda taught vedanta; Yogananda taught yoga, which he also called Self-Realization; Krishnamurti simply dismissed all labels. If pushed, perhaps all three would have been happiest to be characterized as nonsectarian seekers of Truth. I have, perhaps quixotically, forced them under a common Hindu umbrella in order to emphasize their common background and context and to underline their uniquely Indian contributions to the alternative religious options on the American scene. If one takes the label of Hinduism at its face value, as I have, as a catchall category for the complex labyrinth of Indian worldviews, then it certainly applies to these three teachers.

If they were Hindu, they were also more than that. The modernizing trajectory constructed by Roy, Tagore, Sen, Ramakrishna, and Vivekananda developed a momentum that would push it far beyond a united India. As Larson notes in *India's Agony over Religion,* Hindu nationalism transformed into an internationalist movement. The question became, for the gurus studied here and their followers, not "what does it mean to be Hindu?" but, rather, "given all that we have learned, and all that has changed, how then should we live?" They drew on Indian traditions to answer this question, but the answer itself ended up bigger than a continent. And so they went West.

NOTES

1. Bourdillon, *Report on the Census of Bengal, 1881.*
2. Kopf, *British Orientalism and the Bengal Renaissance,* 22.
3. Broomfield, *Elite Conflict in a Plural Society.* The first few chapters of this work outline the rise of the bhadralok class.
4. Larson, *India's Agony over Religion,* 139–140.

5. Ibid., 129.

6. Ibid., 133–134.

7. Ibid., 139.

8. D. Tagore, *Autobiography of Maharshi Debendranath Tagore,* 38.

9. Ibid., 5. The quote is taken from the book's introduction, written by Satyendranath Tagore.

10. Nikhilananda, *Vivekananda,* 24–25.

11. Dutta and Robinson, *Rabindranath Tagore,* 31.

12. Devi, *One Life's Pilgrimage,* x.

13. Borthwick, *Keshub Chunder Sen,* 26.

14. Kopf, *The Brahmo Samaj,* 223.

15. Borthwick, *Keshub Chunder Sen,* 228.

16. Nikhilananda, *Vivekananda,* 98.

17. Ibid., 112.

18. Ibid., 141.

19. From the pamphlet *Vedanta in America and the West,* The Vedanta Societies of Boston and Providence, undated.

CHAPTER 3

American Soil

During the time of the Hindu Renaissance, American experience paralleled the Indian struggle to reconcile religion with science and changing social conditions. A common, and mistaken, myth concerning American religious history is that the United States was purely Christian from the landing of the *Mayflower* until the "summer of love," when wild forces of secularism, liberal humanism, and paganism were unleashed onto a complacently Protestant nation. The United States has always been primarily Christian, but it also has a venerable history of religious dissent and innovation stretching into the colonial past. If it were not so, Hindu teachers would not have found the eager audience that they did.

The Enlightenment deists of the Revolutionary era planted seeds of religious tolerance and pluralism in American society that began to blossom during the mid-nineteenth century. It is remarkable that only 150 years passed between the Salem witch trials of 1692 and the premier event in the Spiritualism movement in 1849, Margaret Fox's first public (and commercial) exhibition of her ability to contact the spirits of the dead. In an earlier time and place, Fox would have been killed rather than paid for her talent.

The last half of the eighteenth century paired widespread religious complacency with Enlightenment ferment among the upper, educated classes—who would, of course, immortalize their minority opinion concerning "Republican Religion" in the architecture of the new State, both in the Declaration of Independence and the Constitution.

Ironically, the separation of church and state coincided with religious revivalism. The major trend during the nineteenth century was renewed interest in Christianity, fueled by the rise of denominationalism and the increase of religious options. Radical religious alternatives flourished alongside the massive sweep of the Second Great Awakening and the proliferation of mainstream Protestant denominations. Unitarianism, mesmerism, Spiritualism, Harmonialism, Communitarianism, Transcendentalism, and Swedenborgianism competed at the fringes of the religious marketplace, while within Protestantism liberal traditions grew in strength and respectability.

The scholar Peter Williams has defined *liberal religion,* in the American context, as

> the impulse to reject dogma in favor of free inquiry; to bring to bear the forces of reason in making religious judgments, while not necessarily denying the reality of supernatural forces; to be suspicious of religious authority that conflicts with individual reason; to replace a preoccupation with the metaphysical aspects of theology with an orientation toward living rightly and doing good in the world; and to exhibit an optimistic stance toward the possibilities of transforming the world into a saner and more humane place through the development of human potential by education, self-cultivation and a beneficent social environment.[1]

The worldview Williams describes so eloquently feels so familiar to contemporary liberal intellectuals that we rarely pause to note how recent a creation it is. As we saw in the previous chapter, the modernizing Hindu Renaissance was based on the same liberal principles: a rejection of dogmatic tradition and superstition where they conflicted with science or reason, a new orientation toward ethics and social action, and belief in progress as inevitable. But whereas liberalizing tendencies were confined in India to a Westernized elite, in the United States they enjoyed a much wider popularity.

THE UNITARIAN MOVEMENT

The vanguard of liberal Protestantism through the nineteenth century was New England's Unitarian movement. William Ellery Channing's Baltimore address of 1819 is still often used to define the position of early Unitarianism. In the address, Channing advocated the rejection of biblical literalism, the value of human reason in interpreting scripture, the unity of God, the rejection of the Trinity, the single human nature of Jesus, the centrality of ethics (as opposed to dogma) in the religious life, the moral nature of God, God's parental rather than judgmental nature, Jesus' mission to rescue humanity from sin through moral example rather than substitutionary atonement, human free will, and the rejection of revivalism and "enthusiastic" religion. Channing also frankly addressed the likelihood of human error in religious formulation and the corresponding need for religious tolerance:

> We find, that on no subject have men, and even good men,
> engrafted so many strange conceits, wild theories, and fictions of
> fancy, as on religion; and remembering, as we do, that we our-
> selves are sharers of the common frailty, we dare not assume
> infallibility in the treatment of our fellow-Christians, or encour-
> age in common Christians, who have little time for investigation,
> the habit of denouncing and condemning other denominations,
> perhaps more enlightened and virtuous than their own. Charity,
> forbearance, a delight in the virtues of different sects, a back-
> wardness to censure and condemn, these are virtues, which,
> however poorly practiced by us, we admire and recommend.[2]

While Channing saw Unitarians as Christian, debates raged within and without the Unitarian Church over whether or not this was true, or even desirable, over the course of the century. The conservatives held that in order to be a real Christian one must believe that Jesus is God; since Unitarians deny the divinity of Christ, they are not real Christians. Rammohun Roy, on the other hand, considered Unitarians to be Christian because they placed Jesus at the center of their devotional life. Roy was a Unitarian for several years but left the church because he found it to be culturally claustrophobic in its obsession with Jesus. Most Unitarians continued to focus their attention on the story of Jesus and the Christian Bible, even while insisting that Jesus was less than God. Yet seeds of a post-Christian religious worldview are clearly present in Channing's Baltimore address.

ALTERNATIVES TO CHRISTIANITY

Other Americans were moving away from traditional forms of Christianity. Take, for example, the followers of Emanuel Swedenborg (1688–1771). Swedenborg was born in Sweden to a Lutheran bishop. During his youth, he traveled widely in Europe and studied the natural sciences, contributing to a wide range of fields. In his mid-fifties, Swedenborg experienced a profound spiritual crisis, during which he was visited by an angel who commanded him to write down the true spiritual meaning of the Bible, which God would dictate to him. His visions told him that the future held a dissolution of traditional Christianity and the emergence of a worldwide spiritual consciousness, which he called the New Jerusalem.[3] Swedenborg believed that his teachings represented the Second Coming of Christ.

Swedenborg believed in the oneness of God and that the Trinity stood for three essential principles of God—love, wisdom, and power—rather than three persons. His cosmology was Neoplatonic: God is the only true substance, and the world is created out of Divine Being rather than from nothing. His theory of correspondence, which influenced the Transcendentalists, maintained that every physical manifestation has a spiritual counterpart and that the material and spiritual worlds mirror and interpenetrate one another. In a like manner, the Bible had both a "literal" sense and a corresponding hidden "spiritual" sense that only Sweden-borg was privy to and which was dispensed through his writings. He believed in free will and that the free choice of morality over sin causes one to go to Heaven rather than Hell. He believed that spirits and angels are in constant communion with the living. He believed, foreshadowing Vivekananda's neo-vedanta, that "the Lord himself flows into each man."

After Swedenborg's death, followers established a church based on his teachings. Most of his followers were English or American. The institutionalized Swedenborgian church, how-ever, was probably not as influential in America as the un-churched circulation of his writings. Ralph Waldo Emerson, Johnny Appleseed, Benjamin Franklin, Thomas Jefferson, and Helen Keller were all influenced by Swedenborg. Indeed, his voluminous and cryptic spiritual writings seem to have contained something for everyone, and they influenced not only the Tran-scendentalists but the Spiritualists and New Thought movement as well.

In Transcendentalism, an educated, liberal New England elite expressed a belief that the everyday world was infused with spirit and meaning in a more universal way than doctrinal Christianity could capture. In Spiritualism, the same sentiments were ex-pressed in a populist tradition. The Spiritualist movement was not an organized religion but, rather, a grassroots surge of interest in the communication with the spirits of the dead through the spe-cial skills of mediums, who traveled the country giving paid per-formances. Mediums normally went into a trance and were then possessed with the spirit of a dead person, sometimes a famous personage and sometimes, by request, a deceased relative of an audience member. The Spiritualist movement was triggered by the spirit-rappings of the Fox sisters in 1847 and peaked in popu-larity around 1860. During the 1850s many such frauds were debunked; even one of the Fox sisters later admitted that their "raps" had been nothing more than the cracking of toe joints. Spiritualism did not disappear from the American landscape, however, surviving continuously to the present day in less fashionable circumstances. Its popularity surged in the 1870s and again in the 1980s under its new name of channeling.

Spiritualism was largely a form of carnival entertainment for the audience and a means of employment for the medium, as scholar Ann Braude shows in her book *Radical Spirits,* but it noticeably shaped American religious sentiments. Americans estranged from traditional Christianity were reassured concerning the survival of the personality in a spiritual form after death and the eventual reunion with dead loved ones. Since most mediums were women, it gave American women an unprecedented chance to be at center stage in an important social sphere; women became accustomed during this time to occupying a podium and men grew used to seeing them there. The unorganized nature of the movement encouraged a personalized, noninstitutional, voluntaristic approach to faith. For example, most Spiritualists were also Christians and saw no conflict between the two.

THE RISE OF
THE NEW THOUGHT MOVEMENT

By the turn of the century, the main philosophical platform (to the extent that there was one) of Spiritualism had been absorbed into New Thought, a label used to denote a loosely affiliated group of thinkers, institutions, and ideals centered around "the overriding significance of spiritual reality, the unity of all religions, the harmony between science and religion, and the ability of the individual to harness the Divine Nature in order to affect all manner of change—including the change from sickness to health."[4] To quote Warren Felt Evans, a leader of the movement, New Thought was meant to denote the underlying philosophical truths of "a variety of phenomena, passing under the names of Mesmerism, Psychology, Biology, Animal Magnetism, Pantheism, Hypnotism, and even Psychometry, that are reducible to one general principle—the influence or action of mind upon mind, and the communication of spiritual life from one person to another."[5]

Historian of American religion Sidney Ahlstrom lumped New Thought into his larger category of Harmonialism, which included Christian Science and Aldous Huxley's Perennial Philosophy: "Harmonial religion encompasses those forms of piety and belief in which spiritual composure, physical health, and even economic well-being are understood to flow from a person's rapport with the cosmos. Human beatitude and immortality are believed to depend to a great degree on one's being 'in tune with the infinite.'"[6] Ahlstrom pointed out the similarities between Christian Science and New Thought, but they had notable differences as well. Christian Science was hierarchical and dogmatic, insisting on strict adherence to its authority and teachings. It also emphasized the reality of sin and the redemptive nature of Jesus Christ, who alone could bridge the gap between human and divine. As a result, Christian Science did not influence the development of Asian religion in America to the extent that New Thought did. Unlike Christian Science, New Thought posits no essential division between God and humanity; human mind is "God within." God is abstracted into Universal Love, Life, Truth, and Joy, while evil and pain are but "the tests and correctives" that appear when one's thought does not reflect the full glory of God. Christian Science founder Mary Baker Eddy, however, maintained that humans, being frail and lost, needed the redemptive power of Christ to rediscover their innate perfection. Eddy did quote from Hindu scriptures in the first edition of *Science and Health,* but the references were removed in later editions.

One of New Thought's prime movers was Warren Felt Evans (1817–1889), who promoted spiritual healing, positive thinking, and harmonial religion. The compatibility between Evans' message and Vivekananda's later reformulation of vedanta for the Western world is striking. "The highest form of existence," wrote Evans,

> is that of a true religious life, which, in its essence, is a harmonious union of goodness and truth, love and wisdom, benevolence and faith, in the character and activity of the individual.

> Where intellect and love are harmoniously united and blended,
> and act in perfect concordance, the resulting product is spiritual
> power. The omnipotence of God is the union of infinite wisdom
> and infinite love.[7]

Vivekananda probably would have been offended by Evans' statement that Christ is "the highest example in human history of the
perfect union of the intellect with the religious nature, and the
resultant spiritual power." However, stepping outside traditional
Christianity, Evans held that Jesus' life was not a unique event but,
rather, of the same nature (if more perfected) as the lives of Con-
fucius, Buddha, Zoroaster, and Muhammad and that the true calling of every individual was to realize the same union of human
and divine nature that Christ showed. Jesus, Evans felt, believed
that matter was "unsubstantial *appearance,* and mind was the only
reality." Sickness and evil were therefore illusions based on incor-
rect perception of divine perfection.

New Thought's harmony with Americanized modern Hinduism is illustrated by John Y. Fenton's characterization of Export
Hinduism, which could almost be used to describe New Thought
word for word:

> Export Hinduism is generally very optimistic about human pos-
> sibilities, holding that the true deep self within each person can
> be awakened and put one in touch with the power of the uni-
> verse at large. The true reality of each person is the same as or
> part of universal reality. This reality is the true basis of all reli-
> gions, but transcends them all. There is no possible conflict be-
> tween science and religion because each points in its own way
> to the same ultimate reality.[8]

This affinity is not coincidental; New Thought leaders as early
as Evans showed interest in Asian religions. According to historian
of American religion Carl T. Jackson, Evans began studying Oriental philosophy late in his career, perhaps around 1881. His readings were eclectic and not very scholarly, relying heavily on
Theosophical works. By the time his final book, *Esoteric Christianity*

and Mental Therapeutics, was published in 1886, Evans was peppering his text with Sanskrit words like *karma* and *akasha.* By 1901, New Thought journals were running articles concerning Hinduism—primarily Vivekananda's vedanta—so frequently that "a reviewer of Max Muller's books might confess that 'We are so accustomed, nowadays, to hear the philosophy and practice of vedanta expounded by Hindoo teachers, and the processes of Oriental thought are so familiar to us, that we forget how fifty years ago Indian religion and literature was an unexplored field.'"[9] Although New Thought interest in yoga and vedanta died down after about 1910, ties between the two movements remained strong: Yogananda often reads more like a New Thought champion than an Indian yogi. New Thought institutions, such as Unity, flourish to this day; the sensibilities and vision of the movement passed on to the Positive Thinking School in the mid-century and still animate New Age discourse.

THE FREEMASONRY MOVEMENT

Yet another religious alternative in Victorian America was provided by Freemasonry—at least if one were male and white, and preferably native-born, Protestant, and middle class. Since the 1920s, the Masons have worked hard to tone down their religious heritage and present a secular face. Prior to 1920, however, Freemasonry was more likely to function as an alternative religion to its members, offering a distinct set of creeds and rituals that had more in common with deistic and unitarian traditions than with traditional Protestant theology.

Although members trace the historic roots of the society back to the building of King Solomon's temple before the Christian era, it probably took shape in the eighteenth century in Britain. It was popular during the Revolutionary era; George Washington, Benjamin Franklin, and John Paul Jones were Masons. Freemasonry contributed to the symbolism of American civil religion and to the Revolutionary focus on freedom of religion. The society was vigorously attacked in the early nineteenth century and decreased significantly in size and influence. The movement recovered its impetus after 1850, claiming 550,000 members by 1879, 1,000,000 by 1900, and peaking in popularity around 1930, when it could claim over 3,300,000 American members—12 percent of the native-born, white, adult male population. By 1870, over 7,000 lodges dotted the American landscape from coast to coast.[10] By 1885, Freemasonry's prestige and social acceptance could be publicly symbolized by the Masonic cornerstone-laying ritual that accompanied the construction of the Statue of Liberty.

While most Masons were also Christians, one did not have to be a Christian to be a Mason. Only one suborder of Masons, the Knights Templar, required allegiance to Christ and, in principle, freethinkers and Jews were welcome in the society—although in practice Jews were infrequent members and, in more conservative temples, freethinkers were encouraged to keep their views to themselves. Masons were required to profess belief in God, "The Great Architect of the Universe"; eternal life after death; and the ethical principles of equality, charity, fraternity, and morality. As a mythological alternative to Jesus, Masonic mythology offered Hiram Abif, the master builder of Solomon's temple who was murdered for his virtue and miraculously resurrected. This 1900 statement from the *Los Angeles Freemason* summarizes the Masonic religious ethos:

> Masonry is the world's religion, in that it contains the foundation of all faith and practice; for Jew and Christian, Mohammedan and Parsee, Roman and Protestant may enjoy the privileges it affords. One thing all must believe—there is a God. After that the manner of serving God, the form and doctrine is left to each individual. He reads the message from his Father and obeys it according to his understanding and agreeably to the dictates of his own conscience.[11]

Vivekananda, incidentally, flirted with Freemasonry during his college years.

Freemasonry supplemented its malleable creed with a formal ritual structure. The society was rigidly hierarchical, and members traveled through the ranks gaining prestige, secret initiatory knowledge, and privileges. The head of each lodge was the elected Most Worshipful Master, who answered only to the state's Grand Lodge and presided over all ceremonies seated on an elevated, thronelike dais "in the East." Three degrees of Masonic membership served as rites of passage to three stages of life: youth, middle age, and old age. Elaborate pageants were acted out, often with colorful costumes and always with a formalistic exactitude so that the ritual experience of every Mason was uniform. The building of Solomon's temple was taken (reminiscent of Swedenborgian correspondences) to represent the individual's quest to create a moral and perfected life out of the roughly hewn material that nature has provided.

The American fascination with the pomp and romanticism of secret societies was exploited to its fullest potential by the Theosophical Society. Unlike Freemasonry, Theosophy followed Spiritualism and New Thought in allowing women access to public power. Theosophy's institutional impact on the American scene was small, but it nonetheless provoked wide interest among an alternative network of sympathizers and curious onlookers.

THE THEOSOPHICAL SOCIETY

The Theosophical Society was founded in New York City in 1875 by Madame Helena Petrovna Blavatsky (1847–1933) and Colonel Henry S. Olcott (1832–1907). Originally a small study group devoted to Western occult and esoteric mysteries, by 1900, Theosophy was a premier conduit in the delivery of Asian religious ideas to the American religious counterculture. In 1878, Blavatsky and Olcott turned their interest East and, in 1879, moved to India, where they excited interest among English and Indian intellectuals by championing the dignity and truth of Asian religions. Success in India backwashed to the United States and Europe. By 1896, there were 103 American branches with roughly 6,000 members. The Theosophical Society played an important role in disseminating information about Asian religions in the United

States; it also contributed to the radical chic of such ideas at the turn of the century among educated, prosperous liberals. Understanding the Theosophical Society is also fundamental to understanding Krishnamurti's career.

Madame Blavatsky is perhaps best remembered as a marvelously eccentric and colorful confidence woman. Her father was an officer in the Russian army; her mother, a Russian noblewoman, was a popular novelist and social radical. Helena was a headstrong, tomboyish child. In 1849, she married a middle-aged widower and vice-governor of Armenia, Nikofer Blavatsky. The union was unhappy, and she left him almost immediately. Her exact biography during the next twenty-five years is unclear, but it seems that she traveled widely, had a child who died, and supported herself by holding seances. She later claimed to have traveled to Tibet during this period, but that is unlikely. She did, however, spend some time in Cairo, where she organized a spiritualist society in 1871–1872. After dissatisfied customers made claims that her mediumship rested on fraudulent stage magic, she left Egypt. In 1873 she sailed for New York City. By this time,

> Her youthful beauty had given way to obesity, but she was a colorful character who made a strong impression on those who knew her. She dressed in loose wrappers and wore around her neck a tobacco pouch in the form of an animal head. She smoked incessantly and captivated listeners with marvelous tales of travels in exotic places. A close associate said she would "sometimes color her language with expletives of all sorts, some witty and amusing, some unnecessarily violent, that we should all have preferred her not to make use of. She certainly had none of the superficial attributes one might have expected in a spiritual teacher."[12]

In contrast, the steady and pedantic Colonel Olcott was the perfect foil for Blavatsky's bohemian charisma. Olcott was brought up in a strict, Presbyterian home in New Jersey. As an adolescent, he dabbled in spiritualism, Freemasonry, and mesmerism, but for most of his middle years practical matters dominated his life. He studied agriculture, writing a best-seller on sorghum. During the Civil War, he successfully investigated corruption among army contractors. After the war, he built a successful law practice and tried his hand at journalism. Despite these accomplishments, his home life was unhappy. He went through a divorce in the mid-1870s. "Olcott later described himself during this period as 'a man of clubs, drinking parties, mistresses, a man absorbed in all sorts of worldly public and private undertakings.' His acquaintance with Madame Blavatsky was to change that and give him a new sense of purpose, mission, and service to others."[13]

In its broad outlines, the aims of the Theosophical Society were similar to those of the later Vedanta Society; Vivekananda may have drawn inspiration from it. The Society promoted the study of paranormal phenomena and religious philosophy, and it advocated religious and cultural toleration. In 1896, its goals were defined as (1) the formation of a universal human brotherhood without distinction of race, creed, sex, caste, or color; (2) the encouragement of studies in comparative religion, philosophy, and science; and (3) the investigation of unexplained laws of nature and the powers latent in man.[14] Despite the broad contours of its official rhetoric, in practice Theosophy was quite prescriptive both in dogmas and in ritual action, becoming increasingly narrow-minded as the years went on.

The core Theosophical doctrines were largely drawn from Blavatsky's writings, which were in turn a plagiaristic mishmash of esoteric and mystical ideas. A fundamental tenet was that all religions are the distorted relics of an ancient, pure, and universal religion. "The secret doctrines of the Magi, of the pre-Vedic Buddhists, of the hierophants of the Egyptian Thoth or Hermes, and of the adepts of whatever age and nationality, including the Chaldean kabalists and the Jewish *nazars,* were *identical* from the beginning."[15] By 1885, Blavatsky was focusing on three basic principles in the "secret doctrine": "(1) the existence of an absolute Reality, the infinite and eternal cause of all; (2) the periodicity of the universe: its appearance and disappearance in cycles; and

(3) the identity of 'all Souls with the Universal Over-Soul': the pilgrimage for every Soul or spark through the cycle of incarnation."[16] These tenets were inspired by exposure to Asian religions.

THE DEVELOPMENT OF HINDUISM IN THE UNITED STATES

These movements—Swedenborgianism, Spiritualism, New Thought, Freemasonry, and Theosophy—had helped to shape, by 1900, a far-flung network of alternative religious seekers. Overlapping membership was high; an individual might be involved with several different alternative religious groups simultaneously or serially. The published journals and books of these societies reached a much larger audience than actual membership numbers would suggest. Many members of more-mainstream religious institutions experimented with these lifestyles, subscribing to journals or attending the occasional lecture. Altogether, this fluid group made up an informal network of seekers who were interested in crafting or discovering new religious options that would speak directly to their concerns in a way that Christianity no longer could. In general, the Americans who sympathized most with Asian religions were of this background; most had experimented in the religious counterculture at some length before turning to Hindu movements. Carl T. Jackson notes that this pattern of interchange is reflected in the groups that Paramananda was invited to speak before:

> Despite their diversity, closer inspection of the hundreds of groups Swami Paramananda spoke to reveals a definite pattern. With few exceptions, there are no references to mainstream Christian churches or organizations, while the names of groups on the perimeter of American religion repeatedly recur. Perhaps half of the religious bodies Paramananda addressed were allied with the New Thought movement, with the other half—led by Unitarians, Theosophists, and Rosicrucians—coming from the liberal, outer fringe of American religion.[17]

Between 1893 and 1910, Hinduism (more precisely, neo-vedanta and yoga) became yet another interlocking piece in this counter-cultural system. This evolution would not have occurred if the basic pattern of a conglomeration of overlapping alternative religious movements with interchangeable clientele had not already been in place and if the early missionaries had not chosen to work within this framework. Hinduism in the United States during this time period did not bill itself as a thing apart, calling for religious conversion but, rather, as *one plausible option* for the modern, rational seeker of religious truth. The new groups were therefore able to make use of an existing network of institutions (such as halls in which to give lectures) and target audiences. In turn, they strengthened the entire network by reiterating the shared values of universalism and individual choice.

An important event in the development of Hindu alternatives on the American scene was the World's Parliament of Religions, held in conjunction with the Chicago World's Fair in 1893. Seventeen delegates from around the world lectured on their own religions. The overwhelming majority of participants were Protestant, but Catholicism, Judaism, Eastern Orthodoxy, Islam, Hinduism, Buddhism, and other religions were also represented. The speakers were encouraged to state their own beliefs in their own words, although without "employing unfriendly criticism of other faiths." Writes Richard Seager, "The goal of the Parliament as set forth in two mission statements was 'to unite all religions against all irreligion'; to set forth 'their common aim and common grounds of union'; to help secure 'the coming unity of mankind, in the service of God and man'; and 'to indicate the impregnable foundations of theism.'"[18]

Despite the liberal and tolerant tone of the mission statements, the event demonstrated a fair amount of ambivalence concerning religious unity. Many of the Christian speakers were unabashed in their belief that Christianity was the best and truest religion; if truth lay elsewhere at all, it was in a primitive and partial form. John Henry Barrows, the Presbyterian pastor who headed the Parliament's organizational committee, expected the

Parliament to be an opportunity to know the "heathen mind" better in order to more readily "supplant their religions with Christianity."[19] The "unity" envisioned by the event's organizers was a Christian unity in which inessential cultural and sectarian differences would be seen for what they were, and discord would be replaced by a union in and through Christ's salvation.

Seager understands the Parliament as representing the triumph of pluralism over unity:

> The Parliament was a liberal, western, and American quest for
> world religious unity that failed. Given the foregoing discussions,
> it can be no great mystery as to why it failed. The Parliament,
> however noble its goals and aspirations, was tainted by the same
> parochialism, ethnocentrism, imperial pretensions, and hege-
> monic intentions as the entire Exposition. In philosophic terms,
> it failed because the premises for its universalistic agenda turned
> out to be particularistic. In crude theological terms, it failed
> because the God of the organizers of the Parliament turned out
> not to be quite the same as the Gods of the Asians. . . . Having
> failed as a liberal quest for religious unity, the Parliament unin-
> tentionally turned out to be a revelation of the plurality of forces
> on the American and world scenes. As a result it was a harbinger
> of the rise of the idea of religious pluralism.[20]

This overstates the case. The Parliament did fail to achieve the parochial Christian unity that the Evangelical delegates seem to have hoped for. On the other hand, the Asian delegates were equally interested in the idea of unity; they simply conceived of it on a more truly universal basis. Eastern and Western delegates at this particular event both harbored optimism concerning a future science of religion, in which universal truths would triumph over sectarian superstition. They merely disagreed over what those truths were. The truly pluralistic worldview, in which two individuals can disagree irrevocably over basic values while acknowledging that they are both equally justified in their position, was still decades away in a postmodern future.

The Parliament's failure to establish Christianity as the pinnacle of that coming world unity was largely due to the popularity and effectiveness of the Asian delegation. Thirty Asian delegates represented Buddhism, Hinduism, Jainism, Confucianism, Brahmoism, and Parsi Zoroastrianism. Of these, a core group of politicized, Westernized representatives from British India were particularly successful in capturing the imaginations of the crowd and the press.

Swami Vivekananda, representing his own version of reformed and modernized vedanta, was for many the highlight of the Parliament. A strong orator, Vivekananda combined the fervor of charisma with the educated sophistication of a gentleman and thoroughly captivated his audience. Perhaps the combination of his exotic dress and fine diction symbolized an ideal of unity between the familiar and exotic. Speaking to the theme of unity, Vivekananda remarked at the close of the Parliament that

> if the Parliament of Religions has shown anything to the world it is this: It has proved to the world that holiness, purity and charity are not the exclusive possession of any church in the world, and that every system has produced men and women of the most exalted character. In the face of this evidence, if anybody dreams of the exclusive survival of his own religion and the destruction of the others, I pity him from the bottom of my heart, and point out to him that upon the banner of every religion will soon be written, in spite of resistance: "Help and not Fight," "Assimilation and not Destruction," "Harmony and Peace and Not Dissension."[21]

HINDU GROUPS IN THE UNITED STATES

Vivekananda's successes were widely reported in both the American and Indian press. When he returned to India in 1897, he was overwhelmed by the crowds that turned out to honor him as a national hero who had successfully defended their faith and country. After 1893, a steady trickle of Indian religious teachers journeyed to the United States. Most were monks in the Vedanta Society, which remained the biggest and best-organized Hindu group in the United States until Yogananda's Self-Realization

Society became popular in the 1920s. By 1930, at least a dozen Hindu gurus were teaching in the United States. To illustrate this point, a sampling of Hindu groups in the United States before 1965 follows.

Baba Premanand Bharati's Krishna Samaj. Bharati came to the United States in 1902 from Bengal as a disciple of Chaitanya's Krishna Consciousness movement. He formed his Samaj in New York City and lectured in eastern cities before moving to Los Angeles. He died in 1914.

Yogi Hare Rama's Benares League. He taught in the United States from 1925 to 1928, advocating a combination of yoga, vedanta, and universalism.

Sri Deva Ram Sukul's Hindu Yoga Society. Sukul, an Indian living in Chicago, started this group in the 1920s. In 1927 he started *Practical Yoga,* a quarterly journal, and issued a ten-part course in what he termed "Yoga Navajivan." Sukul helped popularize yoga, teaching an amalgam of **raja yoga, tantra,** and **kundalini.** He also taught his followers to chant the Gayatri mantra. He settled in California and counted Mae West among his disciples. He died in 1965.

Swami Bhagwan Bissessar's Yogessar. Bissessar claimed to be a "high caste Hindu" educated at "Eton College and Oxford University" who had then completed his education in the Himalayan Mountains "at the feet of the Masters, studying and absorbing the Ancient Wisdom of India." His promotional brochure described Yogessar as his own interpretation of a combination of Eastern and Western philosophies, designed to teach humanity the way to Nirvana.

Srimath Swami Omkar's Sri Mariya Ashrama. A Madrasi Hindu, Omkar established a Peace Retreat in southeastern India in the memory of Swami Rama Tiratha, who in turn had tried to combine Hindu and Christian mysticism. An American branch, the Sri Mariya Ashrama, was established in Philadelphia in 1923.

Kedar Nath Das Gupta's Dharma Mandala. The inaugural meeting in the United States was held at Carnegie Hall in 1928; the society's constitution advocated the cultivation of **dharma** (defined within the constitution as "that which promotes spiritual growth and evolution and leads to realization of the unsurpassable Good, the Supreme Worth") and greater cooperation and understanding between East and West.

Pandit Acharya's Temple of Yoga. Teaching in the United States from the 1920s through his death in 1949, Acharya founded the Yoga Research Institute in New York City but later moved to Long Island, where he ran the Temple, the Prana Press, and Hope Inc. He wrote several books and is remembered for his attempts to reformulate yogic terminology into more scientific jargon.

Rishi Krishnananda's Para-Vidya Center. Krishnananda came to the United States in 1920 and founded his center in Los Angeles in the 1930s; it later moved to New York City. He taught **hatha yoga** and a philosophy of self-realization based on the Upanishads.

Swami Brahmavidya's Transcendent-Science Society. Also known as Premel El Adaros, Brahmavidya seems to have been a Westerner but claimed to be the U.S. representative of the South India Brotherhood and the disciple of A. P. Mukerji. Founded around 1920, this society was one of the earliest American examples of the adoption of guru worship.

Swami A. P. Mukerji. A "Yogi of the South India Order," Swami Mukerji published the following books, first from London and later under the auspices of the "Yogi Publication Society" in Chicago: *Your Inner Forces; or, Hints on Soul Unfoldment* (1912); *The Doctrine and Practice of Yoga* (1922); and *Magnetic Force: How to Unfold the Psychic Forces Latent Within You* (1922).

Yogi Sant Rama Mandal's Universal Brotherhood Temple and School of Eastern Philosophy. Founded in San Francisco in the 1920s, Mandal taught the by-then usual blend of yogic postures and breathing, meditation and mantras, vegetarianism, and kundalini.[22]

This influx of Indian teachers was all but brought to a close by the restrictive immigration laws of 1917, 1921, and 1924, which made it nearly impossible for Asians to immigrate to the United States. The American thirst for Asian gurus, however, went underground without disappearing. When immigration laws relaxed again in 1965, interest in Asian religions immediately soared to new heights. In the interim, established groups like the Vedanta Society and the Self-Realization Fellowship continued to flourish, despite the restrictions that immigration laws placed on their ability to bring in freshly recruited teachers from India.

AMERICAN-BORN GURUS

In addition to teachers of Hinduism that were actually from India, there were a variety of American-born gurus teaching Hindu ideas with greater and lesser degrees of sincerity. Competing with South Asians for a market share were a variety of colorful impostors— Westerners outfitted as swamis in order to take advantage of the fad for Oriental wisdom. One of these was Pierre Bernard, founder of the American Order of Tantricks. Also known as Oom the Omnipotent, American-born Bernard exemplifies the legend of the con artist capitalizing on the Orientalist fantasies of unsuspecting widows. Like Tantra, his teachings included sexual practices. What else he may have known about Hinduism is unclear.

A more ambiguous example of this genre was William Walker Atkinson, a champion of New Thought who had a double life as the influential Yogi Ramacharaka. Atkinson had been a businessman and lawyer before becoming involved in New Thought in 1900; thereafter he became a prolific defender of the movement. Between 1900 and 1910, he churned out such characteristic New Thought titles as *Thought Force, The Law of the New Thought, Memory Culture, Thought Vibration, Self-Healing by Thought Force, Practical Mind-Reading, The Secret to Success, The Subconscious and Superconscious Planes of Mind, The Art of Logical Thinking, and The Psychology of Salesmanship*.[23] At the same time, as Yogi Ramacharaka, he penned *Hindu-Yogi Science of Breath* (1903), *Hatha Yoga* (1904), *Fourteen Lessons in Yogi Philosophy* (1905), and others in the same genre. Yogi Ramacharaka also offered a mail-order class and editions of the Bhagavad-Gita and the Upanishads. Even publishing insiders in the New Thought movement, like Horatio Dresser, sometimes believed Atkinson and Ramacharaka to be two separate individuals.

According to Carl T. Jackson, Atkinson/Ramacharaka was a surprisingly readable and thoughtful exponent of Hindu philosophy. Yogananda was probably influenced by his approach, which included grafting New Thought onto vedanta and explicating Indian ideas in "ordinary English terms." Like Ramacharaka, Yogananda packaged his teaching in mail-order lessons.

In *The Inner Teachings of the Philosophies and Religions of India,* Ramacharaka advocates a modern blend of Eastern and Western approaches, culled through reference to reason and personal experience:

> We belong to what is known as the ECLECTIC SCHOOL of Hindu
> Philosophy. . . . Eclectic, you know, means Selective; Chosen
> from various sources and systems . . . and is the very reverse of
> "Dogmatic" and "Sectarian." . . . We have many points of agree-
> ment with the Monistic school of the Vedanta; and points of
> common thought with Patanjali's Yoga schools; and also some
> points of agreement with Buddhism; but at the same time we
> take exception to many points put forth by each school."[24]

Atkinson must have chosen his pen name shrewdly, with the intention of increasing his readership and income by falsely assuming an Indian identity. And yet, he seems to have had true sympathy for the ideas he propagated.

In sum, after 1893, dalliance with Hindu ideas and gurus was acceptable—even fashionable—in certain liberal, educated circles. In 1941, Krishnalal Shridharani poked gentle fun at the Orientalist craze in his autobiography, relating an amusing anecdote in which an eccentric gentlewoman mistakes him for a swami simply because he is Indian by birth. He gives brief portraits of two so-called swamis, Swami Sulaiman and Yogi Tincanwalla, noting wryly that "a Tincanwalla's name can only belong to a Parsi, and thus he can hardly call himself a Yogi, any more than a Baptist preacher could call himself an Archbishop of Canterbury. . . . To a Hindu 'Swami Sulaiman' sounds as incongruous as 'Pope Bernstein.'"[25] Shridharani's witty observations are all the more keen for his being an ordinary citizen with an open eye, rather than a scholar or seeker. "There are fakirs galore in India, to whom God's name is a salable commodity to be bartered to the superstitious masses," he goes on, "but they are called Bahvas and always distinguished from Yogis and Rishis. With an understanding of all this, it is perhaps easier to grasp why the sensitivity of one brought up in the Hindu tradition is shocked when he finds some of his own countrymen in the United States dragging spiritual qualities down to the market place." Real swamis, Shridharani states from a traditional rather than modern Hindu position, are Hindu by birth, live remote and ascetic lives, do not charge for their services, and are given titles of respect by the faithful and never the teacher himself: the "designation comes unsought and falls in his lap like a ripe mango."

For all his reservations about the guru scene, Shridharani cautiously admits that the best Indian teachers have something of real value to offer Americans:

> Yet there is a case, as there is a place, for this transplanted clergy. They have gone a long way toward establishing a real community of religions. They have also brought the wisdom of the Hindus to a distant shore, and, unlike the Christian missionaries in the Orient, without any intention of proselytizing "the heathens." And very likely their greatest contribution lies in answering a dire American need. The uncertainties of an industrial economy, the speed and noise of the modern city, the dreadful stresses and strains of modern times have had their effects on countless Americans. To a few of these victims of modern "civilization" the Swamis do bring a serenity of mind by teaching the wisdom of a people who for centuries have lived peacefully in face of want.[26]

As an Indian, Shridharani fretted about the ways in which his own sacred traditions were being warped and watered down in the American marketplace. For Americans, however, what was "really" Hindu was of little importance compared to what worked for them. Swimming in the alternative stream of competing religious alternatives that I have mapped here, they were not interested in converting to traditional Hinduism. Instead, they wanted to mine the whole world for additional treasures that they could add to their toolbox of religious options. The most successful of the Indian teachers understood that and ran with it.

Thomas Tweed's article on the life of Marie de Souza Canavarro illustrates this mix-and-match approach to religious search. Canavarro (1849–1933), says Tweed, was "a paradigmatic spiritual seeker in an age of wandering."[27] She turned away from the Catholicism of her birth toward Theosophy, Buddhism, Baha'i, and, finally, Paramananda's Ananda Ashrama of the Vedanta Society. She did not see these associations as competing episodes in her religious development but, rather, an ongoing struggle to overcome sectarian narrowness and find instead a spiritual way of life that could include the best in all traditions and speak directly to her own experience of truth. To seekers like Canavarro, Christianity no longer seemed like the most plausible religious option:

> Between, say, 1880 and 1910 a significant number of Americans of European descent, most of them urban dwellers and middle class, began to find their inherited Judeo-Christian traditions unsatisfying for one reason or another. The acids of Darwinian theory and Biblical criticism, as well as the increased awareness of Asian religions, began to corrode the foundations of their faith. Some also complained—using pragmatic criteria to test religions—that Christianity had treated women unfairly and religions intolerantly. A portion of the disillusioned abandoned all religions. Most found a way to hold on to inherited faiths. Yet thousands of Americans turned to Asian traditions, especially Vedanta Hinduism and various forms of Buddhism. They did so for a variety of reasons. The alleged tolerance of Hinduism and Buddhism attracted many, and the foundations of the Indian worldview—with, for example, rebirth and karma instead of a creator and divine commands—seemed more compatible with the latest finding in the natural sciences. That worldview seemed more rational.[28]

It seemed more rational and also more tolerant. Canavarro's attraction to Paramananda was probably due to Paramananda's championship of religious inclusivism as his vedantic doctrine. Paramananda offered not a new religion but, rather, a new way of being religious, in which human universals of love and tolerance outweighed doctrine and ritual. "Many of these teachers of wisdom from abroad are more than lecturers, and yet can hardly be called founders of new cults," noted Wendell Thomas in 1930. "A fairly new religious form seems to be developing in America: something between a sacred community and a secular audience . . . a religious class that appeals chiefly to chronic 'seekers.'"[29]

Let us turn now to some concrete examples of this "new religious form."

NOTES

1. Lippy and Williams, eds., *Encyclopedia of American Religious Experience*, 579.
2. Gaustad, ed., *A Documentary History of Religion in America to the Civil War*, 289.
3. Taylor, "Swedenborgianism."
4. Gaustad, ed., *A Documentary History of Religion in America Since 1865*, 240.
5. From Evans' *The Mental Cure* (1869), quoted in Lippy and Williams, eds., *Encyclopedia of American Religious Experience*, 904.
6. Quoted in Ahlstrom, *A Religious History of the American People*, 1019.
7. From Evans, *The Divine Law of Cure* (1886), quoted in Gaustad, ed., *A Documentary History of Religion in America Since 1865*, 240.
8. Lippy and Williams, eds., *Encyclopedia of American Religious Experience*, 690.
9. Jackson, "The New Thought Movement and the Nineteenth Century Discovery of Oriental Philosophy," 528–529.
10. Dumenil, *Freemasonry and American Culture: 1880–1930*.
11. Ibid., 49.
12. Campbell, *Ancient Wisdom Revisited*, 6.
13. Ibid., 8.
14. Washington, *Madame Blavatsky's Baboon*, 69.
15. From Blavatsky, *Isis Unveiled* (1878), quoted in Campbell, *Ancient Wisdom Revisited*, 39.
16. Ibid., 42.
17. Jackson, *Vedanta for the West*, 62.
18. Seager, ed., *The World's Parliament of Religions*, xviii.
19. Ibid., 53.
20. Ibid., xxix.
21. Vivekananda, *The Complete Works of Swami Vivekananda*, Vol. 1, 24.

22. This list was compiled from Melton, "How New Is New? The Flowering of the 'New' Religious Consciousness since 1965"; Melton, *Encyclopedia of American Religion;* and Thomas, *Hinduism Invades America.*

23. Jackson, "The New Thought Movement and the Nineteenth Century Discovery of Oriental Philosophy," 538.

24. Ibid., 539.

25. Shridharani, *My India, My America,* 97.

26. Ibid., 99.

27. Tweed, "Inclusivism and the Spiritual Journey of Marie de Souza Canavarro," 44.

28. Ibid., 43.

29. Thomas, *Hinduism Invades America,* 185. As its title suggests, this book is not very sympathetic to Hinduism, especially given that it purports to be an academic history of Hinduism in America. Nonetheless, it remains the only such history for this time period. Despite his prejudiced tone, Thomas does display a grasp of the reforming and modern character of American forms of Hinduism, and he rightly distinguishes them from orthodox Indian Hinduism.

CHAPTER 4

Swami Paramananda

He's a twentieth century Swami,
For he drives a motorcar,
And those who've heard the Swami's word,
From near and from afar
Are loudest in their praises
Of his versatility;
Knows no defeat, each task he meets
With great facility.
We all attest his prowess
In the culinary art;
He milks the goats;
The best of poets,
He reaches every heart.
And here is the keynote,
The Swami's words we quote:
"If first you tune your vina well,
You'll strike no discordant note."[1]

This ditty, one of many comic songs sung at Ananda Ashrama, captures the spirit of the enterprise better than volumes of prose; to quote Sister Devamata, "It is peculiarly descriptive of the Swami with its intermingled humor and gravity." It also captures the gist of Paramananda's teaching: not doctrine, but a sacramental life in which work, play, and worship become indistinguishable. For Paramananda, the key to this transformation was **bhakti,** devotional and sacrificial love.

Although a monk for the rather conservative Ramakrishna Math and Mission, Paramananda was experimental, individualistic, playful, and egalitarian—in short, vividly, floridly Americanized. His unusual techniques often irritated his fellow monks, but his personalized approach was largely responsible for the success of his ministry. Many of his followers were strong-willed, well-educated American women with yearnings toward religious heroism and a vigorous distaste for the status quo—Srimata Gayatri Devi described the Sisterhood as made up of "rugged individualists, pure 'pioneer stock.'" Paramananda was peculiarly well suited to speaking to this sort of person.

Photographs of the Swami portray a cheerful and informal man. Unlike many of the posed, and imposing, photographs of the monks of the Ramakrishna order, Paramananda is often portrayed in action: hiking, playing sports, traveling, reading, playing with children and animals. He was handsome: tall and slender with boyish good looks, delicate features, a full mouth, and merry eyes. He was fond of fine clothes (always bought at bargain prices, we are told), and photographs show him in dapper suits in the latest fashion, in knee breeches, and wearing stylish caps. He liked sports, games, and cars, and was at least as fond of American pop songs as he was of Indian ragas. But, for all of his robust, democratic American style, his acquaintances were nonetheless impressed with his spiritual depth and personal charisma. It is said that, as a young monk, Paramananda stayed in a wealthy Bengali home in which the other young men were fond of gambling. Rather than condemning them, Paramananda joined in—and won. As the days progressed, the casual conversation slowly turned to spiritual matters, with the monk excitedly addressing religious issues when asked but not pushing the subject. Within a few weeks, the cards were forgotten altogether and the evening gatherings had become vedanta classes. This story, apocryphal or not, neatly illustrates the gentle manner in which the Swami preferred to work: in the world, but not completely of it.

Swami Paramananda

PARAMANANDA IN INDIA

Paramananda was born in 1884 in a small village in East Bengal, now Bangladesh. His father, Ananda Mohan, was progressive, although he found the Brahmos too radical in their rejection of Hinduism to join the society. He was a champion for women's rights and education and had little respect for caste restrictions. Paramananda's mother passed away when he was nine years old; Ananda Mohan reacted by becoming increasingly withdrawn from the world and spiritually minded. Paramananda was a sunny, loving child, well liked, and his father's favorite. Everyone assumed that he would go to university and shore up the family's flagging fortunes. Paramananda, however, was fascinated by the renunciant's life from an early age. He often read aloud to his father from religious texts; one that was particularly compelling for him was a collection of the *Sayings of Sri Ramakrishna.*

At sixteen, Paramananda had a mystical experience reminiscent of those of Vivekananda and Tagore. He never divulged the contents of the vision but was visibly affected for days afterward, staggering "around like a drunken youth, abstracted, changed in manner and mien. The world for him was no longer a playground but a prison, barring him from that beatific realm he had glimpsed."[2] Paramananda pled with his father to be allowed to make a pilgrimage to the Belur Math, and on his seventeenth birthday he left for Calcutta with a group of devotees from the village to see Vivekananda, newly returned from the West, and to celebrate Sri Ramakrishna's birthday. His first meeting with Vivekananda electrified him:

> I found myself face to face with a being quite different than anyone I had ever seen before, or even imagined in my vivid consciousness. He looked at me with his big, luminous eyes, which seemed to speak volumes without a single word. I was not formally introduced to the great master, but as my eyes met his lustrous spiritual gaze, I knew the feeling which swept me from head to foot was indelible.[3]

Paramananda returned briefly to the village, announcing that he planned to join the order. His family was bitterly opposed, and finally he ran away to join the Math. He would remain a monk of the Ramakrishna order until his death at the age of fifty-six.

This standard account of Paramananda's youth displays several key elements of the hagiographic style of modern Hinduism, which mixes traditional motifs with new elements. Indian saints are usually remembered as being well liked, bright, and mischievous in their youth, echoing the boyhood of Krishna. In a more traditional narrative (which Yogananda employs), the child is recognized very early on as a spiritual figure, with portents and miracles. Ramakrishna fits this traditional pattern, experiencing ecstasy at a very young age. Paramananda, like Vivekananda and Devendranath and Rabindranath Tagore, follows a more modern pattern in which spiritual realization is concurrent with reaching adolescence and the age of reason. The youth (not a child, like Ramakrishna, but a more sophisticated young man) starts his pilgrimage with the visceral realization that spirituality is something to be experienced firsthand, rather than accepted because of hearsay or dogma. The meeting with the guru is then the climax of this first act. It is often foreshadowed (Paramananda's attachment to *Sayings of Ramakrishna*) and often originally opposed by family (who are always eventually won over by the spiritual power of the young seeker).

PARAMANANDA'S EARLY YEARS IN THE UNITED STATES

By 1901, Vivekananda had all but retired, his former crusadership replaced with a more whimsical, withdrawn piety. He was fond of the new novice and impressed with his humble, cheerful disposition. Vivekananda initiated Paramananda himself, one of the last initiations he would perform before his death in 1902. He also assigned the novice to Swami Ramakrishnananda, then living in Madras with the hope of setting up a Mission outpost there. The choice was well made, for Ramakrishnananda's simple devotion to the Mother complemented Paramananda's loving, gentle nature. Paramananda spent most of the next five years in Madras, until in 1906 the order sent him to the United States to assist Swami Abhedananda's mission at the New York Vedanta Society.

In 1906, the two main Vedanta centers in the United States were in New York and San Francisco. They had both been founded by Vivekananda, experienced a few years of rapid decline after his departure for India, and both were revived by 1906 by successful monks, Swami Abhedananda in New York and Swami Trigunatita in San Francisco. Paramananda would, during the next two decades, establish active centers in Boston and near Los Angeles. Until 1930, the Ramakrishna movement in the United States clung to these few permanent centers, supplemented by a variety of smaller and more ephemeral beachheads in cities including Washington D.C., Providence, Chicago, and St. Louis. Between 1926 and 1936, the movement experienced a new wave of growth that led to permanent centers in cities such as Hollywood, Seattle, Portland, and Chicago.

Paramananda's three years in New York were a difficult introduction to his duties as a Vedanta monk in the United States. Abhedananda's style was diametrically opposed to that of his young assistant. A brilliant public speaker and intellectual, Abhedananda was also somewhat aloof with his disciples, preferring lectures to counseling. He was also a firm believer in modern organization, incorporating the society and instituting dues. While the New York Society grew considerably under his leadership, a group of disgruntled senior members wished the society had remained more like it originally had been under Vivekananda's direction, with a small core of enthusiastic disciples in direct contact with the guru. Paramananda's more intimate style was exactly what they were looking for, and bitter factionalism erupted between partisans of the **bhakta** (devotional) Paramananda and those of the **jnani** (intellectual) Abhedananda, culminating in Abhedananda's request at the end of 1908 that Paramananda leave the center. Paramananda moved to Boston, where he continued to work for the remainder of his life.

Paramananda's immediate popularity among American devotees, and the tension that his success produced between him and Abhedananda, speaks to what the American vedantists wanted and needed in a spiritual advisor. Of the two, Abhedananda was the better philosopher, theologian, and speaker. Like Vivekananda, he had an English-style education and a firm grasp of both Eastern and Western philosophy.[4] He was also a more organized administrator. Under his leadership, the New York Society greatly expanded its membership. Abhedananda routinely spoke to very large audiences. None of this precluded Paramananda's greater popularity with their shared audience; in fact, discord between Abhedananda and powerful members of his congregation preceded Paramananda's arrival and continued after his departure for Boston, culminating in the virtual collapse of the New York center in 1910. The Ramakrishna Math then ordered Abhedananda back to India; he refused, severing his ties with the institution. He taught in America independently until 1921, and then returned to India where he founded his own organization and repaired his ties with the Ramakrishna Math.

Abhedananda's failure in New York stemmed from his inability to establish warm personal relationships. He lacked the personal accessibility that a powerful inner core of American vedantists had come to expect from their experiences with Vivekananda. They objected, for example, to Abhedananda's extended absences from the center and the way in which a flood of new members diluted the original communal atmosphere of the New York Society. Ironically, Vivekananda had almost certainly lectured and traveled just as vigorously as Abhedananda, but he simultaneously managed to impart the impression of intimacy and concern.

In contrast to Abhedananda, Paramananda had a natural ability to make slight acquaintances feel loved, appreciated, and understood, and this ability meant more to the congregation than intellectual and administrative abilities. In a departure from the social scientific norm, I wish to call this ability *charisma,* using the colloquial rather than the sociological sense of the word (a choice that is discussed in Chapter 7). Paramananda was charismatic, as was Vivekananda before him; Abhedananda was not, and his congregation did not forgive him for it.

Boston served as Paramananda's base from 1909 until 1923. From 1923 until his death in 1940, he divided his time equally between Boston and California. It is difficult to summarize the daily routine of the Boston community, for there were changing residences, pastimes, and membership due to the mercurial whims of the young and disorganized Swami. For his first public lecture in Boston on January 24, 1909, Paramananda hired "a two-hundred-seat hall on Huntington Avenue and placed a two-line listing in the church page of the local newspapers: "VEDANTA PHILOSOPHY. Lecture, 'The Need of Religion' by Swami Paramananda of India.'" Fifty people attended the first week, but by the fourth Sunday "the hall was full, and many people were turned away."[5] Paramananda quarreled with Boston's vedanta enthusiasts early on; he was opposed to a large and formal organization and recruitment campaign, preferring instead to work with small groups that grew steadily.

A SCANDAL IN BOSTON

As discussed in the preceding chapter, by this time Asian religions were quite stylish in some avant-garde circles. This did not preclude, however, a considerable amount of prejudice and antipathy toward Hindu movements in mainstream society. Hostilities erupted in Boston soon after Paramananda's arrival, sparked by a media scandal concerning the will of Sara Bull. Mrs. Bull, the widow of a celebrated Norwegian violinist, ran a prestigious Boston salon that featured guests such as William James, Julia Ward Howe, Irving Babbitt, and the young Gertrude Stein.[6] She dabbled in Theosophy and New Thought before turning to vedanta in the mid-1890s. Mrs. Bull proved to be one of Vivekananda's staunchest (and most financially generous) supporters. She took vedanta very seriously, even joining a small group of American disciples on pilgrimage in northern India with Vivekananda in 1898. She not only helped pay for his American work, but also underwrote much of the expense of the construction of the Math's Belur headquarters outside Calcutta.

Mrs. Bull did not care for Abhedananda and was probably largely responsible for staging the failed coup in which Paramananda had been urged to take over the New York Society. He had visited her in Cambridge and was fond of her, and originally moved to Boston at her invitation. However, they fell out soon after his arrival. Mrs. Bull could be a very domineering woman and seems to have believed that Paramananda would be willing to implement her detailed plans for the new Boston Vedanta Society in exchange for financial backing. Instead, Paramananda insisted on full autonomy, and the two parted ways. The disagreement centered on how formal and organized the society would be; Paramananda wanted to let his mission in the city grow organically, at its own pace, rather than immediately facing a huge overhead and empty auditorium.

Two years later, Mrs. Bull died and left most of her $500,000 to the Ramakrishna Math and Mission in India. Her daughter contested the will, claiming that her mother was of "unsound and disordered mind" and under "undue influence." The case became a major newspaper scandal: "Maids and butlers offered lurid accounts of the goings on at 168 Brattle Street, how Indian swamis were received there, how their mistress kept a dimly lit meditation room decorated with 'pictures of fat swamis,' where she and her friends burned incense and sat in a suspicious hush which the servants called 'seances.'"[7] The will was overturned. Although the bad press hurt Paramananda's growing reputation as a gentlemanly representative of a venerable tradition, he was not discredited to the extent that he would have been if Mrs. Bull had been financing his Boston work. His name was never mentioned in court.

The Sara Bull scandal generated a series of outraged publications impugning the motives of American swamis, who were often portrayed as more interested in the bodies and pocketbooks of their wealthy, female devotees than in their souls. Racist sentiments were evoked, with references of "swarthy" priests exerting their irresistible charms over "clean-hearted" white women. A widely read representative of this genre was Elizabeth Reed's *Hinduism in Europe and America,* published in 1914. While some "swamis," like Oom the Omnipotent, probably did seduce their disciples, there is no evidence that any of the Vedanta Society leaders of this time period did so.

It is fair, however, to say that Paramananda was subverting bourgeois gender roles in a way that many people found alarming. In general, the Ramakrishna Math and Mission has taken a conservative position on women's rights; Ramakrishna warned his disciples against the twin evils of "women and gold." Vivekananda, however, radically rejected sexism, and Paramananda was the only vedanta representative in the United States to do the same. Both leaders offered women equal opportunity to devote their lives to

monasticism and full-time preoccupation with spiritual, philosophical, and social concerns. In doing so, they rejected the bourgeois Victorian assumption that a woman's place was always, and
strictly, in the home. Consider, for example, this letter from
Vivekananda, written to a young American woman contemplating
marriage:

> You ought not marry. . . . There are two sorts of persons in the
> world—the one strong-nerved, quiet, yielding to nature, not
> given to much imagination. . . . There are others, again, with
> high-strung nerves, tremendously imaginative, with intense feel-
> ing. . . . Of these alone what we call geniuses are made. . . . per-
> sons of this class, if they want to be great, must fight to be so—
> clear the deck for battle. No encumbrance—no marriage—no
> children, no undue attachment to anything except the one *idea,*
> and live and die for that. . . . You and Isabel are made of this
> metal—but let me tell you, though it is hard, *you are spoiling your
> lives in vain.*[8]

While Vivekananda's either/or option may seem harsh, it is
admirable that it never occurred to him that this woman was
unsuited to a life of heroic action in the world. Vivekananda and
Paramananda offered women with very few career options an
opportunity to embark on an exciting and exotic vocation in
which their gender would not be considered a relevant issue.
Paramananda even outstripped Vivekananda's dedication to
women's rights by giving all three of his top leadership roles to
women. Even though his followers were disproportionately
female, there were men available to whom he could have dele-
gated these tasks, if he had been so inclined.

Although Elizabeth Reed's charges of sexual impropriety were
based on ignorance and prejudice rather than on fact, it should
be granted that Paramananda was an attractive man, and his emotional ties with his close devotees were intimate. Even without sexual intimacy, it is probable that many of his female disciples
sublimated their romantic longings onto his idealized figure. For
some, a celibate life under the loving protection of a male guru

may have been a sort of psychological halfway house between traditional marriage and full independence.

Despite the unpleasant innuendos that followed Mrs. Bull's death, Paramananda's supporters continued to grow in number and distinction. By 1910, the financial patronage of the wealthy Katherine Sherman provided enough money to rent a small studio in an artsy district, where "Boston's Vedanta Centre gradually took shape. The Swami set up an impersonal altar in the studio and filled out the Sunday afternoon public services with readings from various Scriptures, music and meditation. He conducted two evening classes weekly, and a Saturday morning class on 'The Bible in the Light of the Vedanta.' On Monday afternoons he gave individual interviews to those who sought personal spiritual guidance."[9]

THE BOSTON VEDANTA CENTRE

After a few years of hardship and poverty, Paramananda was attracting enough wealthy patronage to establish an ashram in the prestigious Fenway area. The stately house and chic address improved his social standing; eleven years later, the community moved to even more impressive quarters. By 1914, Paramananda was not only speaking to fringe organizations like the Swedenborgians; the Unitarians, the Women's Educational and Industrial Union, and the First Parish Club also invited him to speak. He continued to shy away from aggressive solicitation of funds, but the money he received from his patrons was by that time supplemented by fees for speaking engagements and book sales. Between 1912 and 1914, the Boston Centre issued 10,000 books and pamphlets. In 1912, the Centre began issuing the magazine *Message from the East;* in its first issue, Paramananda reiterated his tolerant and ecumenical stance:

> In the name of the Supreme Being of the Universe we send out
> the Message of the East with the hope and prayer that it may
> bring a clearer understanding between East and West and that
> its spirit may so touch our hearts as to awaken therein Divine

harmony and peace. Uncharitableness, fanaticism and denuncia-
tion do not belong to the spiritual realm or, indeed, to true civilization; hence we should strive diligently to transcend them.
God grant that . . . we shall always welcome the message of Truth
with wholeheartedness, free from bias and prejudice, no matter
whence that message comes. Truth is truth whether it comes
from the East or the West. May we with the sword of wisdom
therefore cut down all the fictitious barriers that divide race
from race, country from country, creed from creed, and find
beneath them the underlying bond of unity.[10]

When in Boston, the Swami gave two Sunday services and
classes on Tuesday and Thursday evenings. The sisters, women
who lived in the Centre dedicating their lives to the Swami's work
as celibate renunciants, attended worship services with him daily.
Interestingly, Paramananda had both a public chapel and private
worship room. The public chapel was quite abstract in its presen-
tation—the altar centered on a plaque showing converging lotus
petals and the Sanskrit character Om, "a truly universal sign and
symbol of the divine."[11] Off the main room was the sanctuary or
shrine room, in which images of the deities were offered **puja** in
a more traditional, Indian manner. This, however, was a private
practice of the inner community, not one that was widely touted.
The chapel was modern, Western, and deeply Victorian. This
compromise illustrates Paramananda's ability and willingness to
adapt creatively to his new environment; he had a keen political
sense for when to placate American norms and when to stand firm
in his own tradition. A description of a dedication ceremony given
in 1929 illustrates the Westernized bourgeois propriety of the
community's public face:

> There was special music—voice, cello, flute and organ, and
> Negro spirituals sung by a professional colored quartet. This last
> was a striking feature of the program. Also Mr. Einar Hansen,
> one of the first violinists of the Boston symphony orchestra,
> played several numbers. In the morning the Swami gave to an

overflowing congregation the glowing message of "Universal Tolerance and Love."[12]

The sisters entertained guests, held services in the Swami's absence, cared for the shrine room, meditated and studied, cooked and cleaned. They operated the small press that published books, pamphlets, and the journal *Message of the East.* They also played: theater-going, ping-pong, kite-flying, and motoring. Here is Levinsky's summary of daily life in Paramananda's monastic order:

> Upon arising, each one was to meditate at her private altar in her own room. Then they gathered before the shrine for group worship, conducted by the Swami or, in his absence, Sister Devamata. After breakfast they set about their duties: maintaining the large house, chapel, and surrounding garden; publishing and distributing the *Message of the East,* as well as the ever-expanding list of books which bore the Swami's name; shopping and cooking for the community; and ministering to the shrine, which included dusting the altar, polishing the sacred vessels, arranging floral offerings, and preparing fruits and sweetmeats for the Lord. They met again for noon service, then dinner. In the afternoon, they might return to their tasks, or visit a sick member of the congregation, or take care of their personal washing and ironing, or practice the organ, or have a singing lesson, or take a drive with the Swami in his Franklin Sedan. Vesper service came at sundown. After a light supper they would gather in the community hall and listen to the gramophone, or Paramananda would read to them or sing Bengali songs, losing himself in the strains of love and longing for God.[13]

It is a pretty picture, if cloyingly Victorian to the modern reader.

Paramananda, so much the man of his time, embraced upper-class Edwardian values: chastity, purity, propriety, stiff-upper-lipness, cheer, and dignity. Pictures of his community sometimes strike one as just a little too precious—the group gathered around the piano singing hymns and drinking tea. Although he admired

Emerson and Tagore and revered the natural world as divine creation, he was uncomfortable with the biological dimension of human nature. For Paramananda, the life of the spirit was an ethereal thing, too fragile to be sullied by this coarse animal world. Perhaps it is this distaste for embodiment that makes it easy to imagine that he kept his vows of chastity and that his romance with the sisters was entirely sublimated. There is no hint of tantra in Paramananda's sentimentalism.

The sisters did not engage in any social service, other than modest financial support of Indian projects. Perhaps it is not surprising that Paramananda, haunted by memories of India's poverty, was not terribly moved by America's social ills. None of the three movements that we will survey emphasized social service, concentrating instead on the interior spiritual progress of the members and service to the community, its ideals, and their propagation.

Paramananda visited California in 1915. The audience there was receptive, but the nearby presence of other vedanta missions, and his Boston work, made moving west problematic. However, he continued to lecture in California frequently—especially when the Boston winters became too harsh. Of the many reasons California has become the American epicenter of Asian influence, its climate has not been entirely irrelevant; more than one Indian Swami has complained bitterly of the northeastern snows and felt more at home in the sun. In 1923, Paramananda purchased 140 rural acres outside La Crescenta in the foothills of the San Gabriel Mountains, 20 miles northeast of Los Angeles. He moved the bulk of his most devoted followers there and began a campaign to transform the land into both a working farm and a spiritual community. Paramananda enjoyed the outdoors and considered the natural world God's cathedral.

Throughout his public career, Paramananda traveled continually, giving lectures in most of the country's major cities. He normally punctuated his Boston–La Crescenta commute with speaking engagements in Cincinnati and Louisville. "In 1920, Paramananda traveled 22,000 miles by train and motorcar, circling the continent twice. Los Angeles. Seattle. Tacoma. Louisville. Buffalo. Philadelphia. New York. Cincinnati four times. . . . Sometimes he found himself addressing the most unlikely audiences, such as the Women's Suffrage Victory celebration in Los Angeles, or a crowd of nine hundred Masons in Buffalo. . . . During one cross-country tour in 1920, he gave twenty lectures in nine days."[14] He also traveled and spoke in Europe and Asia. He pioneered in radio preaching, broadcasting from Los Angeles in the 1930s. Public services routinely drew hundreds, and public lectures even more. His books reached thousands.

Despite all of this frenetic public activity, Paramananda was happiest and at his best in a smaller, more intimate setting. He had misgivings about the Western model of evangelism in which as many people as possible were exposed to his message. Instead, his ideal was that of the forest hermitage in which a chosen few lived in close proximity with the guru. He was distressed at the way Americans wandered in and out of his movement, and the bulk of his energy seems to have been directed toward shepherding his flock of monastics and the more dedicated lay supporters. This core group does not seem to have risen above a dozen at any given time.

PARAMANANDA'S DISCIPLES

Sister Devamata

Paramananda had met his first disciple in his early days in New York. Laura Franklin Glenn was forty at the time:

> A woman of brilliant intellect and culture, she had been born in Cincinnati of a prominent family, descended on her mother's side from Benjamin Franklin. After graduating from Vassar, for ten years she lived in Europe, studying at the Paris Sorbonne and other European academies. Religious and idealistic by nature, she tried a period as a lay sister in an Episcopal convent.[15]

Glenn heard Swami Vivekananda speak in New York in 1896 and
began regularly attending his lectures. While "troubling over her
aimless future," Glenn had a vision of two figures, one of whom
said: "Do not grieve. You have work to do for me." She later identi-
fied the figures as Sri Ramakrishna and Swami Paramananda. She
was initiated by Paramananda in 1907, becoming Sister Devamata.

Sister Devamata would become one of the mainstays of Paramananda's work. During their first year together, Devamata
copied out passages of Paramananda's letters to her into a notebook, which was published in 1907 as his first book, *The Path of
Devotion*. Much of what Paramananda wrote from that time
onward was transcribed and/or edited by Devamata, who also
wrote Paramananda's first biography, *Swami Paramananda and His
Work*. Much of our knowledge of Paramananda has been passed
on through her. In addition to writing and speaking well, Devamata was well versed in vedantic philosophy and had an unwaver-
ing devotion to her guru. She also studied in Madras under
Ramakrishnananda for almost two years, from late 1907 to Sep-
tember 1909. She had already known Vivekananda from his work
in New York; this trip gave her the opportunity to make pilgrim-
ages and to meet Ramakrishna's wife, Sarada Devi, and many of
the other monks. Paramananda depended on her to teach in his
absence, a role that would later be shared by other sisters.

In the early days of the community, Devamata used her experience as an Episcopal lay sister to model the lifestyle of the renunciants in her charge. She does not seem to have been a very
creative thinker and drew heavily on her memories of convent life
to recreate a proper spiritual community. She designed a habit
based on the classic Western model. She policed the novices, functioning from 1909 to 1922 as housemother for a well-meaning but
unruly pack of aspiring sisters. Both she and Paramananda were
in agreement that the communal life should be warm and joyous,
but at the same time dignified and orderly. Even with Devamata's
enforced order, the monastery was only barely able to accommodate so many colorful and willful personalities. Quarrels were not
uncommon.

Devamata's approach was different from Paramananda's. Paramananda did not believe in disciplinary actions; instead, he pleaded with his disciples to discipline themselves, to voluntarily become more and more holy in their daily lives. Srimata Gayatri Devi later described the approach as an "honor system," "which combines considerable personal freedom with self-imposed discipline. . . . One expects the best from oneself without pressure or fear of authority."[16] Devamata, in contrast, was a disciplinarian who watched carefully over the novices. Many of the sisters remembered resenting Devamata's authority at the time and appreciating it later; evidently, the unconscious division of labor between the swami and the senior sister was beneficial, setting up a system of authority that scapegoated Devamata while leaving Paramananda free to perform his role as the benevolent child of God. Her efficacy during those years is apparent in the contrast to the atmosphere of the community following her illness and semi-retirement; it was much more hectic and rancorous than the Boston Centre would have dreamed of being under Devamata's watch. During these years Paramananda treated her as an equal, and she often argued with him; behind her back, the sisters called her "But Swami." As the years went on, she seemed to become harsher rather than mellowing:

> Devamata was a woman tyrannized by "shoulds," for herself and
> others. . . . The foible of the strong is that they use their own
> strength as the parameter to judge all others; this lack of empa-
> thy for human weakness becomes their fatal weakness. Expect-
> ing perfection from others, Devamata became annoyed by their
> every lapse.[17]

In 1922, Devamata suffered a near-fatal illness; the doctors diagnosed encephalitis and said that nothing could be done. Devamata lived—which she and the community attributed to divine intervention—but never fully recovered, being partly paralyzed and confined to a wheelchair. She continued to write but had to relinquish her role as housemother.

Devamata's authority was eventually taken over by two other women: Sister Daya and Srimata Gayatri Devi. Like Devamata before them, they carried out all the official functions during the swami's frequent absences, conducting public worship and giving lectures and classes.

Sister Daya

Sister Daya, born Georgina Jones Walton, first met Paramananda in 1919 during one of his earlier speaking tours in California. She had been born in 1882, the child of a wealthy Nevada senator and a socialite. She moved to New York at twenty, working in a settlement house and writing poems; she later dramatized Sir Edwin Arnold's *The Light of Asia*. While there, she joined the Theosophical Society, where she met her husband; they moved back to California together in 1914. The marriage was not a happy one. Daya became increasingly uncomfortable with the occult aspects of Theosophy while her husband became increasingly engrossed in them, and a miscarriage and ongoing health problems crushed her hope of becoming a mother. By 1919, she was describing her state of mind as a "parched desert." Daya's description of her first encounter with Paramananda is worth quoting at length:

> I was asked to the dinner in order to meet this wise young teacher from the Orient with his age-old wisdom. My spiritual need was very great and my heart was crying out for genuine guidance.
>
> I looked forward to the meeting with an eagerness I myself could hardly understand. . . . I stood in the small parlor, waiting and listening for the Swami's approach. At last I heard his footsteps outside: firm, light and rhythmic, neither slow nor hurried. In another moment I had opened the door and he was in the room, his very presence like a light, conveying strength, beauty and peace.
>
> There was just one moment for greeting, one moment to introduce myself and ask a question which somehow I felt I could not ask after the others came into the room. Breathlessly,

and without preamble I blurted out, "Swami, tell me, how does the supreme vision come?" He looked at me tenderly and replied, "It comes gradually, just like a sunrise."[18]

Six months later, she had left her husband for the Boston Vedanta Centre. The Los Angeles Examiner ran a story with the headline "L.A. Society Woman Takes Veil of Indian Cult; Sister Daya Must Work as Servant." In fact, Daya's lack of preparation for household chores became a community joke; her cooking was so inedible that for years she voluntarily washed dishes rather than spoil the dinner. The rest of her life was devoted to the swami's work, with the exception of two years of withdrawal from 1937 to 1939.

Sister Daya was a perfect antithesis to Devamata's strict organizational genius. Hagiographic descriptions of her bring to mind Julie Andrews' character in *The Sound of Music*—loving, dynamic, disorganized, and spontaneous:

> Even in her mature years, she could become a little girl. At the seashore, with her head thrown back in excitement and glee, she would run to meet the high waves or spend hours gathering sea shells of many shapes and hues. Then with utmost care she would transfer them to the trunk of her car and take them home. On these occasions she would live in timelessness, often returning home late for her scheduled assignment, suddenly rushed and conscience-stricken.[19]

This anecdote shows how Daya was able to make real, in her own life, Paramananda's prayer for each individual: She transformed her dry, parched heart into one of joyous abundance. Nothing pained Paramananda more than the unhappiness of his disciples, and nothing gave him more satisfaction than to inspire a playful interlude. For example,

> He would surprise his community with the most ludicrous costumes, delighting some and shocking others. One time he was Hamlet, in long cloak and turndown collar, wandering about the house with a melancholy and philosophic mien. Another time he appeared on the landing as a European prince, bedecked

with jewels. Still again, he would scurry about as a French chef,
in tall hat and apron, waving a fan and exclaiming "It's very
warm in the kitchen! It's very warm in the kitchen!"

. . . "It is very hard to stay gloomy long near him," wrote
Georgina Walton four months after moving into the Centre. "He
begs us all to be happy. He says that the Vision of Blessedness
does not come to a depressed heart."[20]

This emphasis on the joy latent in the present moment infuses
Paramananda's biography and his writings. If Paramananda's goal
had been to cultivate merely the impression of sanctified bliss, one
could hardly imagine him imitating French chefs. He really
believed that innocent fun was holy, in and of itself, and that a
lighthearted and childlike person could find God sooner than a
serious and depressed one.

Another example of Paramananda's joyous approach to the
spiritual life is that of Mr. Doble. He and his wife began attending
the Vedanta Centre when he was deeply depressed by "a severe
financial crisis."[21] In order to draw him out of himself, Paramananda challenged him to a kite building and flying contest.
Soon, Mr. Doble had forgotten his business troubles and was
deeply engrossed in the project, down on his hands and knees on
the floor, constructing his kite. The contest was held at Revere
Beach: "The ostensible object was to bring down the other man's
kite, but the rivalry was forgotten as the two men, clad in knickers
and caps, ran along the shore maneuvering their creations amidst
the billowy clouds."[22] Paramananda's object was to draw Mr.
Doble out of his depression by re-engaging him in the world of
immediate life, rather than abstract anxieties concerning the past
and future. When Paramananda talked of "selflessness," he meant
this kind of practical orientation rather than any kind of subtle
metaphysics. He taught that the spiritually mature person directs
her energy outward, rather than floundering in self-absorption.

Srimata Gayatri Devi

Alongside Devamata and Daya, the third member of Paramananda's flock to assume a leadership role was his niece, Sri-

mata Gayatri Devi. Under Paramananda's guidance, she would become the first Indian woman to teach Vedanta in the West. Born in 1906, Gayatri was raised in a happy, progressive household in Dacca, in what is now Bangladesh. An idealist with big dreams from a young age, Gayatri was strongly influenced by Rabindranath Tagore and Gandhi as well as her beloved uncle and the Ramakrishna Math and Mission. When her father arranged for her to be married, she unhappily wrote to Paramananda and asked him to veto the plan; he cabled his opposition to the wedding, but it arrived too late. The marriage was unhappy but short; her husband died three years later in 1926. Paramananda, in India at the time, urged Gayatri to accompany him back to America, a proposal that shocked her in-laws, who considered her obligated to remain with them. She agonized over the decision, but in the end left to start a new life in America—an adventure that ended only with her death in 1995.

Gayatri Devi's personality comes across as more elusive than that of either Daya or Devamata, perhaps as a result of her Indian upbringing. She reports that during her first year with Paramananda she struggled with a skeptical attitude and a saucy tongue, but the other sisters describe her as modest, humble, and self-effacing. She was the only sister who never seemed to offend anyone; in a community often fraught with interpersonal irritation, this gracious and loving woman made friends everywhere. The Swami kept a close eye on her, spending more time personally tutoring her than any of his other charges. By the time of his death, he relied on her to carry on his work. All of the sisters assumed that Gayatri Devi would follow him as their spiritual leader. She made up for a lack of mercurial wit and intellectual brilliance with a self-sacrificing devotion to the cause and a huge heart. She did not have Paramananda's charisma but did possess all the organizational skills and sincerity of purpose that a second-generation movement could hope for. "She was a wise woman," one acquaintance of hers told me. "She definitely had a spiritual presence." Another observer said that Gayatri Devi "did possess her own charisma and engendered both devotion and respect from many who knew and followed her," adding that she combined "motherly devotion and sharp intelligence."

The wisdom of Paramananda's faith in Gayatri's leadership abilities is most clearly illustrated by the skillful way she handled the crisis with the Ramakrishna Math and Mission immediately following his death. By 1940, Vivekananda's organization had coagulated into a reactionary bureaucracy. Paramananda had been having uneasy relations with his parent organization for decades. Tensions often erupted between him and the other monks working in the United States. Most of the criticism revolved around the degree of freedom and authority he gave to his female followers. On one occasion Paramananda, Gayatri, and several other sisters visited Akhilananda's Providence Vedanta Society. Paramananda had hoped that Gayatri would be able to speak to the congregation, but she was denied access to the pulpit, causing the swami to blurt out, "Just think! You are the only Indian woman doing something in this country, and not one of them will recognize it. . . . Swamiji [Vivekananda] would have understood."[23]

Equal treatment of women was not the only cause of tension between Paramananda and the Belur Math. Some of the monks objected to Paramananda's interest in the finer things of life; on his visits to India, his opponents ridiculed his numerous pieces of luggage. He had little regard for the written bylaws of the Math. For example, although he considered ritual worship at the shrine an integral part of the community's life, he took creative liberties in streamlining the complicated processes involved. In *Vedanta in Practice*, Paramananda defends his approach with this allegory: An Indian holy man is distracted by his cat during his meditation, so he confines it in the next room. This goes on for a long time, until both master and cat pass away, leaving behind a disciple. The disciple, seeking to imitate his guru, then expends considerable effort trying to find the same kind of cat to tie up. Of this sort of ritualistic mindset, Paramananda says,

> We often make a similar blunder and, mistaking the non-essential for the essential, waste our forces in vain. Most of our religious disharmonies are the direct result of unassimilated ideas. Great souls do things with a certain purpose in view and their followers, not understanding the true spirit of their actions, misinterpret

them, often to their own hindrance. Rituals and ceremonies should not be our main object in worship, but should be regarded only as helps towards the goal.[24]

In this passage, one can see how Paramananda defends a rationalized approach to spiritual practice and projects his orientation onto the great religious teachers of the past: "Great souls do things with a certain purpose in view." It is sometimes argued that premodern or primitive religious specialists work from a prerational state of mind, with no conscious understanding of the symbolism they employ or why those symbols should move people as they do. I am inclined, however, to agree with Paramananda. Putting aside petty officials in established religions, the "great souls" have always, in any age, been reflective about their motives and purpose, and this clarity of thought is part of what produces charisma. As Paramananda points out, the actions seem mysterious and magical to the followers, but have rational explanations from the viewpoint of the religious virtuoso. The quotation above also illustrates Paramananda's "industrial age" mentality: sorting the essential from inessential acts in order to increase productivity and efficiency.

While Paramananda's Americanized approach bolstered his work, it alienated more conservative fellow monks. Paramananda did not like formality in personal relations any better than formality in ritual, and once he offended Swami Prabhavananda by introducing him casually as "a fellow countryman." (Prabhavananda's Hollywood bookshop refused to stock Paramananda's works until after Prabhavananda's death in 1976.) When the intellectual and traditional Swami Akhilananda was assigned as Paramananda's assistant in 1926, relations were so divisive that he left acrimoniously after a year to start his own center, replaying Paramananda's own drama with Abhedananda in New York twenty years earlier.

When Paramananda died, the entire community rallied around Gayatri Devi's leadership and refused to accept a new swami from the Belur Math. Gayatri begged the Math to acknowledge Paramananda's three centers (in Boston, Cohasset, and La

Crescenta) as a Sisterhood, but the Math refused and the centers were forced to withdraw from the organization. The crisis was painful for Gayatri, but she was certain that she was following the wish of her guru: "I can truthfully say that that story is written in the black letters of a soul's dark night, which lasted several months and seemed like aeons. We did not separate happily; instead, we obeyed the order issued by the authorities involved."[25] Gayatri, the first female head of a Hindu community in the United States, continued to lead the communities until her death in 1995.

Following Gayatri's death, the community went through a difficult period of reorganization. By 1999, Ananda Ashrama and the Vedanta Centre of Cohasset had stabilized and rebounded under the leadership of Reverend Mother Sudha Puri Devi. As of the summer of 2000, Mother Sudha oversaw five monastics, including one novice, and a robust lay membership of almost 1,000 members.

PARAMANANDA'S SPIRITUAL MESSAGE

Having reviewed the history of Paramananda's American work and the key personalities involved, let us retrace our steps and consider in turn his teachings. His message changed little during his thirty-six years in the States. Doctrinally, Paramananda faithfully taught Vivekananda's vedanta with only a few shifts in emphasis. He believed that the essence of all things is One and that it is equally valid to conceptualize that One as impersonal (as the Supreme, Reality, Truth, or Self) or personal (as Mother or Lord). He called this spiritual essence, at different points in his poetry, the Abiding Presence, the Spirit of the Universe, the Spirit of Love, the Breath of Our Life, the Cosmic Source, the Divine Spirit, Love, Abode of Peace, and the Inner Light. His favorite name, though, was Mother:

> If we would worship Him we must do so through some form.
> All, however, cannot Love Him in the same form or approach
> Him in the same relation, because we have varying tendencies.
> Of all the relations we know in the world, however, the relation

of the mother with her child is the holiest and highest, as well as the most universal. . . . Our Mother is the Mother of the whole universe."[26]

It is worth pausing to reflect on how extraordinary these words must have seemed to American readers when published in 1912, eight years before the Nineteenth Amendment granted suffrage to all American women. Of the many contributions that Hindu gurus made to the American religious counterculture in the first half of the century, perhaps this is one of the most radical. While Paramananda uses masculine pronouns for the Divine in this quote, and in the half of the essay that precedes it, from this statement on he uses feminine pronouns for the Supreme Being throughout.

The words Paramananda used to refer to God pointed only in the general direction of a phenomenon, a perception that Paramananda experienced as real: "Some call him Father, some Mother, others Master, or Lord, or Friend; but all worship the same Supreme Being, from whom the whole universe has come forth."[27] Paramananda reports that this presence has to do with bliss, compassion, life, light, perfection, wisdom. Paramananda's Mother is "free of all grief, impurity, all ignorance" and is the "source of all light, wisdom and blessing."[28]

Paramananda taught that the higher soul of the individual is divinely perfect; only ignorance and lack of will keep the individual from realizing this. Like Ramakrishna, Paramananda seems to have conceived the relationship between the individual soul and the Supreme Self as **bhedabheda,** both different and not different:

> Since Thy asking I have emptied my heart of self.
> Now it is full! Yea, it is full of the inexpressible.
> At Thy Will, I have cast off self, yet I am!
> I have given up life, yet I live!
> Yea, I live now, not separate
> But in wholeness of Thy life.[29]

The true self of the individual is one with the Mother, but the perception of difference is not illusory. At issue is the definition of *real*. When Paramananda and other neo-vedantists used the word *real,* they used it to refer to things that were permanent and unchanging. Distinctions between objects are "unreal" in the sense that they are finite and temporary. The unity between things is infinite and permanent and therefore "real." While Indian philosophy can get very technical and hard to follow on these issues, Paramananda was not a philosopher by nature and was content with the basic gist outlined here.

Through concentration, discipline, devotion, and self-sacrifice, any individual can shift the center of his or her consciousness out of the false, egotistical self and into the expansive, universal Self. Doing so brings a continual flood of bliss, peace, happiness, and power. "By meditating on the Supreme Being of the Universe, by worshipping Him, by offering all our prayers to Him . . . the Yogi attains to that state of consciousness which is the goal of all spiritual practice—the state of complete illumination."[30] Paramananda called his method of disciplining the mind "meditation." America's religious counterculture uses this word to refer to a wide spectrum of activities, none of which nicely correspond with the standard dictionary definitions of "to meditate," for example, to reflect on, contemplate, consider at length, or plan in the mind. All of these synonyms suggest intellectual activity, and meditation is being used here to mean a type of mental activity that bypasses intellectual analysis. In religious circles, "meditation" refers to mental exercises designed to train the mind to function in a different and more effective manner. The goal is generally to quiet the practitioner's banal, incessant, half-conscious, internal dialogue so that the mind becomes peaceful and clear, like a deep pool. Different schools have different meditative techniques. Some, like Krishnamurti, seek a state of total mental relaxation in which all intellectual functions cease. Others, like Paramananda, seek to concentrate the mind into a single focused and sustained image to the exclusion of all other thoughts. The latter practice is more common among devotional theists, who often understand meditation as a silent remembrance of the Divine combined with a patient yet expectant waiting for spiritual revelation. For the theist, prayer is talking to God. Meditation is listening.

Paramananda describes meditation as "a constant remembrance of the object we meditate upon."[31] Although Paramananda was familiar with meditation techniques that focused attention on the Self—the Divine within—he normally recommended that the disciple focus attention on an external Lord. Even if the ultimate vision showed the internal soul and the infinite oversoul to be one in essence, Paramananda thought that beginners, at least, were more likely to benefit from the adoration of an idealized Other. "When we maintain this kind of [constant] remembrance in relation to the Supreme Being, then all the bonds of the heart break and it becomes illumined by the presence of the Self. Through meditation we feel the nearness of Divinity. There is *no other way* to reach Him" [italics added]. Or again, "The thing necessary is for us to feel intense love in our hearts for this Supreme Self or God; otherwise He is not attainable."[32] In *Vedanta in Practice,* published in 1908, Paramananda called this final goal of the spiritual life "self-realization." Yogananda almost certainly read the booklet, and this may have been where he got the phrase.

Paramananda's emphasis on devotion as the truest path toward spiritual realization suggests that he rejected Vivekananda's four-fold path of *jnana* (intellect), *bhakti* (devotion), *karma* (service), and *raja* (physical discipline). Vivekananda held that each individual personality is best suited to one of these four paths. While I do not believe that Paramananda consciously rejected Vivekananda's doctrine (he did not like to think of himself as an originator but, rather, as a faithful interpreter), he downplayed the jnana and raja paths.

Paramananda did teach Vivekenanda's interpretation of Patanjali's school of yoga, which he called raja yoga. In Vivekananda's raja yoga, ethical behavior, spiritual and psychological disciplines, traditional postures, and breathing exercises are employed simultaneously to produce **samadhi,** a state in which the true self transcends ego identity and merges with the universal

Self. Paramananda taught simple physical postures and breathing exercises that he believed aided meditation and promoted physical well-being. Unlike Yogananda, however, he characterized these practices as being of limited usefulness:

> It is not possible for me to take up here any intricate methods of breathing, although the various methods of controlling the breath and thereby restoring the equilibrium of the body were made a great science in Indian psychology. It recognized that this body is the instrument through which we have to work out our salvation. If it is out of order, it becomes a serious hindrance. When the body is disturbed, it is difficult to forget it; and if we are constantly thinking of the body, we have not time to think of higher things. A healthy person is one who is least conscious of the body.[33]

Attention to the body, then, is a preliminary step that clears the way for the real work, rather than a path toward God that is of equal weight to the devotional life.

Likewise, Paramananda does not reject outright the jnana and karma paths toward God:

> The first class—the workers—by entire unselfishness, by giving their labor freely without thought of personal gain, making every deed an act of worship, are purified in heart and attain realization. The second class—the *Bhaktas* or devotees—by worshipping the Lord with intense single-hearted devotion reach union with the Divine Object of their worship and attain realization. The third class—the *Jnanis*—take the hardest way to reach the goal. Rigid self-control and constant self-denial alone can carry them on the way. Only the strong, mentally and physically, can travel by this road; but he who is determined and perseveres to the end arrives at realization of the Self. He sees It dwelling in every living thing, and thus seeing the Self everywhere and knowing his oneness with It, he cannot hate or injure any being.[34]

He does, however, recommend bhakti as a more universal path; jnana is "the hardest way." Although he enjoyed intellectual pursuits—he wrote a book comparing Emerson and Plato—Paramananda was skeptical of the usefulness of book learning for spiritual growth, and this skepticism is related to his personal feeling that bhakti is more effective than jnana. Perhaps his beliefs on this matter stem from his youthful contact with Vivekananda. Vivekananda had been stridently jnani as a young man, but around 1897 had a conversion experience, after which he withdrew into semiretirement and renounced his intellectualism, trading it for simple devotionalism. It was after this conversion that Paramananda met him.

Regardless of the path used to reach the goal, once there the "self-realized" individual does not lose conscious touch with the phenomenal world (as Ramakrishna did while in samadhi) but functions as a saint, moving in society in perfect rhythm with the Spirit and imparting blessings and healing. Paramananda emphasized loving service to others and wholehearted devotion to the Supreme:

> Love is a divine essence.
> Its inbreathing is life.
> What is opposed to love is enemy of life.   •
> Those who love truly, they live;
> For love abounds in unending life.
> Live and love!
> Love and live!
> Where love reigns death can never be.
> Love is mother of both joy and peace;
> From that heart where love always lives
> peace and joy will never part.[35]

The key to loving other people was to be entirely in love with the Mother. If the devotee could continually remember love for the Divine, loving service to humans (who are, after all, Her children and our siblings) would inevitably follow. Compassionate action in the world was not merely optional, or something to do in addition to worship, but a natural outcome of the worshipful attitude. This did not necessarily imply service to the world in general but, rather, service to the concrete individuals that life throws in one's path. Paramananda did not insist that his followers devote their lives to helping strangers, but he did insist that they behave lovingly toward the people around them. Loving real people is both more difficult and more effective than loving the abstract stranger. It is easier to smile at the old woman you are helping across the street than at the old woman with whom you share a room.

For Paramananda, the transcendence of self had less to do with esoteric or intellectual change; rather, it required a simple change of focus from narcissistic preoccupation with the ego to engagement with the outside world and other people. Levinsky gives this example:

> One stormy evening, for example, Sister Seva, troubled with some grievance, voiced her complaint to the Swami while he gazed meditatively out of the window, which was all jeweled by the rain. When she had finished, his only reply was, "See how beautiful the raindrops look as they run down the screen!" "Have you ever noticed," he would say, "that when the barrier of self is removed from someone who has been struggling, suffering, and is full of discontent, that he becomes a different person altogether? The whole picture changes."[36]

For Paramananda, transcending the ego was not an esoteric doctrine for the few but a psychological orientation that could be achieved by anyone given enough patience, discipline, and love:

> Here is the true secret of happiness: Forget yourself and think of others. I don't know that I have ever expressed it this way before, but I feel it is the true way. In my life, my moments of greatest happiness have been when I have forgotten myself completely in serving others. When you feel dull and heavy and depressed, it is because you are thinking of yourself. . . .

My greatest consolation and inspiration have been when I have found something in myself to give, even when I have been in the depth of misery, whether physical or otherwise. When somebody comes to me in distress and I am instrumental in just doing something for them, that all goes away. I am electrified; that is the secret.[37]

It would be a mistake to confuse here the struggle against narcissism with the disavowal of individualism. Paramananda strove to keep self and other in creative tension, rather than sacrificing either to an extreme. Paramananda encouraged his disciples to express themselves creatively and to follow their intuitions and inclinations in crafting a personal method of serving God and humanity. In this he followed the lead of Rabindranath Tagore, whom he admired; Tagore was an eloquent defender of the Romantic spiritualization of the particular—of "eternity in an hour." For example, if Sister Seva could forget her pain by noticing and celebrating the patterns of raindrops on the window, then in like fashion a sister's annoyance with Seva's imperfections could be overcome by noticing and celebrating her uniqueness as an individual. Perfection meant realizing the unique role God had created for each individual, rather than disregarding singularity in favor of uniformity:

It does not make any difference what you call yourself; be something that satisfies your own soul. Do not always look around to see whether your friend or your neighbor or the public approves; gain the sanction of your inmost being. The recognition that you desire from others, seek it from within. Be strong; stand up; never deny the fact that you have in yourself the power to put this ideal into practice. Once you learn to love and cherish the God-part within you, your very countenance will show how your life is transformed. Awaken that love in your soul and you will be invincible.[38]

Universal love, in this passage, lends strength and authenticity to individuality, rather than effacing it.

Individual transformation, according to Paramananda, was not spontaneous but the fruit of sustained discipline and concentration. He saw the spiritual path as a painfully difficult one, if unimaginably rewarding at the end. He was not naive about the difficulties of life in general or of the monastic life in particular, and continually pushed his followers toward a disciplined, courageous attitude. He wanted his disciples to think of themselves as soldiers, recalling the language of St. Paul. Also like Paul, Paramananda believed that the hard-won rewards of the disciplined spiritual fight were the fruits of the spirit, tangible results: "But at last through the earnest struggle of the soul, a channel is opened. . . . In him alone we see true fearlessness, uprightness, purity, truthfulness, and the absence of all anger and passions. Through self-control he becomes peaceful and happy."[39] The struggle may be hard, but the victory is inevitable.

Although technically a monist, Paramananda often used dualistic imagery to get his point across. His conception of evil is entirely practical, exhibiting the timeless indifference to philosophical subtleties that true believers can pull off with grace and security. "Indian conception does not admit two forces—one, God, and the other, devil. . . . When the sun shines, the darkness vanishes."[40] The "good" is "real" in the sense that it is infinite and changeless, whereas evil is always finite in both space and time and therefore "unreal." That being said, there is nonetheless a very sharp distinction in Paramananda's thought between good and bad; the spiritual life consists mainly in learning how to distinguish one from the other and, having done so, to choose the good.

Paramananda believed that the Divine is a real, tangible presence and that the goal of spiritual life is learning how to attune one's soul and life to the power and compassion of the Spirit:

> At the core of the Swami's teaching was the principle of living "in rhythm": "If you are in right rhythm, all things will flow under your hand." Accidents, he taught us, were almost always due to lack of right rhythm.
>
> "One must *feel* in the world of religion," the Swami would often say. "Spirituality is a matter of feeling." For this reason he

told us we should try to create an atmosphere of beauty and holiness, especially in places of worship, so that the mind may be attracted to contemplation and inner awareness. Nothing should be done mechanically. A sense of sanctity should enter into everything. He taught us that even the hair on our head was not our own—nor our hands nor our feet, nor any part of us. They were God's and should be treated as such. They should be kept clean, pure and worthy. Our bedrooms, too, were to be cared for as though they were a shrine. "If your rooms were untidy," he would say, "and I should come in, how would you feel? There is One far loftier than I who may come night or day. So we must be ready."[41]

As in many strands of Asian religious philosophy, the monism that Paramananda taught does not lead to nihilism or moral relativism. Instead, it is assumed a priori that the "real"—the Divine essence that lies at the heart of all things, unifying them—is fundamentally good, the source of all bliss and compassion. Evil, while "unreal" in a philosophical sense, is entirely real in the everyday world of practical affairs, as the outcome of ignorance and hatred and as a field of human practice that the spiritual seeker must avoid. In other words, although everything is in theory and at root unified, not all actions are equally good and desirable. Evil is not to be hated or feared, merely avoided whenever possible.

Paramananda's dual emphasis on sacrificial love and optimistic, moderate self-discipline does much to explain why he was particularly drawn to the Buddha and Christ; while always a child of the Mother, Siddhartha and Jesus were his favorite templates for the well-lived life:

If you were to ask me, are you a Christian? I should say no. If you were to ask me, are you a Buddhist? I should again say no; yet I can say sincerely from my heart that I am a devout follower of both these ideals, and to me there is no difference between them. All great faiths are the expression of the one great cosmic Spirit coming down to man to show him his relationship with the Divine.[42]

Whether or not the Buddha was, in fact, an expression of one great cosmic Spirit is irrelevant. Many Buddhists would take issue with this statement. Perhaps the Buddha would have too; or perhaps he and Paramananda would have contentedly ambled over the California foothills in amiable silence, had they been contemporaries. Without meaning to belie the historical and contextual particularity of each and every individual religious quest, I wish to draw attention to the underlying attraction of Paramananda's universalism. In a world containing too many religions, a frightening and overbearing variety of philosophical options, Paramananda clung to the very simple idea that there is, under it all, a single reality, and, if the descriptions of it differ, the fault lay in the descriptions rather than the substance. This is why he thought of himself as a Universalist first and a Hindu second.

> I am not seeking to establish a new cult or creed. There are
> plenty of creeds already existent; another would be only one too
> many. Nor am I interested in a new dogma or in occult myster-
> ies. I have only one fundamental interest uppermost in my heart
> and that is interest in humanity, its betterment, its unfoldment,
> its all-embracing unity. With these lofty and noble ideals we have
> established this work.[43]

"The one great cosmic Spirit" was as real to Paramananda as he was to himself, as real as Sister Daya, as real as the ashram's fruit trees. He was unshakably certain that it was the source of all love, mercy, and hope. Therefore, wherever human history and behavior demonstrated the fruits of the Spirit, he saw Spirit and was too busy acting and loving to bother much about how to critically analyze that experiential reality.

PARAMANANDA'S LEGACY

If one symbol could summarize Paramananda's American mission, it would be his Temple of the Universal Spirit, constructed at the La Crescenta Ananda Ashrama in 1928. Paramananda had been dreaming for years of constructing it, as had Vivekananda before him: "[Vivekananda] very much wanted to build a 'Temple Universal' where people of all faiths would gather to worship the Godhead through the symbol *Om,* representing the undifferentiated Absolute."[44] Rabindranath Tagore, who Paramananda admired, had built a similar temple on the campus of his Bengali college.

Set against the natural splendor of the ashram's forested hills, the peaceful courtyard complex still stands as a tribute to Paramananda's universalizing vision. Devamata's loving and proud description makes it sound grand; in truth, much of the temple's charm lies in its simplicity and the way it seems to spring naturally from the mountain.

> Over the high doors of the Temple is the inscription in illuminated letters, "Truth is One." The same note of universality is sounded in every detail of the interior. In each leaded window is a stained glass inset depicting an historical place of worship representative of some one of the great religions of the world— Christianity, Buddhism, Hinduism, Mohammedanism, Judaism, Shintoism; the Greek, Chinese and Egyptian faiths. This was conceived by the Swami as an expression of his fundamental conviction that as the same light passes through all these windows—symbolic of different creeds—so the one Truth shines in and through all religions.
>
> Beneath the windows and alternating with them are arched niches further symbolizing the ideal of universality. Each niche contains passages from some one of the great Scriptures of the world, written in illuminated letters. Over each quotation is a symbol of the faith represented. At the east end of the Temple is the sanctuary where a beautiful altar stands with this inscription above its arch, "Where I Am There is Peace." On either side of the steps leading to the sanctuary, against the wainscoted wall, are pictures or statues of great spiritual teachers. Thus the whole Temple proclaims the sole tenet of the Swami's creed, "Truth is One; men call it by various names."[45]

Paramananda had dreamt of this temple for much of his adult life, and its final construction gave tangible, symbolic form to so many of his themes: the graceful order of human civilization balanced against the forces of nature; the unity and harmony of all religions; the unity of truth; his continuing focus on his vedantic background, balanced against his religious tolerance; and the easy interdependence of the social, spiritual, and intellectual spheres.

The Vedanta Society movement in America was the most organized, public, and successful Hindu movement in America before 1965. Many of its other swamis had careers that were just as successful; interested readers should turn to Carl T. Jackson's excellent history of the movement, *Vedanta for the West*. I have focused on Paramananda because his hagiography celebrates a life that was particularly successful at balancing traditional and modern, Indian and American, heritages into a synthesis. Doubtless, behind the hagiography lies a biography fraught with greater ambiguity and troubling mistakes. Nonetheless, Paramananda's intimates and social acquaintances alike insisted overwhelmingly that he was saintly in his nature. It seems that he was able to use a very modern, tolerant, abstract belief system to live a remarkably kindhearted and joyful life. As we will see in subsequent chapters, Yogananda was kind and sincere, yet his beliefs were not compatible with a scientific worldview, whereas Krishnamurti, for all his intellectual prowess, had difficulty maintaining intimate relationships. Paramananda, in contrast, sought to balance rationality and compassion whenever possible, while opting for the latter where a balance could not be reached.

NOTES

1. Devamata. *Swami Paramananda and His Work,* 309. A vina is a musical instrument from India.
2. Levinsky, *A Bridge of Dreams,* 34. I have drawn heavily on this delightful book.
3. Levinsky, 37.
4. Jackson, *Vedanta for the West,* 50.
5. Levinsky, *A Bridge of Dreams,* 127.
6. Ibid., 90.

7. Ibid., 119.

8. Nikhilananda, *Vivekananda: A Biography,* 202.

9. Levinsky, 156.

10. Ibid., 174.

11. Devamata, *Swami Paramananda and His Work,* 183.

12. Ibid., 103.

13. Levinsky, 231.

14. Ibid., 224.

15. Ibid., 94.

16. Devi, *One Life's Pilgrimage,* 23.

17. Levinsky, 256–257.

18. Daya, *The Guru and the Disciple,* 2–3.

19. Ibid. Quoted from the introduction by Gayatri Devi.

20. Levinsky, 232–233.

21. Ibid., 243.

22. Ibid., 244.

23. Ibid., 549.

24. Paramananda, *Vedanta in Practice,* 39.

25. Devi, *One Life's Pilgrimage,* 15–16.

26. Paramananda, "God as Mother," 156.

27. Ibid., 156.

28. Paramananda, *Vedanta in Practice,* 17.

29. Paramananda, *Soul's Secret Door,* 54.

30. Paramananda, *Vedanta in Practice,* 17.

31. Paramananda, *Vedanta in Practice,* 70–71.

32. Ibid., 78.

33. Paramananda, *Spiritual Healing,* 29–30.

34. Levinsky, 87.

35. Paramananda, *The Vigil,* 72.

36. Levinsky, 243.

37. Ibid., 245.

38. Quoted in Devi, *One Life's Pilgrimage,* 152.

39. Paramananda, *Vedanta in Practice,* 35.

40. Paramananda, *Christ and Oriental Ideals,* 28.

41. Daya, *The Guru and the Disciple,* 6–7.

42. Ibid., 18–19.

43. Levinsky, *A Bridge of Dreams,* 154.

44. Nikhilananda, *Vivekananda: A Biography,* 188.

45. Devamata, *Swami Paramananda and His Work,* 61.

CHAPTER 5

Paramahansa Yogananda

Paramahansa Yogananda's *Autobiography of a Yogi* is a minor countercultural classic; from its publication in 1946 to the present day, it has intoxicated readers with its magical worldview. The *Autobiography* describes a world in which gurus levitate, raise the dead, live for hundreds of years, bilocate, read minds, and materialize palaces. Intertwined with these miracles is a philosophy of yoga that is a brilliant mixture of tradition and modernity, a magical and ancient worldview that has been rearticulated for the consumption of modern masses. Plot and philosophy are held together, transformed by an exuberant joy of being, an infectiously narrated ambiance that suggests, even to the most callous reader, a sense of the way life ought to be, even if it is not.

This underlying sweetness can make it difficult for the skeptic to interpret Yogananda's seemingly outrageous claims. It is sometimes assumed that there is a correlation between a religious teacher's goodness and factual reliability, but the study of Yogananda suggests that this does not always need to be the case. From the social scientific perspective, Yogananda makes claims concerning the spiritual world that can seem very hard to accept at face value. For example, he says, "Among the fallen dark angels, expelled from other worlds, friction and war take place with lifetronic bombs or mental mantric vibratory rays."[1] Such a statement is more difficult to reconcile with the scientific worldview than a statement concerning ethics like "love one another." Yogananda taught that he had literal, reliable information concerning the nature of the universe; he taught that he was fully enlightened and, therefore, perfect and not capable of error. He also presented himself as a miracle worker and the observer of many miraculous events. While some scholars think that it is most appropriate to simply accept these statements, since we cannot know for certain whether they are true, a critical scholar applying the social scientific perspective might question whether these claims should be taken as the literal truth. These difficult choices concerning interpretive strategy were less important in the preceding chapter, since Paramananda did not claim to be perfect and rarely referred to miraculous events that seem at odds with the scientific worldview. Since Yogananda stressed these events so strongly, however, we can no longer skirt the issue of how to best understand miracle stories in the academic study of religion.

We can start by noting that one of the following statements must be the case, and which one we pick will determine our interpretive strategy:

1. The miracles Yogananda describes are literally true.

2. They did not "really" happen as Yogananda perceived them, but he genuinely believed that they did and is therefore entirely honest in his account of them.

3. They did not "really" happen, and Yogananda knows this, but he is using these stories as metaphorical pedagogical devices. In other words, he is engaging in a mode of discourse in which literalist definitions of truth and falsity are irrelevant.

4. Yogananda just plain lied.

In the end, each student must make his or her own decision concerning which of these four options is the most likely. It is possible

Paramahansa Yogananda

that each was true at different points over the course of Yogananda's life. It is also reasonable to withhold judgment on this matter altogether, as scholars do when they employ the phenomenological approach to the study of religion. When I suggest psychological and sociological theories concerning how to interpret miracle stories from a critical perspective, I only intend to expand each reader's interpretive options and to remind the reader that events can look quite different depending on one's point of view.

The following account of Yogananda's life is based solely on hagiographic accounts, as scholarly biographies are not available.

YOGANANDA'S EARLY LIFE

Yogananda was born Mukunda Lal Ghosh in 1893, the year Vivekananda went to Chicago. His parents were Bengali bhadralok and his father a railway executive. He was raised in Calcutta, and his autobiography describes his childhood with classical piety; like Krishna, he was playful and beloved. He did poorly in school but wished from an early age to follow a religious life. His affectionate and doting mother died when he was eleven, leaving him in the care of a stern, ascetic, and religiously minded father.

Yogananda's childhood was filled with visions, small miracles, and portents, such as the following, which occurred when he was about eight:

> Shortly after my healing through the potency of the guru's picture, I had an influential spiritual vision. Sitting on my bed one morning, I fell into a deep reverie.
>
> "What is behind the darkness of closed eyes?" This probing thought came powerfully into my mind. An immense flash of light at once manifested to my inner gaze. Divine shapes of saints, sitting in meditation posture in mountain caves, formed like miniature cinema pictures on the large screen of radiance within my forehead.
>
> "Who are you?" I spoke aloud.
>
> "We are the Himalayan yogis." The celestial response is difficult to describe; my heart was thrilled.
>
> "Ah, I long to go to the Himalayas and become like you!" The vision vanished, but the silvery beams expanded in ever-widening circles to infinity.[2]

Yogananda's parents were disciples of Lahiri Mahasaya of Banaras, a minor historical figure responsible for propagating **kriya yoga,** a system of physical yoga postures and breathing techniques that was specifically designed to be practiced effectively by householders rather than world-renouncers. Kriya claims to scientifically streamline the art of yoga so that spiritual progress can be made in a fraction of the time that was previously needed and thus be democratically available to everybody. This would have had obvious appeal for Yogananda's father, a civil servant with a comfortable income and large family. Young Yogananda was also exposed to Sri Ramakrishna and his disciples, as well as the Tagores. His college experience and his family's lifestyle and connections placed him at the heart of the Renaissance movement.

Lahiri Mahasaya claimed to have received the secrets of kriya yoga from his guru, Babaji, an ageless and deathless (yet embodied) person living in the Himalayas who possessed supernatural powers. The similarities between Babaji and the Theosophical Mahatmas should be noted. According to tradition, Babaji had "rediscovered and clarified the technique after it had been lost in the Dark Ages . . . a revival of the same science that Krishna gave millenniums ago to Arjuna, and that was later known to Patanjali and Christ, and to St. John, St. Paul, and other disciples."[3]

To the secular eye, kriya appears to bear the stamp of the modernist trajectory. Its basic techniques form an efficient and easily understood version of yoga in the Patanjali tradition: ritual postures, body purification, breath control, and concentration exercises. While maintaining prescribed breathing patterns and posture, the practitioner "mentally directs his life energy to revolve, upward and downward, around the six spinal centers," causing a "revolution of energy around the sensitive spinal cord." These practices were "a simple, psychophysiological method by which human blood is decarbonated and recharged with oxygen," thus speeding up the natural maturation process of the human spirit and leading to spiritual transcendence over mental and physical obstacles. Kriya yoga is an "instrument through which human evolution can be quickened" through breath mastery; the end of this evolutionary process is reabsorption into the Cosmic consciousness, and to reach this end "the life force, which is ordinarily absorbed in maintaining heart action, must be freed for higher activities."[4]

Kriya reflects modernization in three of its distinctive features: its democratic appeal; its emphasis on science; and its promise of speedy, painless progress. Unlike traditional forms of yoga, often restricted to a small elite of twice-born males, kriya was meant for everybody. Householders, sudras, even the unclean **mleccha** foreigners were invited into the kriya fold. Also, it was presented not as an esoteric tradition but, rather, as a spiritual science, a program of self-improvement based primarily on experience and the perfection of technique through scientific principles of experimentation and the accumulation of reliable data. The scientific method had produced a technique that was so accurate, foolproof, and powerful that anyone could make use of it, even women and businessmen; one "half-minute of Kriya equals one year of natural spiritual unfoldment." Other forms of spiritual practice mixed science with superstition and spurious practice, making their execution burdensome and overly time-consuming. Kriya was the "jet plane" of spiritual growth. "Through gradual and regular increase of the simple and foolproof methods of Kriya, man's body becomes astrally transformed day by day and is finally fitted to express the infinite potentials of cosmic energy, which constitutes the first materially active expression of Spirit."[5]

Kriya offers a simple form of practice that is easy to memorize and carry out, and it promises salvation based entirely on its straightforward program. Personal choices that might confuse the anxious seeker are kept to a minimum; at the same time, the language emphasizes freedom—a formula that would prove to be a powerful draw to individuals overwhelmed by the choices offered in the modern, pluralistic world. Lahiri Mahasaya had died shortly after Yogananda's birth, but the family maintained strong ties to the movement.

As an adolescent, Yogananda experimented with a variety of gurus and practices—including, according to his brother, Spiritualism, tantra, and hypnotism (more on that later).[6] In 1910, at the age of seventeen, he became a formal disciple of Sri Yukteswar, an initiated disciple of Lahiri Mahasaya. Yukteswar was born to a wealthy businessman in Serampore, not far from Calcutta. He married, had a daughter, and invested his family's fortune in land. During middle age, he became a follower of Lahiri Mahasaya. After his wife's death, he turned full-time to the spiritual life and converted his mansion into a hermitage. Sri Yukteswar was a stern, stately man and exerted a maturing influence on his young disciple. Yogananda's master "always spoke plainly and upbraided sharply. No trifling lapse into shallowness or inconsistency escaped his rebuke. . . . I am immeasurably grateful for the humbling blows he dealt my vanity."[7] Despite Yogananda's own interpretation of his life as filled with mystical portents, there is little indication that Yukteswar favored this pupil. He did not choose Yogananda as his spiritual heir.

After only six months of discipleship, his guru graced him with his first experience of "cosmic consciousness," or ecstatic union with the Divine. This experience is the goal of kriya. One day, while Yogananda was attempting to meditate but failing to organize his scattered thoughts, his guru called for him. Sri Yukteswar struck him gently on the chest, triggering a mystical state. Yogananda felt as if he had left his body; he felt a spiritual unity with all things, and he felt that he had acquired piercing spiritual vision that allowed him to "discern the inward flow of sap" in the roots of plants and trees through the suddenly transparent soil. He was ecstatic:

> An oceanic joy broke upon calm endless shores of my soul. The Spirit of God, I realized, is exhaustless Bliss; His body is countless tissues of light. A swelling glory within me began to envelop towns, continents, the earth, solar and stellar systems, tenuous nebulae, and floating universes. The entire cosmos, gently luminous, like a city seen afar at night, glimmered within the infinitude of my being. The dazzling light beyond the sharply etched global outlines faded slightly at the farthest edges; there I saw a mellow radiance, ever undiminished.[8]

The trance state ended abruptly, and Yogananda was returned to "the humiliating cage of a body." Yukteswar cut short his grateful prostrations, saying in his characteristically wry and practical manner, "You must not get overdrunk with ecstasy. Much work yet remains for you in the world. Come, let us sweep the balcony floor; then we shall walk by the Ganges."[9] Yogananda took to heart his guru's nonchalant attitude toward the miraculous, incorporating it into the everyday world until mundane tasks became tinged with magical energy.

Yukteswar demanded that Yogananda go to college; perhaps he realized that this would boost his student's authority in the world. Although an indifferent student, he passed his A.B. examinations at Calcutta University in 1915 and shortly thereafter took **sannyas** from Yukteswar, becoming a monk. He started a small ashram in 1916, expanding it to a residential school in 1917, and in 1918 moved the organization to bigger and more rural property in Bihar, where a local maharaja financed the project. The ashram-school seemed to have been quite a success, staying open long after Yogananda himself had left for America. From 1935 onward, he donated money to it from his American work.

THE SELF-REALIZATION FELLOWSHIP IN THE UNITED STATES

In 1920, Yogananda sailed for Boston, where he had been invited to address the International Congress of Religious Liberals, sponsored by the American Unitarian Association. His father bankrolled the trip and he left with his guru's blessings to spread kriya yoga to the West, just as Lahiri Mahasaya had wished and foretold. Babaji himself appeared to Yogananda on the eve of his departure in order to encourage him. Later, Yogananda revealed that Jesus Christ himself had appeared to Babaji, requesting that yogis be sent to Christian lands to remind his people of the true spiritual path.[10]

"Because of Father's generous check," Yogananda was able to stay on in America after the Congress. "Three happy years were spent in humble circumstances in Boston. I gave public lectures, taught classes, and wrote a book of poems."[11] While in Boston, he met Dr. M. W. Lewis and his wife, Mildred. Dr. Lewis would become his first American disciple; for years he led the Boston fellowship after Yogananda moved west. The couple seems to have dabbled in religious alternatives prior to meeting the Swami, and Mildred first ran across Yogananda at a lecture given by a leader of the Rosicrucian order in 1920, only months after Yogananda's arrival in the United States. Dr. Lewis went to visit Yogananda at his room at Unity House, a New Thought institution. The mild-mannered dentist was skeptical, but Yogananda then

> showed Doctor the light of the spiritual eye and of the thousand-petaled lotus in the brain. Looking directly into Doctor's eyes, Paramahansaji asked:
> "Will you always love me as I love you?
> Doctor replied in the affirmative.
> Then the Guru said, "Your sins are forgiven and I take charge of your life." He added, "I want you to promise that you will never avoid me." Doctor promised.[12]

This exchange reveals Yogananda's authoritarian leadership style, which will be discussed in greater detail in Chapter 7.

In 1923 Yogananda began giving lecture tours across the country, and in 1925 his disciples purchased Mount Washington Estates in Los Angeles, which became the headquarters for his Self-Realization Fellowship. His soul had called him to Los Angeles, which he considered "the Benaras of America."[13] He gave yoga classes and lectured at clubs, colleges, and churches. And his Fellowship prospered:

> His magnetism was irresistible. On January 25, 1927, in Washington, D.C., after a lecture attended by 5,000 people, the *Washington Post* reported, "The Swami has broken all records for sustained interest." For some time a famous photographer kept a life-size photograph of the Master on the street outside his shop. President Calvin Coolidge received Yogananda at the White House. On April 18, 1926, in New York's famous Carnegie

Hall, the Master held a crowd spellbound for an hour and a half, repeating with him the simple chant, "O God Beautiful!"[14]

In 1925, he was able to raise $45,000 in three months from his disciples for the purchase of Mount Washington, an indication of how quickly he was able to establish a circle of devotees. He seems to have originally hoped to make Mount Washington a "how-to-live" school along the lines of his school in Ranchi, but there was not enough public interest in the project. After a few years, the plan was dropped and Mount Washington became a monastery and administrative center.

Yogananda spent the rest of his life in America, lecturing, writing, and teaching yoga. Until 1935, he toured the country frenetically on the lecture circuit. His tours were well organized:

> Swami Yogananda, who had come to America in 1920, was lecturing to thousands every night; his public healing meetings and prayer affirmations were a sensational success throughout the country. Before Yogananda would enter any city, a staff of volunteers would go before him and prepare the way by advertising in newspapers and on billboards, arranging as many meetings as possible in clubs and liberal churches.[15]

Unlike Paramananda, who disapproved of the "circus-like" techniques of his fellow countryman, Yogananda had a genius for marketing and was not afraid to use it. "Using Madison Avenue techniques such as promotional letters and prominent newspaper and billboard advertisements, Yogananda offered, for $25, a three-part correspondence course on spiritual techniques. Paramananda's followers were shocked to see pictures of Swami Yogananda smiling down on them in the Boston trolley."[16]

Yogananda was an energetic speaker. Several disciples later related that, during a lecture, they would feel as if the Swami had been looking directly at them in particular or spoken specifically to their needs. His style was conversational; he liked to make the audience laugh. "He sometimes actually came running out onto the lecture platform, his long hair streaming out behind him, his orange robe flapping about his body as if with kindred enthusiasm. 'How is everyone?' he would cry. 'Awake and ready!' came the eager response, in which he led them. 'How *feels* everyone?' Again the shout: 'Awake and ready!'"[17]

From 1935 to 1936, Yogananda traveled in Europe and returned to India. He checked in on the Ranchi School and renewed his interest in the project. Around this time he organized his Indian support base into the Yogoda Satsanga Society (YSS); in 1938, YSS dedicated an ashram at Dakshineswar that still serves as its headquarters. During his stay in India, Sri Yukteswar died—and was resurrected. While sitting in a Bombay hotel room, Yogananda was roused from his meditation by a beatific light, and he beheld the flesh-and-blood form of Sri Yukteswar. "From cosmic atoms I created an entirely new body, exactly like that cosmic-dream physical body which you laid beneath the dream-sands at Puri in your dream-world," he explained. "I am in truth resurrected—not on earth but on an astral planet. Its inhabitants are better able than earthly humanity to meet my lofty standards. There you and your exalted loved ones shall someday come to be with me."[18] Yukteswar then revealed to Yogananda much more concerning his new astral home, life, and death, including the little-known fact that astral beings consume "luminous raylike vegetables." Able to materialize and dematerialize into this plane at will, Yukteswar promised Yogananda that he would always be available to him.

After his return to Mount Washington, Yogananda became increasingly withdrawn from the public sphere, spending more time training his band of monastics and less time with the public, although he continued to lecture frequently until his death in 1952. During this period, his institution expanded in property, adherents, and in formal bylaws. During Yogananda's absence in India, disciple James Lynn had purchased a large estate on the ocean in Encinitas, California, for his guru. Yogananda spent much of his time there afterward. In the late 1930s, he attempted to make the Encinitas Center a "spiritual village," or place where householders in his movement could live communally, but the plan failed.

In 1936, Self-Realization Fellowship (SRF) Centers in Boston and Los Angeles were joined by a new group in London. A "Church of All Religions" was opened in 1942 in Hollywood, soon to be followed by a center in San Diego (1943) and Long Beach (1947). By 1948, Yogananda was giving sermons in the San Diego and Hollywood churches on alternate Sundays. In 1949, Yogananda was given another beautiful estate in the Pacific Palisades section of Los Angeles. The twelve-acre site boasted a beautiful lake and became known as the Lake Shrine; a Mahatma Gandhi World Peace Memorial, purportedly containing a portion of Gandhi's ashes, was dedicated there in 1950. Yogananda was also given a desert retreat at Twentynine Palms, California; during his last few years, he often went there to escape public life.

The center of SRF's mission work, however, was not congregational but postal. A magazine, *East-West,* was started in 1925; it is still published today as *Self-Realization: A Magazine Devoted to Healing Body, Mind and Soul.* As early as 1924, Yogananda was offering mail-order lessons in kriya yoga; the back page of *The Science of Religion,* published by him in that year out of Boston, advertises correspondence courses in both "'Yogoda' or Tissue-Will System of Physical Perfection" and "Highest Techniques of Concentration." Significantly, considering Yogananda's strong ties with the New Thought movement, correspondence courses in yogic techniques were by then standard fare for New Thought followers. In 1910, the New Thought journal *Nautilus* had advertised a yoga correspondence course by Sakharam Ganesh Pandit of Bombay, with lessons mailed every Thursday.[19] W. W. Atkinson, under the pen name of his alter ego, Yogi Ramacharaka, also offered correspondence courses. Yogananda continued to refine and edit his lessons throughout his lifetime, and they are still available today through SRF.

Compared to the traditional guru-disciple relationship, with its long initiation period and personal dimension, the mail-order method of transmission is robustly American and democratic. Anyone with the money and time could now learn these techniques in the privacy of their own home. Yogananda clearly understood the modernizing implications of this creative marketing technique:

> In the Atomic Age, yoga should be taught by a method of in-
> struction such as the Self-Realization Fellowship Lessons, or
> the liberating science will again be restricted to a chosen few. It
> would indeed be a priceless boon if each student could keep by
> his side a guru perfected in divine wisdom; but the world is com-
> posed of many "sinners" and few saints. How then may the multi-
> tudes be helped by yoga, if not through study in their homes of
> instructions written by true yogis? The only alternative is that the
> "average man" be ignored and left without yoga knowledge.[20]

Interestingly, in the same text Yogananda states that "because of certain ancient yogic injunctions, I may not give a full explanation of kriya yoga in a book intended for the general public. The actual technique should be learned from an authorized **Kriyaban** (Kriya Yogi) of SRF." Not being initiated into kriya yoga, I do not know what sort of information a kriyaban might dispense that goes beyond that offered in the printed lessons. The lessons themselves concentrate on simple meditation, breathing and posture techniques, instructions in "plain living and high thinking," and devotional material.

Not that the lessons were considered the end goal:

> In the overall plan of his work, Paramahansa Yogananda saw
> individual students first receiving the SRF lessons, and practicing
> Kriya Yoga in their own homes; then, in time, forming spiritual
> centers where they could meet once or twice weekly for group
> study and meditation. In areas where there was enough interest
> to warrant it, he wanted SRF churches, perhaps with full- or part-
> time ministers. And where there were enough sincere devotees
> to justify it, his dream was that they would buy land and live to-
> gether, serving God, and sharing the spiritual life together on
> a full-time basis.[21]

Ideally, "on a full-time basis" meant "in monastic community." At Mount Washington, the core group of disciples lived in celibacy with strict division between the sexes; the men's dormitories were in the basement, while the guru and the female devotees lived upstairs. Yogananda expected rigorous physical discipline from his renunciants, including celibacy and a minimum of food and sleep. His authority was absolute, and he sometimes upbraided his followers vigorously: "Often, in his training, he would push our equanimity to the limit, to see which way we would break. If we rebelled, or if under the strain we grew upset, it meant we had failed the test."[22] He does not, however, seem to have abused his power. All public accounts portray Yogananda as a loving, trustworthy man.

YOGANANDA'S DISCIPLES

Rajarsi Janakananda

Like Paramananda, Yogananda was successful in inspiring absolute faith in a core group of intelligent and interesting people. Of his devotees, perhaps his favorite was James J. Lynn (1892–1955), who later became known as Rajarsi Janakananda. Lynn was born in a small town in Louisiana to a tenant farmer, the fourth of six children. He was a self-made man in the most mythic sense of the phrase. He dropped out of school at the age of fourteen to work for the railroad. By seventeen he was working as a railroad auditor, a job with large responsibilities for someone his age. About this time, he moved to Kansas City, which would be his home for most of his adult life. By studying at night, he not only finished high school but passed the bar at age twenty-one and became a certified public accountant at twenty-four. In 1929, he bought the underwriting company that he had been working for with a high-risk loan, and made good on it. By diversifying his assets—in citrus ranches and oil, among other things—Lynn weathered the Depression well. In his obituary the *Kansas City Times* called him one of the richest men in the city.

By 1932, the year he met his guru, Lynn had realized that his wealth was not making him happy. "I had always been interested in truth and religion, although I had never accepted any church," he said in 1937. Further,

My life was business; but my soul was sick and my body was decaying and my mind was disturbed. I was so nervous I couldn't sit still.

After I had met Paramahansaji and had been with him a little while, I became aware that I was sitting very still; I was motionless; I didn't seem to be breathing. I wondered about it and looked up at Paramahansaji. A deep white light appeared, seeming to fill the entire room. I became a part of that wondrous light. Since that time I have been free from nervousness.[23]

Lynn met Yogananda in Kansas City, where the swami was giving a lecture. The two must have immediately impressed one another; a few weeks after their first meeting, Yogananda wrote Lynn a letter that a cynical person might interpret as sycophantic. "On your human life the immortals have put their invisible hands. . . . I too rejoice that the Spirit has taken the flute of your life to play the divine song of Self-realization and to lure other children back to His home. . . . I send you my deepest love, and my covenant to be your friend forever. . . . You are a Hindu yogi of Himalayan hermitages of the past, appearing in this life as an American prince, a Western maharaja-yogi who will light the lamp of Self-realization in many groping hearts."[24]

At the time, the Depression was taking its toll on Yogananda's ministry and Yogananda was in great need of cash.[25] In fairness, however, Lynn was not just rich but also brilliant and sincere. By 1937, Yogananda had taken to calling his friend "St. Lynn" and holding him up as an ideal for other devotees:

"I know how religiously Mr. Lynn conducts his life. He doesn't drink or smoke. He follows a simple diet of vegetables and fruit juices. He leads a celibate life. He doesn't go to the movies. For recreation he sits on the grass and meditates on the Divine. His whole existence is an exalted one, even though he attends to heavy business duties and is required to travel extensively in connection with his business responsibilities. He has had many temptations thrown in his way, but he has not succumbed to them. He has felt that Joy within which is greater than anything the world can offer."[26]

Kriya yoga was originally designed by Lahiri Mahasaya as a path for the householder who worked in the world. By combining worldly and spiritual success, Lynn embodied the goals of the movement. I have mentioned that Yogananda paid close attention to New Thought beliefs and incorporated their organizational techniques, such as mail-order lessons and aggressive advertising. He also borrowed heavily from the glib, jingle-laden rhetoric of New Thought; one of his most popular lectures was "How to Be a Smile Millionaire." However, it would be unfair to say that Yogananda merely echoed New Thought; in some ways, he challenged, expanded, and subverted the movement, and his use of Lynn as a public ideal is an example. Like New Age today, New Thought had within it a tendency to migrate toward the "gospel of wealth," the idea that right living automatically led to material prosperity because of God's justice. One can imagine that this line of reasoning would have been especially noxious to an Indian, used to seeing daily examples of impoverished saints and wealthy sinners. "St. Lynn" turned this paradigm on its head; he started out as not only very wealthy but self-made as well, the epitome of American worldly success. Yet he was unhappy: "My soul was sick and my body was decaying and my mind was disturbed." It was only by turning to the spiritual life that he found happiness, and once he had done so his money was no longer important to him.

Circa 1950, Lynn moved to California to be near his guru. After Yogananda's death in 1952, Lynn became president of SRF and was thereafter known as Rajarsi Janakananda. The death of a founder is a crucial time for a new religious movement, and Rajarsi carried the group through the crisis with grace. After Rajarsi died in 1955, Daya Mata became president, a post she holds to the present day.

Sri Gyanamata

If Rajarsi was Yogananda's ideal male disciple, then Sri Gyanamata (1869–1951) served that role for the women. She was born Edith Anne Ruth D'Evelyn in Woodbridge, Canada. Edith was a religiously minded child: "I can still see the little white English church amidst the pine trees. When I was about four years old I used to stand on the kneeling bench in the church in order to bring my head above the top of the pew, and I sang the hymns with all my heart."[27] Her father died when she was four; her mother, considered unconventional and strong-willed, then remarried and the family moved to Madelia, Minnesota. Edith was bright but quit school after eighth grade. She was unimpressed with her adolescent suitors and went on with life, not planning to marry. At thirty, however, she met and married Clark Prescott Bissett, a young divinity student who had been conducting summer services at Edith's Episcopalian church. They seem to have had a sweet, companionate relationship.

Soon after the marriage, Mr. Bissett left the ministry and entered law school in Minneapolis. Their only child, Rex, was born during these years. The family then moved to Seattle, Washington, where Bissett first practiced law and then became a professor of law at the University of Washington. He flourished as a teacher, and Mrs. Bissett also thrived in the university atmosphere. She read widely in philosophy and religion, attended lectures, and had a prestigious social life; at one point, Rabindranath Tagore was a dinner guest at the Bissett household. As time went on, she and her son gravitated toward Eastern thought. The **Bhagavad-Gita** impressed her strongly.

In 1924, Yogananda came to Seattle on a lecture tour. As usual, he stayed in the city long enough to give large public lectures and a series of smaller classes for intensely interested students. Edith was worried that her husband would be censured at the university if she went to hear a long-haired yogi (perhaps a similar scenario had already taken place in the past), so she sent Rex in her stead, and with Yogananda's permission he transmitted the teachings to his mother. Rex suffered from a nervous condition that Edith thought might be improved through yoga. The following year, Yogananda returned to Seattle and came to dinner at the Bissett home, and Edith was finally able to meet her future guru. Edith's first words to Yogananda were "Bless me, that I may realize God." They meditated together, and Yogananda revealed that she had been his disciple in a past life. He then inspired in her a mystical state in which she directly experienced God as **Om** —the sound that represents, in Hinduism, the oneness and sacredness of all things. As long as she remained in Seattle, she kept a vase of orange flowers on the spot that Yogananda had stood as he revealed this to her.

Yogananda also performed what could alternately be interpreted as a miracle or a parlor trick that first evening at the Bissett's, and it left a lasting impression on Edith:

> A curious and significant incident occurred during that first meeting: Many guests were seated at the dinner table, and on the table was a novel saltshaker. Its leaded base caused it to spring upright whenever it was pushed over. Several of the guests played with it in turn, but no one could make the toy stay on its side.
>
> "Then," Gyanamata recalled, "after several of the guests had tried it, the Master took the saltshaker and examined it thoughtfully for a few minutes. He pushed it down with his finger— it came up. He pushed it down again and again, looking at it intently—each time it came up. Once more he pushed it down, and when he raised his finger, finally it stayed down! Everyone was astonished. But he simply said, "The mind was determined that it should stay down."[28]

This is a good example of the way in which Yogananda was able to cultivate the impression among his followers that, for him, magic was an everyday, ordinary thing. A simple episode, which in a different context might be forgotten or brushed off, is instead magnified as proof of the mind's power over material objects. Materialistic explanations are not sought and, in fact, are avoided (could it be, for example, that the saltshaker tended to spring up, but could be balanced in such a way that it would not?). Later that evening, after Swamiji departed, the guests tried repeatedly to imitate the trick, to no avail. When it was Edith's turn, however, she pushed the saltshaker down and it stayed down. "Everyone exclaimed, 'She's done it, too!' But I knew that 'I' had not—the Master's vibrations were still with me."

Although she did not see her guru again for five years, Edith never lost faith in him. She meditated, wrote to him, and studied his writings. Once, when very ill, she wrote to the Master and asked for his prayers. "He was in New York at the time, and I in Seattle. I figured out how long it would take for my letter to reach him, and just at the time I felt he should get the letter, I felt his healing vibrations as I sat in my meditation chair—they shook the chair. . . . The tremendous roar of Aum [Om] rolled over and under the house. . . ." Edith was healed.[29]

Although Edith was often sick and frail, she remained cheerful and hardworking, performing household duties, helping her husband with lectures, and caring for others more sick than herself. In 1930, the Bissetts spent the winter in La Jolla so that Edith could be near Yogananda. Finally, in 1932, Mr. Bissett brought his wife to Mount Washington and asked Yogananda to let her live there permanently. He died soon after. Edith took her final vows of monastic renunciation later that year, becoming Sister Gyanamata.

For twenty years, the elderly Gyanamata was an institution in the community. From 1932 to 1936 she functioned as abbess at Mount Washington, overseeing the spiritual development of the nuns and sometimes taking charge of the entire community while Yogananda was away. After 1936, she moved to Encinitas to be near her guru. She wrote inspirational letters to younger members and performed whatever services she could as her health failed. When she died at eighty-two, her last words were "What joy! What joy! Too much, too much joy!"

Daya Mata and Swami Kriyananda

Two other influential members were Daya Mata and Swami Kriyananda. Daya Mata was born Faye Wright in Salt Lake City, Utah, in 1914. Even in grade school India fascinated her, and she first read the Bhagavad-Gita at fifteen. In 1931, when she was seventeen, she attended a lecture given in Salt Lake City by Yogananda.

"Recalling her first impressions, she has said, 'How can I describe it to you? When I saw him standing there on the platform, I became absolutely transfixed. He was speaking of the spiritual potential of will power and of love for God. I was enthralled. Instantly recognizing him as one who knew God and who could show me the way to Him, I resolved, 'Him I shall follow.'"[30]

Like Rex Bissett, Faye attended not only the lecture but the series of classes that Yogananda also offered. At the time, she was suffering from a chronic blood disorder, and bandages covered her swollen face. Yogananda told the class that within seven days no trace of her illness would remain, and so it was. Although Faye's family at first protested, she left two weeks later for Mount Washington. Her entire life would be devoted to Yogananda's cause.

Little biographical information concerning Daya Mata is available from SRF; its historical archives are not open to the public. To a greater degree than Paramananda, Yogananda encouraged his disciples to erase their own personalities in order to better merge with and concentrate on the Divine. During her early years, she depended on Sri Gyanamata and was lonely after the elder renunciant moved to Encinitas. Daya Mata took dictation at many of Yogananda's lectures and helped the publications department turn the notes into published texts. It was not uncommon for her and a few of the other devoted sisters to work around the clock. Of her work, she later said

> When I first came to the ashram many years ago, I had one
> dream, and that was to devote myself, as many hours a day as
> I could, to long and deep meditation. There was no thought in
> my mind to do organizational work. I served in the kitchen, in
> the gardens, in the office, as well as fulfilling my duties as secre-
> tary to Guruji [Yogananda]; I did everything that was asked of
> me, but there was no desire other than to get to God, to have
> His divine contact as fast as I could. But I noticed that as often as
> I tried to remain only on the meditative level of activity, Master
> pulled me back into the work. For a long time this troubled me,

until one day he said to me, "You must realize this: seeking God means also to serve Him in mankind. You cannot be wholly immersed in God's divine consciousness until you have learned how to balance your life with meditation plus right activity."[31]

With the exception of her father, her family's initial reservations melted into participation. Her mother and sister joined her at Mount Washington, becoming nuns. By 1935, her brother, Richard, was serving as Yogananda's secretary; he traveled with Yogananda during his 1935–36 trip to Europe and India in this capacity. By 1948, Daya Mata was assuming more and more institutional leadership within the organization. Yogananda called her his "nest egg" and dated the beginning of his monastic order from her arrival in 1931. Daya Mata became the third president of SRF in 1955.

Yogananda was often strict with his young disciple, just as his guru had been with him when he himself was an adolescent:

> Daya Mata tells a story dating back to when she was a teen-ager, and new on the path. At first, in her association with the Master, he had treated her lovingly, like a daughter. But once her feet were planted firmly on the path, he prepared to teach her the superior merits of impersonal love. To her now, feeling for him as she did the affection of a devoted daughter, he seemed all at once distant, even stern.
>
> One evening in Encinitas, he addressed her with what seemed unusual aloofness. She went out onto the bluff behind the hermitage, and prayed deeply for understanding. At last she reached a firm resolution. "Divine Mother," she vowed, "from now on I will love only Thee. In beholding him, I will see Thee alone."
>
> Suddenly she felt as though a great weight had been lifted from her. Later she went indoors and knelt before Master for his blessing, as she always did before retiring for the night. This time he greeted her gently with the words, "Very good!"[32]

In 1965, in a talk on the "Qualities of a Devotee," Daya Mata said, "I remember Guruji's saying to a group of us: 'I do not want mediocre devotees on this path. That is why I am hard on you all. I want to see who has the fiber to go all the way to God.' His last personal words to me—how I treasure them!—were uttered three days before his *mahasamadhi* [final conscious exit from the body]. We were coming down together in the elevator here at the headquarters. 'Poor child,' he said, 'I have been very hard on you in this life. I gave you the same hard discipline that my Guru gave me. I saw that you could take it. But remember, he scolded me because he loved me.'"[33]

It is unfortunate that we do not have more information about the process by which Daya Mata was elected president of SRF; it would be interesting to know if there was opposition based on her sex. The strength of SRF to the present day attests to her success as a leader. Part of that success rests on her humility; lesser officials might have used their power to promote themselves, but Daya Mata kept the focus on Yogananda and his teachings rather than seeking self-glorification. Conversations with current members suggest that their main frustration with the contemporary organization is that it has become overly dogmatic and literalist in its application of Yogananda's original vision. This is, of course, a perennial problem for sects struggling on after the death of the founder.

Swami Kriyananda, in 1977, wrote that "of the nuns, Daya Mata was the one I got the opportunity to know best, and also the one from whom I drew the greatest inspiration. I found her always fairminded, gracious to all, humble, childlike in her spontaneity. What inspired me most about her was her utter devotion to God and Guru. She had no desire that I ever observed except to do Master's will."[34] This is a strong statement, considering that in 1962 Kriyananda had been kicked out of the Fellowship while Daya Mata was president. His autobiography, *The Path: Autobiography of a Western Yogi,* was not published by SRF and appears to be one of the more candid accounts available of life as a disciple of Yogananda.

Kriyananda was born Donald Walters in 1926. His parents were American, but he was born in Romania and traveled extensively with his family as a child. He attended two colleges but did not graduate. Donald was enthusiastic as a young intellectual and budding writer, but an indifferent student; his own wry account of his youth portrays a painfully grandiose and arrogant adolescent *philosophe.* After dropping out of college, he held a variety of odd jobs and read widely. Sir Edwin Arnold's translation of the Bhagavad-Gita impressed him deeply: "I fairly devoured it, feeling as though I were soaring in vast skies of pure wisdom."[35]

After finishing it, Donald hurried back to the bookstore's Indian philosophy section to buy another book that he had seen the day that he had purchased the Bhagavad-Gita. It was *Autobiography of a Yogi,* and although he was initially amused by the idea that Asian wisdom could be dispensed via California, he could not stop thinking about the photograph of Yogananda on the book jacket: "The author's photograph on the cover affected me strangely. Never had I met anyone whose face radiated so much goodness, humility, and love."[36] His reaction to the *Autobiography* gives a sense of how powerful the book can be for the right person at the right time:

> I waited until I reached my room in Scarsdale before opening the book. And then began the most thrilling literary adventure of my life. . . . In chapter after chapter I found moving testimony to God's *living* reality, not only in the abstraction of infinity, but in the hearts and lives of actual human beings. I read of how Yogananda's prayers even for little things had been answered, and of how, by placing himself unreservedly in God's hands, his unanticipated needs had always been met. I read of intense love for God such as I myself yearned to possess; of a relationship with the Lord more intimate, more dear than I had dared to imagine possible.
>
> Until now I had supposed that a life of devotion might give one, at best, a little peace of mind. But here, suddenly, I discovered that the fruit of spiritual living is a joy beyond human imagination!
>
> Until recently I had doubted the value of prayer, except perhaps as a means of uplifting *oneself.* But now I learned, and could

not for a moment doubt, that God relates individually, *lovingly,* to every seeker.

Miracles abound in this book. Many of these, I confess, were quite beyond my powers of acceptance at the time. But instead of dismissing them, as I would certainly have done if I'd read of them in most other books, I suspended my incredulity. For the spirit of this story was so deeply honest, so transparently innocent of pride or impure motive, that it was impossible for me to doubt that its author believed implicitly every word he had written. . . . For three days I scarcely ate or slept. When I walked it was almost on tiptoe, as though in an ecstatic dream.[37]

Donald Walters was 22. He had nothing in the world but big dreams and a desire to make them real. A few days after completing the book, he took a bus to California to offer a lifetime of devotion to Yogananda, convinced that he had found his guru.

YOGANANDA'S LATER YEARS

By 1948, Yogananda's work was well established, and he was nearing the end of his life. Although he continued to lecture on Sundays, he no longer toured the country and spent increasing amounts of time in seclusion, often writing or editing his earlier texts. Many disciples were drawn to the organization through the *Autobiography,* and the numbers of renunciants at Mount Washington were swelling. The guru was impressed with Donald's sincerity and initiated him immediately. Donald moved to Mount Washington and often stayed with Yogananda at the Twentynine Palms retreat, doing everything from digging a swimming pool to editing. Soon he was giving sermons as well. After Yogananda's death, Donald took his final vows of renunciation under Daya Mata and became Swami Kriyananda. For the next seven years, he helped streamline the society's organizational structure.

In 1962, Kriyananda left SRF for unknown reasons. In 1968, he founded Ananda Church of Self-Realization and proceeded to implement Yogananda's dream of an intentional community.

Ananda Cooperative Village, near Nevada City in Northern California, exists to the present day. Donald Walters, however, resigned as leader of the organization in 1998, after being dogged for several years by accusations of sexual impropriety. As of 1992, Ananda had five residential branch communities, located in Seattle (Washington), Portland (Oregon), Sacramento, Palo Alto (California), and Assisi, Italy. Their church, established in 1990, is open to anyone who follows the teachings of Yogananda. It is unclear how Ananda will fare during the next few years, as it attempts to make the transition from a charismatic personality cult to a bureaucratic organization.[38]

Paramahansa Yogananda died with the same drama and magic that he lived. He became ill in 1951 and had trouble walking. His own diagnosis was that by taking on the bad karma of his devotees, he had left his physical body open to the attacks of demonic spirits. On March 7, 1952, Yogananda attended a banquet in honor of India's ambassador to the United States and rose to speak afterward. After reciting his poem, "My India," he fell dead of a heart attack. His coffin was left unsealed for twenty days afterward, and the funeral director reported that the corpse did not decay. Several disciples later reported that Yogananda had appeared to them in physical form to offer comfort or advice.

Only a few days before, the guru had predicted his own death to Daya Mata:

> Then Gurudeva said to me, "Do you realize that it is just a matter of hours before I leave this body?" A great pain of sadness went through my heart. Not long before, when Gurudeva had spoken of leaving his body soon, I had said to him, "Master, what will we do without you? You are the diamond in the ring of our hearts and of your society. Of what value is the setting without the beauty of the diamond?" Then came the answer from the great *bhakta:* "Remember this: When I am gone, only love can take my place. Be absorbed night and day in the love of God, and give that love to all."[39]

Perhaps we will never have enough objective, historical information concerning Paramahansa Yogananda to know what he was

really like. I imagine him, however, as a benevolent magician, forever attempting to capture the attention of restless children with
party tricks in order to impart a small amount of good sense along
with the show.

REASONS FOR YOGANANDA'S SUCCESS
IN THE UNITED STATES

Having given a brief overview of Yogananda's life and message, I
want to examine two themes in greater depth: how Yogananda
manipulated theological language in order to create a bridge
between Hinduism and Christianity, and how Yogananda's worldview shaped his understanding of ideal interpersonal relationships.

Yogananda's success in America owed much to his organizational skill, the quality (and occasional wealth) of his followers,
and his exploitation of American interest in the exoticism and
magic of the Orient. These practical strengths were necessary but
insufficient to account for his enormous success. Equally important was the content of his message and program. Both the beliefs
and activities that he promoted resonated deeply with his audience. His magical worldview was just what his disciples had been
yearning for, and his program of yoga, meditation, and charismatic authority really did deliver the goods. Yogananda was a
genius at fostering a social environment that allowed magical
thinking to flourish unchecked, and this was (and is) exactly what
many Americans needed as an antidote to secularization.

In order to provide this service, it was necessary for him to
translate the symbols of kriya yoga into a language that would
speak directly to the hearts of Americans. Yogananda was clearly
familiar with New Thought and liberal Protestantism, and he
incorporated their themes and symbols into his own synthesis.
While it is possible that Yogananda's adaptations had a mercenary
angle, it is equally plausible that his motives were sincere. For all
his miracle tales, Yogananda was a modern guru in many ways. He
believed that he was transmitting basic truths about the universe,
that these truths were authorized by experience and tested

through experiment and observation, and that if new ways could be found to explain and transmit them, the new ways were just as authoritative as the old ones. It would be a mistake to view Yogananda's marketing techniques and personal sincerity as necessarily conflicting. Like a parent looking for ways to make chores more fun, or a teacher embedding math in games, Yogananda's popularizing strategies attracted a reluctant audience toward necessary medicine.

Despite his patriotic love for India, Yogananda was always careful to stress what he saw as the universal aspects of his theology. For example, in 1942 he dubbed the Hollywood Center his "Church of All Religions"—perhaps in a conscious attempt to compete with Ananda Ashrama's Temple of the Universal Spirit. Like Paramananda's Temple, Yogananda's Hollywood Church sported niches containing figurines depicting great religious teachers from around the world that lined the sides of the sanctuary. His Pacific Palisades property became known for his Gandhi World Peace Memorial, and the flamboyant towers at Encinitas along Route 101 he named the World Brotherhood Center. All these names underlined the universalizing aspirations of his message. In his lecture "The Art of Living" (1933), he recommended that his listeners "visit different temples and churches—Protestant, Catholic, Buddhist, Jewish, Hindu, and so on—to develop your appreciation and understanding of all faiths. Look upon each one as the Temple of Our God." But, he goes on to say, you should honor God not only in man-made temples, but "learn to worship and commune with Him in the inner temple of silence."[40]

In a further, and more radical, attempt to appeal to a wider American audience, Yogananda consistently played down the traditional Hindu deities, replacing them with Jesus Christ. In his transcribed lecture, "Personal and Impersonal God,"[41] he presents the familiar Hindu theme of God's double nature as **saguna** and **nirguna,** with and without qualities. However, instead of discussing the personal deities of India, Yogananda discusses Jesus, with the comment that "it is significant that when we think about

God in human form, we visualize him according to our own familiar concepts. . . . Such is man's need for a personal God in a form to which he can easily respond." Yogananda taught—and lived—devotional theism, but he was not concerned about which cultural symbol that devotion poured itself out on. The primary iconography of SRF became its line of gurus—Babaji, Lahiri Mahasaya, Swami Sri Yukteswar, Paramahansa Yogananda, and *Jesus Christ,* newly added to the lineage by Yogananda in order to reach Western audiences more effectively.

At the same time, he de-emphasized the Hindu deities. Kriya yoga, as it was originally taught to Yogananda, is in the Shiva-Shakti tradition, with special emphasis on the deity as Mother—primarily in the form of Kali, given its Bengali roots. Lahiri Mahasaya was born in Bengal, as was Yukteswar. Lahiri Mahasaya's family was **Shaivite,** and Babaji himself is reminiscent of **Shiva**—an ever-young, physically beautiful yogi of the Himalayas. Kriya yoga's debt to Kali seems to be acknowledged in India; in fact, the Indian headquarters of Yogananda's work is in Dakshineswar, famous as the home of Ramakrishna and his beloved Kali Temple. Yet these deities get scant attention in Yogananda's writings. In *Autobiography of a Yogi,* for example, Kali is defined in footnotes as "a symbol of God in the aspect of eternal Mother Nature" (p. 14) and as representing "the Eternal Principle in nature" (p. 50). The latter footnote goes on to describe Kali as "traditionally pictured as a four-armed woman, standing on the recumbent form of the God Shiva or the Infinite; because the activities of nature or the phenomenal world spring from the latent Spirit. The four arms symbolize cardinal attributes: two beneficent, two destructive; the essential duality of matter or creation." This is a remarkably sanitized portrait of Kali, who traditionally represented the Mother Goddess in her destructive aspect and is iconographically portrayed with a lolling tongue, a girdle of human hands, and a necklace of severed heads.

Yogananda did not forget his Divine Mother altogether. Like Paramananda, Yogananda frequently used feminine language for the Divine. God is both Father and Mother; although beyond sex and gender, God appears to devotees in masculine and feminine forms: "Jesus spoke of God as Father. Some saints speak of Him as Mother. In His transcendental aspect, God is neither Father nor Mother, but when we think of Him in terms of human relationship, He may become for us either Father or Mother."[42] Yogananda deserves credit for employing such language; it cannot have been comfortable for his Western audiences. Nevertheless, compared to the Bengali Kali, Yogananda's Mother was a domesticated Victorian housewife.

One can hardly blame Yogananda for shrinking in the face of exposing his deity to needless misunderstanding and ridicule. For him, Kali was simply the Divine Mother, and part of his genius was his ability to rework the symbolism surrounding her in order to better communicate his main point to his audience. According to Yogananda, Truth is One, and God is the same everywhere, regardless of what a person's religious concepts are: "He eventually appears to the persistent devotee in whatever form he holds dear. A devout Christian sees Jesus; a Hindu beholds Krishna, or the Goddess Kali, or an expanding Light if his worship takes an impersonal turn."[43] This sentiment is expressed in the "Aims and Ideals of Self-Realization Fellowship," which are printed at the end of most of their publications. The third aim is "to reveal the complete harmony and basic oneness of original Christianity as taught by Jesus Christ and original Yoga as taught by Bhagavan Krishna; and to show that these principles of truth are the common scientific foundation of all true religions."

In place of Shiva and Kali, SRF presented to the West the sanitized icon of Babaji, the Eastern Messiah. I am not familiar enough with the origins of kriya yoga in India to trace Babaji's historical evolution; Yogananda claims to have accurately transmitted Babaji's lore as he received it from Yukteswar, who in turn learned about Babaji from Lahiri Mahasaya, who is said to have been initiated into the ancient secrets of kriya from Babaji himself. Whether through coincidence or strategy, Babaji's iconography is well suited to the American mass market. Yogananda's description of Babaji, taken out of context, could almost pass for a description of a successful Hollywood leading man of the times:

> The deathless guru bears no mark of age on his body; he appears to be a youth of not more than *twenty-five. Fair-skinned,* of medium build and height, Babaji's *beautiful,* strong body radiates a perceptible glow. His eyes are dark, calm and tender; his long, lustrous hair is copper-colored. [italics added][44]

Babaji is beautiful, young, androgynous, and *white.* Yogananda goes on to say that Babaji bears a strong resemblance to Lahiri Mahasaya, but the iconic representations of the two gurus look nothing alike. Photographs of Lahiri Mahasaya portray a kindly Indian gentleman. Paintings of Babaji look like a rock star, complete with fantastically high cheekbones.

Together, Babaji and Christ are the cosmic redeemers of the universe, twin messiahs:

> Babaji is ever in communion with Christ; together they send out vibrations of redemption and have planned the spiritual technique of salvation for this age. The work of these two fully illumined masters—one with a body [Babaji], and one without a body [Christ]—is to inspire the nations to forsake wars, race hatreds, religious sectarianism, and the boomerang evils of materialism. Babaji is well aware of the trend of modern times, especially of the influences and complexities of Western civilization.[45]

By replacing the traditional Shiva/Shakti iconography with Babaji/Jesus, Yogananda made his movement much more appealing to Americans. Babaji has an exotic edge without being overwhelmingly pagan. Shiva's sexuality is airbrushed out, and the idea of the feminine as divine is pushed into the background. Americans who secretly love and remember the happy Jesus of the nursery, but who cannot reconcile with the judgmental Father of the Church, are provided with a kinder and gentler deity who always loves and never judges.

YOGANANDA'S MODIFICATION OF TRADITIONAL HINDUISM

If Yogananda modified Hindu deities to better suit Western tastes, he also adapted the idea of Jesus to better reflect Hindu teachings. Yogananda's Jesus was not the only son of God, but one of many avatars—the Divine made flesh in order to lead humanity toward perfection. Jesus had incarnated many times before, as an ordinary mortal, but finally became perfected through self-mastery before his appearance in Bethlehem; in his previous life, he had been Elisha.[46] He now exists as a conscious, cosmic spirit who guides humanity and can be seen and talked to by enlightened masters like Yogananda. All of us have the potential to reach the same level of perfection; Yogananda often referred to the perfected mind as "Christ-Consciousness." Like all other great souls, Jesus can be counted on to choose to reincarnate again, in order to help others. Yogananda's Jesus, while on earth, taught reincarnation, meditation, yoga, and vegetarianism.

Yogananda also added the idea of Satan to his cosmological views after coming to the United States: "Master once told an audience, 'I used to think Satan was only a human invention, but now I know, and add my testimony to that of others who lived before me, that Satan is a reality. He is a universal, conscious force whose sole aim is to keep all beings bound to the wheel of delusion.'"[47] Traditional Hinduism also includes tales concerning malevolent spiritual beings. By emphasizing the singular, universal nature of one such being, and using the name of Satan to describe it, Yogananda further modified his religious language in order to speak to the hearts of Americans.

Although Yogananda played down traditional Hindu iconography and mythology when he talked of God, he drew heavily on classic Hindu themes. In addition to reminding his followers that God had both an impersonal and personal nature, he often taught that the Divine should be considered alternately as friend, lover, parent, and master. As impersonal force, Yogananda's God was **satchitananda**—being, consciousness, bliss. The Divine was Cosmic Energy, the source of all wisdom and compassion, the source and sustenance of all. As a personalized force, God played with his devotees, manifesting in various forms. At root, anything or anyone was divine in essence and could be worshipped as a manifestation of the Lord. Yogananda taught that it is better to understand this and to play creatively with our ideas about God; otherwise, our internal images become idolatrous, the end rather than the means. "The Infinite Entertainer forbids that we love Him forever in only select forms of our choosing, lest we fail to appreciate the entertainment of His ever-changing, infinite variety of forms. But to teach us what love is, the Cosmic Lover invites us in the beginning to love Him in any way we please, until through the silent coaxing of His courtship, our love becomes purified."[48]

This quotation, and others like it, form the basis of my interpretation of Yogananda as a benevolent magician. If God himself is the Infinite Entertainer, it cannot be disrespectful to theorize that Yogananda thought that this was an appropriate mode of interaction with his disciples. In Hindu bhakti traditions, the Lord of the Universe is believed to engage in **lila**—playful, joyous creativity. This is not play in the sense of a meaningless game but, rather, in the sense of childlike enthusiasm for life itself. Perhaps, then, it is a mistake to make a big fuss over whether Yogananda's miracles were truly supernatural occurrences or have a natural explanation. Either way, they functioned as reminders that the Infinite Entertainer wants us to be delighted with his cosmic show.

YOGANANDA'S INTERPERSONAL RELATIONSHIPS

In addition to emphasizing devotional prayer, meditation, and the physical disciplines of kriya, Yogananda placed great emphasis on ethics, both as self-discipline and as selfless service to others. "Happiness lies in making others happy," he insisted.[49] His followers were expected to lead chaste and disciplined lives. For all of his rhetoric concerning the miraculously quick and painless effects that kriya would achieve, his expectations for his disciples were rigorous. Yogananda's dedication to balancing his emphasis between internal growth and external behavior undoubtedly contributed to the sense of well-being and accomplishment that many of his devotees enjoyed.

However, if one inquires more closely into Yogananda's rhetoric on love, some difficult questions emerge. At issue is how one wishes to define ideal love. Yogananda taught that the aim of Self-Realization is to realize one's essential unity with the Divine. According to Yogananda, a human being is really a perfect spirit, encased in a finite, imperfect body. In SRF, there is a tendency to associate one's *personality* with the exterior casing that needs to be shed on the road to God. According to Kamala, one of Yogananda's disciples, "All discussion about personality traits, comments on the actions, habits or activities of others, and of one's self, all that makes up the usual small talk, is replaced with quietness."[50] Whether or not this belief is metaphysically correct is not something that I am qualified to judge. I can say, however, that this belief produces corollaries that need to be addressed. Within this worldview one identifies a person with his or her idealized essence and understands this essence as being uniform in all beings. It is this essence that is "loved." Meanwhile, individual characteristics are considered imperfections and rejected. One might consider whether this is an acceptable definition of love or empty rhetoric.

We must proceed carefully here, for many people really are psychologically and emotionally freed by monist concepts. They feel as if the recognition of the essential divine unity in all people helps them to overcome artificial boundaries and prejudices. When a spiritual teaching helps a person to see humanity as a single human family, rather than fragmented competing groups, the new worldview does have the capacity to increase ethical awareness. Vivekananda used the language of vedanta in this way, sparking an intuitive appreciation of the divinity in Everyman. He believed that this would work as a democratic leveler, drawing people closer together.

Humans tend to see members of one's own social group as more like oneself than they really are and to see outsiders as less like oneself than they really are. Perhaps, then, monism is more useful in cultivating ethical sensitivity toward strangers than toward intimates, since it counters this tendency. Among intimates, however, it has the potential to turn sour, promoting a narcissistic blindness to the unique needs and strengths of other individuals.

It is reasonable to argue that, contra Yogananda's position, to deeply love another person is to see, accept, and cherish that person as they really are right now, in their totality. In SRF, the ideal was sometimes pursued at the expense of the real. Donald Walters reports that Yogananda counseled the disciples not to mix too closely with others: "The desire for outward companionship is a reflection of the soul's inward desire for companionship with God. But the more you seek to satisfy that desire outwardly, the more you will lose touch with the inner, divine Companion, and the more restless and dissatisfied you will become."[51] Yogananda held aloofness and seclusion as virtues. Among the monastics, he required a strict separation between men and women:

> So strict was he that he even discouraged many of the normally accepted courtesies that men and women extend to one another. I remember one day, when Master and I were standing out of doors near the entrance to his Twenty-Nine Palms retreat, a young nun came to the door from the car, laden with packages. Observing that she was having difficulty in opening the door, I went over and opened it for her. "You should not have done that," Master told me, after she had gone inside. "Keep your distance," he added, "and they will always respect you."[52]

In this quote, Yogananda demonstrates both his preference for formal hierarchical authority over the relaxed sociability more typical of American culture and his assumption that male monastics stood in a position of authority over female monastics. While these values may conflict with the values of some Americans, they do reflect the worldview of traditional Hindu monasticism and were not invented by Yogananda.

It is also possible that Kriyananda and Daya Mata did not enjoy the full measure of Yogananda's capacity for mature friendship or that they declined to write about it. A different portrait of Yogananda's interpersonal relationships emerges from *Treasures Against Time,* a collection of reminiscences by Doctor and Mrs. Lewis compiled by their daughter, Brenda Lewis Rosser. The volume also includes many unedited letters that Yogananda sent the Lewises over the years; Rosser published the book privately rather than have it edited by the SRF staff. It is therefore an unusually candid portrait of Yogananda's personal life (in one anecdote, Mrs. Lewis recounts Yogananda's youthful habit of coming over to their house, luxuriating in their shower, and leaving soggy towels strewn about the bathroom for her to pick up and wash). The Lewises were among Yogananda's earliest supporters in Boston when he first arrived in 1920 and remained faithful to his mission throughout their lives.

In *Treasures Against Time,* Yogananda comes across as much more loving and informal than in any of the official SRF literature. Apparently, Yogananda had a more amiable relationship with Doctor Lewis than with his wife—perhaps because he was in the habit of asking the doctor for large sums of money, which Mrs. Lewis would have liked to have put to other uses. Still, his letters to "Doctor and Mil" are affectionate and intimate. Yogananda asks after their children, begs them to come visit, rejoices with them when their son returns from war, asks for a photograph of their new house, thanks them for helping cook when he last saw them. The letters span thirty years of friendship, ending in 1951, with "Your invitation 'come again' seems so sweet —it had a magnet call. Poverty and want are good for it makes us appreciate the richest possession is our true friends."[53] It is no wonder, then, that Doctor Lewis was able, in 1959, to lecture movingly to an SRF congregation on the theme of "Divine Friendship":

The greatest [friendship] is the guru-disciple relationship. Because what is the spiritual law of the guru-disciple relationship? The guru introduces his friend to God. He introduces his friend to the friend of all friends, that one eternal Father. That's the greatest relationship. That's the most wonderful thing.[54]

I have dwelt at length on the quality of Yogananda's interpersonal relationships because he made very strong claims about his perfected level of cosmic consciousness, and those claims have been taken very seriously by his followers. "I killed Yogananda long ago. No one dwells in this temple now but Him."[55] His teachings, then, rest not only in his words but in his actions as well; if everything that he did was the action of pure divine will, then every single aspect of his life should therefore be above reproach. This is not necessarily the most useful way to interpret his life.

Perhaps Yogananda's apparent flaws draw attention to a flaw in the universalist project. When one focuses on the search for universal standards for religious truth, it becomes correspondingly difficult to pay attention to context and particularity. The universalizing worldview of modernism privileged abstract ideals of perfection at the expense of the situated perfection of the individual. In other words, perhaps it is a mistake to think of any person—Yogananda included—in terms of whether or not they are a perfect *person,* as if there is some sort of single and universal standard by which we can measure human achievement. Perhaps it is more appropriate to ask, "Was Yogananda perfectly himself? Did Yogananda raise human life to an art form, brilliantly and uniquely, through his own creative performance?"

To this, I would have to answer yes, and yes again.

NOTES

1. Yogananda, *Autobiography of a Yogi,* 479.
2. Ibid., 12.
3. Ibid., 276.
4. Ibid., 279.
5. Ibid., 280.
6. Ghosh, *Mejda.*
7. Yogananda, *Autobiography of a Yogi,* 141.

8. Ibid., 167.
9. Ibid., 167–168.
10. Kriyananda, *The Path,* 217.
11. Yogananda, *Autobiography of a Yogi,* 407.
12. *Dr. M. W. Lewis,* 14.
13. Yogananda, *The Master Said,* 119.
14. Kriyananda, *The Path,* 184.
15. Levinsky, *A Bridge of Dreams,* 263.
16. Ibid., 370.
17. Kriyananda, *The Path,* 324.
18. Yogananda, *Autobiography of a Yogi,* 476.
19. Jackson, "The New Thought Movement and the Nineteenth-Century Discovery of Oriental Philosophy," 523–548.
20. Ibid., 556.
21. Kriyananda, *The Path,* 324.
22. Ibid., 233.
23. *Rajarsi Janakananda,* 37.
24. Ibid., 25.
25. Rosser, *Treasures Against Time,* 129.
26. *Rajarsi Janakananda,* 34.
27. Gyanamata, *God Alone,* 3.
28. Ibid., 13.
29. Ibid., 15.
30. Mata, *Only Love,* viii.
31. Ibid., 131.
32. Kriyananda, *The Path,* 253.
33. Mata, *Only Love,* 31.
34. Kriyananda, *The Path,* 362.
35. Ibid., 159.
36. Ibid.
37. Ibid., 161–162.
38. There are several additional kriya yoga organizations in the United States at present. The Kriya Yoga Center in Washington D.C. was founded by Swami Hariharananda Giri in 1974. Hariharananda traces his lineage to Sri Yukteswar, but through Sreemat Swami Satyananda, who inherited Yukteswar's authority in 1936. The Self-Revelation Church of Absolute Monism in Washington D.C. was founded by a disciple of Yogananda's, Swami Premananda, in 1927. Premananda had been a teacher at the Ranchi School and came to Washington D.C. at Yogananda's request to help with the American work. It is not known why he organized separately rather than as a branch of SRF. The Temple of Kriya Yoga in Chicago was founded by another Kriyananda, born Melvin Higgins. Kriyananda claims to have been initiated into kriya by a disciple of Yogananda, one Sri Sri Shelliji. In addition to yoga, his institution teaches astrology. More recently, Yogananda's disciple Roy Eugene Davis has founded the Center for Spiritual Awareness in Georgia, and the

Amrita Foundation of Dallas, Texas, claims to publish original editions of Yogananda's earliest works (SRF has a tendency to take out Yogananda's quaint turns of speech). I have not checked Amrita's publications against the first editions, and it should be noted that their publication, *The Second Coming of Christ,* is purported to be by Yogananda but does not read like an original work. For more information on kriya organizations, search the Internet on "kriya yoga," or consult Rawlinson, *The Book of Enlightened Masters.*

39. Mata, *Only Love,* 175.
40. Yogananda, *Man's Eternal Quest,* 401.
41. Yogananda, *The Divine Romance,* 371–382.
42. Yogananda, *Man's Eternal Quest,* 373.
43. Yogananda, *Autobiography of a Yogi,* 242.
44. Ibid., 348.
45. Ibid., 347.
46. Yogananda, *Man's Eternal Quest,* 231.
47. Kriyananda, *The Path,* 387.
48. Yogananda, *The Divine Romance,* 370.
49. Ibid., 25.
50. Kamala, *The Flawless Mirror,* 123.
51. Kriyananda, *The Path,* 274.
52. Ibid., 277.
53. Rosser, *Treasures Against Time,* 192.
54. Ibid., 201.
55. Yogananda, *The Master Said,* 152.

CHAPTER 6

Jiddu Krishnamurti

There is no path to truth. Truth must be discovered, but there is no formula for its discovery. What is formulated is not true. You must set out on the uncharted sea, and the uncharted sea is yourself. You must set out to discover yourself, but not according to any plan or pattern, for then there is no discovery. Discovery brings joy—not the remembered, comparative joy, but joy that is ever new. Self-knowledge is the beginning of wisdom in whose tranquillity and silence there is the immeasurable.

—J. KRISHNAMURTI[1]

Krishnamurti was a religious teacher, originally from India, who spent much of his time in the United States from 1922 to his death in 1986. He did not think of himself as a Hindu during his adult life. I have included him here as a counterpoint to Yogananda and Paramananda because his life and teachings help define the limits of American Hinduism and to draw attention to the universalizing tendencies already dominant in its more traditional forms. Some of Krishnamurti's teachings, especially his recommendation of meditation and his nondualism, are drawn from his Indian heritage. However, he refused to frame his experiences within the language, myth, or traditions of India and, instead, struggled to overcome all sectarian boundaries by speaking as universally and plainly as possible about his philosophy. He rejected all religious authority—both scriptures and gurus—and advocated complete personal freedom in life and the religious quest.

Krishnamurti's career contains many paradoxes and confusing points, but in this chapter I focus on the role he played in advancing the ideal of a universal science for spiritual growth. This is his point of contact with Paramananda and Yogananda, both of whom saw themselves as adding Hindu truths to an American melting pot that would eventually lead to a universal religion that could transcend sectarian boundaries. Krishnamurti extended this line of thought to its inevitable conclusion and, in doing so, gave us some useful hints concerning the limitations of the project.

Additionally, Krishnamurti's personal life suggests some interesting trains of thought concerning the American fascination with the "Orient" and the idea of the guru. Although Krishnamurti verbally rejected the role of the guru and consistently advocated personal responsibility and creative freedom in spiritual life, his relationships with his students retained a high degree of ambivalence concerning his status. Krishnamurti gave mixed messages on these issues, especially as he grew older. Even while disavowing his role as a charismatic religious authority, he sometimes acted like one. His role as a lecturer and teacher implied that he possessed special insight, which set him over and above his audience.

Krishnamurti was born in 1895 to an orthodox Brahmin family in South India. His father, Narianiah, held a minor bureaucratic post; his parents blended Theosophy with traditional Hinduism. He was a dreamy, sickly child who did poorly in school and shared his beloved mother's spiritual interests. By some accounts, he was dull as a child, but, in light of his later career, it seems more plausible that he was merely shy and possibly learning disabled (he never developed a taste for literary pursuits). Within his large family, he had a special relationship with his brother Nitya, three years his junior. In 1905, Krishnamurti's mother died, an event that affected him deeply, further isolating him in a private, interior world. He was comforted by visitations from his mother's spirit.

Soon after his wife's death, Narianiah retired from government service. Unable to support the children with his meager pension, he applied for work at the Theosophical Headquarters in Adyar. The family moved near the grounds in 1909. Although

Jiddu Krishnamurti

Theosophists would later describe the family's living conditions during this time as slovenly, it is unclear whether this was actually the case by Indian standards or merely by aristocratic British standards. Theosophical legend also describes the young Krishnamurti as ugly and wasted, but photos from the time portray an adolescent marked by a delicate physical beauty.

BESANT, LEADBEATER, AND THE THEOSOPHICAL SOCIETY

By 1909, the Theosophical Society rested firmly in the capable hands of Annie Besant (1847–1933), who had been elected president in 1907 after Olcott's death. Even before Theosophy, Besant was "a prolific author and perhaps the leading woman orator of her era."[2] She was active in Charles Bradlaugh's National Secular Society and, later, campaigned for socialism and access to contraception. She was good friends with George Bernard Shaw, who fictionalized her in *Arms and the Man*. It was perhaps through Shaw's influence that Besant realized her religious impulse could be channeled in more exciting directions than Anglicanism; about this time she began to distance herself from secularism, as she had previously done with Christianity. On reading Blavatsky's *Secret Doctrine* in 1888, Besant almost immediately converted to Theosophy. By 1889 she was close friends with Blavatsky. Her trust in her new teacher was so great that she publicly repudiated her earlier advocacy of birth control; "Koot Humi had spoken out against it, and the Society's official doctrine was that birth control simply encouraged the indulgence of those animal passions which prevented men from rising to their higher selves."[3]

Koot Humi was one of Theosophy's "Masters." According to Theosophists, these Masters are not spirits but highly evolved humans who live to incredible ages and have supernormal powers: such as clairvoyance, astral projection, and omniscience. The Masters were

> thought to be part of a Great White Brotherhood or White Lodge, who watch over and guide the evolution of humanity and who preserve the truths of the ageless wisdom. Many of the great religious teachers, such as Abraham and Moses, are identified as Masters. Also, the "mighty triad" of Buddha, Confucius and Jesus are thought to be Adepts, as are Solomon, Laotze, Boehme, Cagliostro, Mesmer and many others.[4]

Although Hinduism contains folk tales of **sadhus** who live secretly in the Himalayas and survive for centuries accumulating magical powers, the Theosophical construction of the Master was probably also influenced by the Spiritualist tradition of supernatural communication with the spirits of great teachers.

During the late 1890s, Besant formed an intellectual partnership with Charles W. Leadbeater. Besant and Leadbeater became as close a team as Blavatsky and Olcott had been before them, although in this case the sex roles were reversed: Besant was the diplomat and organizer, while Leadbeater played the role of eccentric mystagogue.

By 1909, Leadbeater still served as Besant's spiritual soul mate, but an unpleasant series of events had threatened his institutional standing in the Theosophical Society. Leadbeater had been accused on several occasions of "improprieties" with pubescent boys. It is not known whether his misbehavior was confined, as he maintained, to recommending masturbation as a harmless exercise, or if he sexually molested the boys, as some of them charged. Regardless of the physical extent of Leadbeater's activities, the charges scandalized the Society and he had been forced to resign in 1906. Besant had reinstated him as a member, bucking considerable disapproval, but he would never again hold a formal office.

The scandal was even more acute in the context of Theosophy than it would have been for mainstream Edwardians, because Theosophy had very strict standards of sexual purity for its inner circle:

> According to theosophical doctrine only the pure in heart,
> mind, spirit and body could become Initiates—and only Initiates were able to visit the Masters. Indeed, initiation altogether
> was a very tall order, requiring perfect physical and mental
> health, an absolutely pure life, complete unselfishness, charity,
> compassion, truthfulness, courage, and indifference to the
> physical world. If Leadbeater were not pure he could not be an
> Initiate, and if he were not an Initiate his visits to the Masters
> could not have taken place.[5]

Since Leadbeater's contacts with the Masters were well publicized, his alleged impurities had a theological dimension as well as an ethical one. Although Krishnamurti denied throughout his life that his relationship with Leadbeater was sexual, he also denied remembering anything concerning his childhood and adolescence for most of his adult life. The circumstantial evidence that Leadbeater may have sexualized his relationship with Krishnamurti, and that this exacerbated Krishnamurti's already difficult biography, is suggestive.

Although we do not know the extent of Leadbeater's sexual activities, it is clear that he was fond of the company of young boys. Before the scandal, he had served as a tutor to the sons of several prominent Theosophists and been involved in a variety of youth activities. After the scandal of 1906, Leadbeater's access to boys was limited; perhaps it is not a coincidence that his search for the new World Teacher escalated at this time.

Theosophy borrowed from Hinduism the idea that divine beings incarnated at various points in human history in order to spread righteousness. Members of the Society expected the imminent arrival of the World Teacher—a return of the perfected divine being who had previously walked on the earth as Krishna and Jesus. From Buddhism, they borrowed the name of the future World Teacher—Maitreya—and developed a distinctive mythology of their own. Theosophy has a baroque hierarchy of spiritual beings; Maitreya was above the Masters but below the Buddha and was hiding in the Himalayas until the time came for him to take possession of a human body and re-enter the stream of human history.

Theosophy had to modify the traditional idea that the Maitreya's soul would incarnate in a human baby at birth because that would mean that Maitreya would be useless to them for years, either as an undiscovered child or as a not-yet glib one. Leadbeater was therefore searching, not for Maitreya himself, but the "vehicle" that Maitreya would later enter and possess as his own substitute body.

In 1909, Leadbeater found the vehicle on the Adyar beach in the form of an Indian boy of fourteen. He recognized Krishnamurti as the vehicle of the future World Teacher because of his pure aura, and soon Krishna, as he was then known, and his brother Nitya were living in the Adyar compound while Leadbeater tutored them.

Leadbeater made every effort to transform the boys into English gentlemen. They followed a rigid schedule of studies and physical activities, learning everything from proper English pronunciation to how to eat with a knife and fork. Krishna continued to be an indifferent student; Nitya was considerably brighter. Krishna, however, showed more promise than Nitya in the occult mysteries; soon he was having visions of the Masters and received his formal Theosophical Initiation. Their father was extremely unhappy that the boys had been taken from him and were being encouraged to give up all Orthodox Hindu ritual; he was also uncomfortable with Leadbeater's history. Besant brokered a compromise in which Narianiah gave her legal custody of the boys with the understanding that they would be kept away from Leadbeater—a promise that went unkept. Narianiah later successfully sued for custody, but by then the boys were in England, rendering the judgment moot.

Besant arrived in London with her charges in 1911, creating great excitement among the Theosophists. The Society had recently published *At the Feet of the Master,* a book said to have been authored by Krishnamurti, but that may have been written by Leadbeater. Also in 1911, Besant had started an international organization called the Order of the Star in the East to promote public reception of the idea that Krishnamurti would become the new World Teacher. She had a passion for organizations and started many, but this one would prove the most successful Theosophical venture of all time. The boys returned briefly to India that year, but were removed again as Narianiah continued his threats of a lawsuit. The brothers lived primarily in England between 1911 and 1922.

Much later, describing his early years in Theosophy, Krishnamurti related an incident from that time which suggests how frightening and disorienting his new role must have felt. He refers to himself in this passage in the third person, which he had a habit of doing from the 1930s onward:

> He [Krishnamurti] was literally worshipped—and he used to shrink from all that. There was a scene, I believe, when returning with Dr. Besant from Europe at a station in India, the train stopped and a huge mob came and wanted to see the boy. He had locked himself in the lavatory and wouldn't come out.

Because he was shy and didn't want any of this. And Dr. Besant had to come and said: "Please come out." And only because she asked, he came out; otherwise, he wouldn't have come. And the train was held up, I don't know for how many hours. Because they all hung on the rails, on the roof, and everywhere. And this boy, neither worship, nor flattery, nor crowds—nothing seemed to touch him. So—he was vague, moronic, perhaps that's not the word, but enough to describe a boy who was absolutely vacant. He would tell everybody: "I will do whatever you want." That used to be his favorite phrase. "I'll do what you want." Even now sometimes it happens.[6]

This probably occurred in 1911, when Krishna was about sixteen. This story is made sadder by the fact that Krishnamurti could not even claim it as his own experience, but had to speak of it in the third person.

KRISHNAMURTI AND THEOSOPHY

As Krishnamurti aged, his relationship with Theosophy became increasingly ambivalent. He loved Besant and several other members (although not Leadbeater, who he did not care for), but the occult visions of his early years of initiation were being replaced by frustration with the claustrophobic social atmosphere and skepticism concerning the Society's esoteric claims. The brothers were well cared for, but their lives were highly structured by others, even after they reached maturity. Even small details, like what they ate and how they could spend their money, were dictated by Theosophical leaders. Krishna was not allowed any privacy; Mrs. Besant had decreed that two Society members must be with him at all times. It also must have been difficult for the young men to comply with the Society's expectations concerning their continued celibacy; it was unthinkable that Krishna, the future World Teacher, would ever become attached to a woman, let alone lose his virginity or marry. He became increasingly sulky and withdrawn, more interested in cars and clothes than in spiritual matters. Yet the pressure to remain within the system was strong; as the World Teacher, he had an aristocratic standard of living and thousands of adoring followers. Without Theosophy, Krishna would have been just another Indian. He could, however, have returned to obscurity without financial worry; in 1913, a wealthy follower had given him an independent income—500 pounds a year for life.

By 1921, Krishna's discomfort had become extreme. At twenty-six, he was developing his own ideas about the spiritual path, and they did not coincide nicely with Theosophy. Krishna did not like complicated rituals, but Besant and Leadbeater were both enamored of them and continually created additional and increasingly baroque ceremonies, vestments, orders, and badges. Nitya, the person that Krishna was closest to in the world and in some ways his only truly intimate friend, had been diagnosed with tuberculosis. Krishna had also fallen in love for the first time, but of course he could not marry the woman. He had tried to begin to take more of a leadership role within the Order of the Star, but had become disgusted with the bickering and petty jealousies that dominated the society. At the end of 1921, Mrs. Besant had sent him back to India to "begin his work," but he found that he hated public speaking and was not particularly good at it, especially in India. He had forgotten the Telugu of his childhood and knew no Indian languages.

In 1922, the brothers moved to Australia, where Leadbeater had relocated in 1914. Through the influence of a new friend, Josiah Wedgwood, Leadbeater was now happily involved with a new spin-off from Theosophy, the Liberal Catholic Church. "The Mass followed the Roman Catholic ritual, but the liturgy, which Mrs. Besant had helped Leadbeater to compose, was in English; there was no confessional; and celibacy was not required of the clergy. The priests as well as the bishops were decked out in gorgeous vestments." Leadbeater and Wedgwood were both now bishops, as well as Theosophical Initiates, and "the old man had more power than ever now, for he was able to create priests as well as give out occult advancements."[7] Krishna's reaction is preserved in a letter to his good friend and foster mother, Lady Emily Lutyens: "Sunday morning I went to the L.C.C. church & C.W.L. was the acting priest. He did it all very well but you know I am not a ceremonialist & I do not appreciate all the paraphernalia with all those prayers & bobbing up & down, the robes etc.; but I am not going to attack it, some people like to so what right have I to attack or disapprove of it? The church lasted 2½ hours & I was so bored that I was nearly fainting. I am afraid I rather showed it. I must be careful or else they will misunderstand me & there will be trouble."[8]

By the end of this tour, Nitya was exhausted and showing spots on both lungs. It was decided that he should go to Switzerland for treatment, but that the brothers would break their journey in California. A Theosophical friend had a house in the Ojai Valley, 80 miles north of Los Angeles, where the climate was said to be beneficial for consumptives. Krishna begged Besant to give him time off from public work: "I told her that my mental body was not developed enough and that I wanted to study quietly and uninterruptedly."[9]

As it turned out, Ojai would become the place that Krishnamurti most thought of as home. He liked California right away; speaking of the University of California, at Berkeley, he wrote:

> There was not that dreadful distinction between men & women which creates that peculiar atmosphere so particular in England & elsewhere. People look one another full in the face, not that sidelong glance so painful in the older countries. I wanted to live there & relive some of my life. The laisser aller [unconstraint] of everybody was my particular delight. . . . I wanted to help them all; I felt so friendly, so amiable, not caring even if they knew my history. There was not that aloofness that exists between the godly Englishman & the humble Indian. That arrogant spirit of class & of color was not to be found there. . . . One breathed the air of freedom of equality which is the equality of opportunity & of ability irrespective of class, creed or color. I was so thrilled that I wanted to carry the physical beauty of the place with me to India.[10]

In Ojai, Krishnamurti and Nitya had their first taste of normal life, away from imposed restrictions and the public eye. The physical landscape charmed them both. As Nitya's health deteriorated, a Theosophical friend sent her sister, Rosalind Williams, to help with nursing. Rosalind, then nineteen and very beautiful, struck up an easygoing friendship with both brothers. She and Nitya fell in love. Nitya began to get better, and Krishnamurti began meditating daily, determined to recapture the mystical certainties of his adolescence. He wrote to Lady Emily that "*I am going to get back* my old touch with the Masters & after all that's the only thing that matters in life & nothing else does. At first it was difficult to meditate or to concentrate & even though I have been doing it for only a week, I am agreeably surprised."[11]

KRISHNAMURTI AND THE "PROCESS"

A week later the "Process" began, as it came to be known among Krishnamurti's intimates. In brief, the Process refers to Krishnamurti's periods of physical pain in the neck, head, and spine, accompanied by mental anguish, amnesia, and dissociation. The first episodes occurred in Ojai in 1922 but continued periodically throughout his life. During them, Krishnamurti would complain of intense pain and feverish chills. At Ojai (though not later) he also was deeply disturbed that everything, especially his bed, seemed dirty and he did not want to be touched or even seen. He would lie in bed for hours, writhing with pain and mumbling feverishly. He would talk in a variety of voices, often as if he was a small boy. He would talk to invisible presences or converse with hallucinatory images of his own past.

Some people have interpreted these episodes in spiritual terms: as the by-product of his rising kundalini, as the Masters readjusting his physical body in order to purify and hone it for their possession and use, or even as evolutionary mutation of his neural system. An argument can also be made that these episodes were dissociative fugues indicative of a personality disorder. Krishnamurti had difficulties throughout his life remembering the past, expressing emotion, and formulating a coherent sense of self. His early life had been painful and traumatic in many ways, a fact generally denied by him and his controlling, overbearing community of followers and promoters. His recent trip had been emotionally exhausting; he had seen both his estranged father and Leadbeater after a considerable period away from them, been separated from his first romantic love, and dealt (or not dealt) with Nitya's declining health. In Ojai, he was suddenly put in the novel position of being isolated with his thoughts about the past; his new experiments in meditation would have heightened his introspective turn. Nitya's withdrawal from him into his romance with Rosalind would have threatened Krishna's most important and intimate relationship.

Regardless of the mechanism causing these episodes, spiritual or secular, in the final analysis the pain seems to have been worth the insight that Krishnamurti gleaned from them. Afterward, memory of the suffering paled in comparison to the memory of the mystical experiences that followed. These experiences included, somewhat paradoxically, both a sense of unity with humanity and nature, and a sense of calling, of being set apart, of finally achieving the unique messianic status that had so long been attributed to him. He wrote that

> I came to myself about noon each day. On the first day while I
> was in that state and more conscious of the things around me,
> I had the most extraordinary experience. There was a man
> mending the road; that man was myself; the pickaxe he held was
> myself; the very stone which he was breaking up was a part of
> me; the tender blade of grass was my very being, and the tree
> beside the man was myself. I almost could feel and think like the
> roadmender, and I could feel the wind passing through the tree,
> and the little ant on the blade of grass I could feel. The birds,
> the dust, and the very noise were a part of me. Just then there
> was a car passing by at some distance; I was the driver, the en-
> gine, and the tires; as the car went further away from me, I was
> going away from myself. I was in everything, or rather every-
> thing was in me, inanimate and animate, the mountain, the
> worm, and all breathing things. All day long I remained in this
> happy condition.[12]

On the next day, both the hysteria and the following euphoria were even more intense:

> That evening at about the same hour of six I felt worse than ever. I wanted nobody near me nor anybody to touch me. I was feeling extremely tired and weak. I think I was weeping from mere exhaustion and lack of physical control. My head was pretty bad and the top part felt as though many needles were being driven in. While I was in this state I felt that the bed in which I was lying, the same one as on the previous day, was dirty and filthy beyond imagination and I could not lie in it. Suddenly I found myself sitting on the floor and Nitya and Rosalind asking me to get into bed. I asked them not to touch me and cried out that the bed was not clean. I went on like this for some time till eventually I wandered out on the verandah and sat a few moments exhausted and slightly calmer. I began to come to myself and finally Mr. Warrington asked me to go under the pepper tree which is near the house. [Mr. Warrington must have been aware of Krishnamurti's intense and positive relationship with nature, and wisely thought that being out of the house in a natural setting would be soothing to him.] There I sat cross-legged in the meditation posture. When I had sat thus for some time, I felt myself going out of my body, I saw myself sitting down with the delicate tender leaves of the tree over me. I was facing the east. In front of me was my body and over my head I saw the Star, bright and clear. Then I could feel the vibrations of the Lord Buddha; I beheld Lord Maitreya and the Master K. H. I was so happy, calm and at peace. I could still see my body and I was hovering near it. There was such profound calmness both in the air and within myself, the calmness of the bottom of a deep unfathomable lake. Like the lake, I felt my physical body, with its mind and emotions, could be ruffled on the surface but nothing, nay nothing, could disturb the calmness of my soul. The Presence of the mighty Beings was with me for some time and then They were gone. I was supremely happy, for I had seen. Nothing could ever be the same. I have drunk at the clear and pure waters at the source of the fountain of life and my thirst was appeased. Never more could I be thirsty, never more could I be

in utter darkness; I have seen the Light. I have touched compassion which heals all sorrow and suffering; it is not for myself, but for the world.[13]

These experiences gave Krishnamurti a renewed interest in Theosophy. He began writing for Star publications, answering letters, and speaking publicly in the Los Angeles area. He also arranged for the Society to buy a bigger house at Ojai for his use. In 1923 he toured the United States, speaking at Theosophical and Star centers and attending the Theosophical Society Convention in Chicago. The Process continued: "He was in constant pain, with a throbbing and burning at the base of his spine. He frequently went out of his body when, Nitya told him, he would groan and weep and call out for his mother."[14] His belief in the Masters was restored, and he began to develop a flair for public speaking. He continued, however, to be uncomfortable with the ritual aspects of Theosophy, as well as the endless and petty politicking.

Finally, in 1925 Krishnamurti's faith in the Masters suffered a crushing blow, although it would take years before he worked this out and came to grips with it. While Krishnamurti was in India, Nitya died in Ojai. He had not originally wanted to leave his brother, but Besant, Leadbeater, and his own visions of the Masters had all assured him that Nitya's life would be spared so that Nitya could aid Theosophy with his work. Krishnamurti continued his Theosophical work, but his faith in it waned from that time onward. Later in life, he maintained that his own experiences with the Masters were nothing more than psychological manifestations of his own desires for occult experience.

KRISHNAMURTI'S BREAK
WITH ORGANIZED RELIGION

Krishna's loss of his brother added a new dimension to his personal faith and his sense of empathy with humanity. In 1926, he wrote in *The Herald of the Star* that an old dream is dead and a new one is being born, as a flower that pushes through the solid earth. A new vision is coming into being and a greater consciousness is being unfolded. . . . A new strength, born of suffering, is pulsating in the veins and a new sympathy and understanding is being born of past suffering—a greater desire to see others suffer less, and, if they must suffer, to see that they bear it nobly and come out of it without too many scars. I have wept, but I do not want others to weep; but if they do, I now know what it means.[15]

In a poem published in 1931, he would again refer to both his personal loss and the newfound emotional maturity later gained from it:

I looked for his face
In every passer-by
And asked each if he had met with my brother;
But none could give me comfort
I worshipped,
I prayed,
But the gods were silent.
I could weep no more;
I could dream no more . . . And then
In my search,
I beheld Thee,
O Lord of my heart;
In Thee Alone
O my eternal Love,
Do I behold the faces
Of all the living and all the dead.[16]

Nitya's death appears to have even further distanced Krishnamurti from his past and any normal sense of self. It was after this point that he began referring to himself in the third person, often as "K." At a Star Congress in December of 1925, while speaking of the World Teacher (another Theosophical name for Maitreya) he suddenly began speaking in the first person: "He comes only to those who want, who desire, who long . . . and I come for those who want sympathy, who want happiness, who are longing to be released, who are longing to find happiness in all things. I come to reform and not to tear down, I come not to destroy but to build."[17] He said shortly afterward that he felt like a shell—impersonal. This sort of dissociation is not uncommon in the aftermath of a tragedy; what was peculiar about Krishnamurti's case was that he had thousands of people interpreting his grief as a messianic sign. Theosophical membership continued to rise, peaking in 1928 at 45,000.

Krishnamurti continued to try to work within Theosophy, but as his views matured he ran increasingly at cross purposes with the Society's elite. He talked more and more of individual freedom and less and less about the Masters. Some, including Wedgwood, whispered that the personality filling Krishnamurti was not Maitreya after all but, rather, a powerful black magician using the "vehicle" to attack the movement. Krishnamurti continued to despise ritual and politics, and became increasingly vocal about his beliefs, even when they were sure to displease his superiors. For example, when Mrs. Besant announced that another prominent Theosophical member, Rukmini Arundale, had been chosen as the vehicle for the World Mother (Mary, in a former life), Krishnamurti dismissed her claims as the "outcomes of his [George Arundale's] fertile brain." He frequently told audiences that they, too, could reach liberation through direct contact with the Beloved, without any need for intermediaries, Masters, gurus, or World Teachers.

By this time, Krishnamurti had fully established a lifelong habit of dividing his time fairly equally between India, California, and Europe, often visiting all three continents annually, giving lectures and hosting private gatherings in each place. In May 1928, he gave his first public lecture in the United States (earlier lectures had been exclusively for Theosophical Society members) to 16,000 people at the Hollywood Bowl. His topic was "Happiness through Liberation." That summer, he gave his first "camp" in Ojai. The camp was probably modeled on the Chautauqua Movement, popular from 1874 to about 1910 in the United States (Greenacre, the adult education summer camp in Maine that Vivekananda spoke at, was also probably inspired by Chautauqua).

The camp was a Theosophical tradition of a week-long, festive seminar of tent camping, campfire talks, and lectures. One thousand people attended the first Ojai camp, and it was held annually throughout the 1930s with varying degrees of success.

Finally, at the annual Star Camp in Holland in the summer of 1929, the tension between Krishnamurti's evolving philosophy and the Theosophical status quo reached its climax. As the head of the Order of the Star, Krishnamurti simply dissolved the organization. His announcement, to more than 3,000 Star members who had come from all over the world to attend the festivities, was magnificent:

> I maintain that Truth is a pathless land, and you cannot approach it by any path whatsoever, by any religion, by any sect. That is my point of view, and I adhere to that absolutely and unconditionally. Truth, being limitless, unconditioned, unapproachable by any path whatsoever, cannot be organized; nor should any organization be formed to lead or coerce people along any particular path. If you first understand that, then you will see how impossible it is to organize a belief. A belief is purely an individual matter, and you cannot and must not organize it. If you do, it becomes dead, crystallized; it becomes a creed, a sect, a religion, to be imposed on others.
>
> This is what everyone throughout the world is attempting to do. Truth is narrowed down and made a plaything for those who are weak, for those who are only momentarily discontented. Truth cannot be brought down, rather, the individual must make the effort to ascend to it. . . .
>
> The moment you follow someone you cease to follow Truth. I am not concerned whether you pay attention to what I say or not. . . . I am concerning myself with only one essential thing: to set man free. I desire to free him from all cages, from all fears, and not to found religions, new sects, nor to establish new theories and new philosophies. . . . If there are only five people who will listen, who will live, who have their faces turned towards eternity, it will be sufficient. Of what use is it to have thousands who do not understand, who are fully embalmed in prejudice,

who do not want the new, but would rather translate the new to suit their own sterile, stagnant selves? . . .

Because I am free, unconditioned, whole, not the part, not the relative, but the whole Truth that is eternal, I desire those, who seek to understand me, to be free, not to follow me, not to make out of me a cage. . . . Rather should they be free from all fears. . . . As an artist paints a picture because he takes delight in that painting, because it is his self-expression, his glory, his well-being, so I do this and not because I want any thing from anyone.[18]

This heroic act was Krishnamurti's finest hour.

In this remarkable speech Krishnamurti did not reject the idea that he was the World Teacher, at least not explicitly; he affirmed that he was liberated, enlightened, perfected. He affirmed that he had a special mission to help others, and that the essence of salvation was gnostic—a matter of understanding hidden wisdom. In these respects, he did not deny the theoretical basis of Theosophy's hopes for him. In dissolving the Order, Krishnamurti was specifically attacking the role of organized institutions in the spiritual life. At the same time, of course, Yogananda and the Ramakrishna Vedanta Society were rushing to embrace Western forms of institutionalization as a useful and practical tool; but then, they had not been intimately exposed to the worst excesses of organized religion in the way that Krishnamurti had.

In rejecting organized religion, however, Krishnamurti did not reject organization. His publication and public speaking career continued unabated after his break with the Theosophical Society. The *Star Bulletin* continued to be published and circulated widely; he continued to publish books of lectures and poetry; the summer camps at Ojai continued; he still toured the world giving lectures and running small-group discussions. None of this would have been possible without his business manager, Desikacharya Rajagopalacharya, known as D. Rajagopal.

Rajagopal was a brilliant intellectual in his own right, as well as an administrative genius. He was born in Madras in 1900. His father was a Theosophist, and Rajagopal was one of a long list of handsome young boys "discovered" by Leadbeater. For a while, during Krishna's rebellious phase, Leadbeater toyed with the idea that it was Rajagopal who would be the next World Teacher, but Besant resisted Krishna's replacement. Rajagopal met Krishna and Nitya in 1920 in England; the brothers were at first disdainful of the new Theosophical star but eventually warmed to him. Unlike Krishna, Rajagopal enjoyed academics and did well at Cambridge (Krishnamurti did not pass the entrance exams). During the 1920s, he established a respectable career for himself doing organizational work for the Society. In 1927, he married Rosalind Williams, and they settled in Ojai. When Krishnamurti left Theosophy, Rajagopal left with him and dedicated his considerable skills to the propagation of Krishnamurti's teachings. He expertly edited all of Krishnamurti's publications until 1968. He also arranged all the practical details of Krishnamurti's complicated life and finances: paying bills, buying tickets, arranging travel plans, dealing with publishers, making excuses when Krishnamurti failed to show up for a booked lecture. Krishnamurti himself was disorganized and impractical and relied heavily on Rajagopal for the execution of all the details of his career.

The 1930s also saw the consolidation of Krishnamurti's basic message, which subsequently remained fairly consistent throughout his career. Krishnamurti taught that God was identical with Truth, and that the pure religious quest consisted of throwing off all false consciousness and engaging in an internal, meditative, and heroic quest for self-knowledge. By honestly confronting the authentic self, the seeker could finally apprehend Truth itself. The perception of reality as it is, rather than as one wishes it was, then produces spiritual regeneration and evolution. Krishnamurti's stance was radical: Introspection can create a conscious unity between the individual and *noumena,* things as they really are, cutting through *phenomena,* things as they normally appear to human beings.

KRISHNAMURTI
AND ROSALIND RAJAGOPAL

The 1930s were a productive and happy time for Krishnamurti, perhaps the happiest of his life. Freed from the restraints of Theosophy, he was nonetheless able to continue to speak and write to a large audience as he saw fit, thanks to the organizational efforts of Rajagopal. According to Sloss, he was also in love.[19] By 1932, Rosalind was unhappy and lonely in her marriage. Her union with Rajagopal had been based on friendship rather than romantic passion, but that friendship dwindled quickly into a distant business partnership, due mostly to Rajagopal's frenetic work schedule, poor health, and emotional and physical absences. Even the birth of their only child in 1931, their daughter Radha, could not draw them together. Rajagopal was out of the country and did not see his daughter until she was six weeks old.[20] This kind of emotional distancing was typical of him.

Krishnamurti's schedule was more relaxed, and he spent a great deal of time with Rosalind and Radha. Krishnamurti and Rosalind had been close for a decade; rumors about them had circulated between Nitya's death and Rosalind's marriage, which some had believed was arranged by the Theosophy elite to defray said rumors. Unlike Rajagopal, Rosalind was never a Theosophist and not interested in spiritual matters. Her interest in Krishnamurti was entirely personal; she always treated him like an equal rather than a guru.

By 1932 they were lovers, and their affair would last for two decades. Krishnamurti delighted in his new freedom and the simple pleasures at Ojai, punctuated by his lecture tours and a steady stream of distinguished guests. In 1938, Krishnamurti became friends with Aldous Huxley, who he met through Gerald Heard. Their mutual admiration was heightened by their mutual commitment to pacifism; both would speak forthrightly against the war in the coming years and be criticized for it. Huxley was experimenting with the Ramakrishna Vedanta Society at the time, as were Heard and his friend, Christopher Isherwood. However, Huxley's critical mind was more at home with Krishnamurti's insistence on personal experience and experiment. The two men shared a love of nature and went on long walks in the hills together. Maria Huxley and Rosalind Rajagopal became close friends as well. Krishnamurti enjoyed the company of celebrities, and his social circle included Frieda Lawrence, Greta Garbo, and Charles Chaplin.

Krishnamurti's travels were restricted during the war years, as was his normally extravagant budget. By 1945, relations at Ojai were getting claustrophobic and strained. At the urging of friends, Rosalind was struggling to make a career for herself apart from Krishnamurti; in 1946 she opened the Happy Valley School in Ojai, a project that would involve her for eighteen years. Krishnamurti was also ill that year, and, although Rosalind nursed him faithfully through it, by the end of the year she was exhausted and irritated with him. Rajagopal was busy, too; in 1945, he had revamped his organizational structure, and the Star Publishing Trust became Krishnamurti Writings, Inc. (KWINC).

In 1947, Krishnamurti went to India on his own; it was the first time in two decades that he had traveled without Rajagopal to coordinate his itinerary. The result invigorated him. He stayed for eighteen months and created a circle of new friends and supporters that would remain important to him for the rest of his life. Among them were two sisters, Pupul and Nandini Jayakar. Although there is no proof that Krishnamurti and Nandini had an affair, he developed a crush on her, which in turn further eroded his relationship with Rosalind. The Process intensified yet again. Krishnamurti later viewed this period as transitional for him: "Full awakening came in India in 1947 and 1948."[21]

After his return to the United States, Krishnamurti tried to resurrect his romance with Rosalind, even taking most of the year off in 1950 in order to stay in Ojai courting her. He told his Indian disciples that he was on retreat and observing silence. But Rosalind's jealousy over Nandini had led her to confide in Rajagopal, who she believed had known all along about her sexual relationship with Krishnamurti. He had not, or at least had preferred actively ignoring it, and relationships between the three of them sunk deeper and deeper into a mire of lies, misunderstandings, and petty accusations. The final split between Krishnamurti and Rajagopal would not come until 1968, when Krishnamurti disassociated himself entirely from KWINC and sued Rajagopal for all of the organization's assets and copyrights. Krishnamurti then set up an alternative organization, the Krishnamurti Foundation. Litigation dragged on through the courts until Krishnamurti's death in 1986.

Despite their growing antagonism for one another, Rajagopal and Krishnamurti continued to collaborate fruitfully through the mid-1960s. During the 1950s, Rajagopal was able to establish business relationships with mainstream publishers like Harper & Row, which greatly increased the circulation of Krishnamurti's writings. Postwar prosperity caused a surge in charitable donations and lecture fees; operations thrived. By 1965, thanks in part to Aldous Huxley's ongoing veneration, Krishnamurti was an established part of American countercultural iconography, especially on college campuses, where he lectured frequently. His legal disputes did little to tarnish his reputation as an awakened spiritual master, since Rajagopal was blamed for everything and cast as a greedy, controlling bureaucrat whom Krishnamurti had fled in order to maintain the purity of his teaching.

During his last two decades, Krishnamurti was ably cared for by his companion Mary Zimbalist, a widow and longtime friend. Her cheerful support must have been a relief after his dealings with the Rajagopals; in an interview after his death, Zimbalist insisted that she saw no difference between the man and the teaching. "One of the many extraordinary things about him was that there was never any shadow in Krishnamurti. He really was what you saw, what you sensed, and infinitely more, but nothing was ever in contradiction."[22] Later in the interview, she added:

> To me his life was proof that a human being is capable of extraordinary intelligence and perception, and a way of living that is different from most human life. It was real in him, it was not something I imagined. Doubtless some will say I am projecting onto him some ideal. But for me it was incontrovertibly evident that this man was what he was talking about and he lived that way. In all the years I was with him I never saw anything that denied that or was inconsistent with a life lived that way. There were no contradictions. At many, many times there was undeniably a sense of something I can only call sacred.[23]

Krishnamurti died of cancer at the age of ninety-one at home in Ojai. The Krishnamurti Foundations in India, America, and England continue to publish and distribute his writings. A library and archives still operate in Ojai.

THE TEACHING
OF MINDLESS AWARENESS

Although he is sometimes portrayed as a secular philosopher and a materialist (and sometimes spoke like one, especially in his last three decades), Krishnamurti clearly believed that the source of his personal power and knowledge was supernatural, the same divine energy that united and animated the cosmos. He talked about this energy, if he talked about it at all, in impersonal and oblique terms. "There is an element in all this which is not man-made, thought-made, not self-induced, "he once told Mary Lutyens, his official biographer. "We are trying with our minds to touch *that*. Try to find out what *that* is when your mind is completely quiet."[24]

Krishnamurti gives the impression of being secular because he rarely spoke of *that*. He thought that dogmatic faith in such things was harmful; only personal experience of spiritual essence justified its contemplation. He therefore encouraged his listeners, first and foremost, to examine their own experiences honestly. Nevertheless, he implied that, once self-examination had reached a mature and subtle level, perception of *that* would necessarily follow. Truth might be a pathless land, but it was a land that existed.

Krishnamurti's Notebook, a printed record of a journal that he kept from 1961 to 1962, begins with "In the evening it was there: suddenly it was there, filling the room, a great sense of beauty, power and gentleness. Others noticed it." This "it" is what I am talking about, the lifeblood of Krishnamurti's message: beauty, power, gentleness, truth, reality, love, all inadequate words for a single power. Krishnamurti attacked belief and dogma concerning this power because he believed that hearsay was a pale imitation of the reality and that this power could be experienced only after one let go of all conditioning and expectations. According to Krishnamurti, this essence is real but discursive cognition is not, being an artificial system. Therefore, the seeker must use right meditation —what Krishnamurti called *mindless awareness*—to reach beyond the rational mind to direct experience of the infinite:

> When the mind is swept clean of image, of ritual, of belief, of symbol, of all words, mantrams and repetitions, and of all fear,

then what you see will be the real, the timeless, the everlasting, which may be called God; but this requires enormous insight, understanding, patience, and it is only for those who really inquire into what is religion and pursue it day after day to the end. Only such people will know what is true religion. The rest are merely mouthing words, and all their ornaments and bodily decorations, their pujas and ringing of bells—all that is just superstition without any significance. It is only when the mind is in revolt against all so-called religion that it finds the real.[25]

Mindless awareness, which Krishnamurti also referred to simply as meditation, was his prescription for how to find the real.

Mindless awareness resembles Zen practice more than kriya yoga. It is not a matter of disciplining the mind to concentrate on a single point or principle, but rather the cultivation of a detached awareness of one's own mental processes. It is not something that involves effort; the ego must learn to observe the mind passively rather than attempt to control it. The ego, or constructed self, is a barrier between the true self and reality. According to Krishnamurti, mindless awareness cannot be taught by another, except indirectly and through suggestive metaphor. Instead, each individual must take personal responsibility for bringing about awareness of reality through a process of rigorous self-examination and experimentation:

> Meditation is one of the greatest arts in life—perhaps *the* greatest, and one cannot possibly learn it from anybody. That is the beauty of it. It has no technique and therefore no authority. When you learn about yourself, watch yourself, watch the way you walk, how you eat, what you say, the gossip, the hate, the jealousy—if you are aware of all that in yourself, without any choice, that is a part of meditation. So meditation can take place when you are sitting in a bus or walking in the woods full of light and shadows, or listening to the singing of birds or looking at the face of your wife or child.[26]

Or again,

> Meditation is constant awareness and pliability, not an adjustment to any standard or mode of conduct. Try to be aware of

your own idiosyncrasies, fancies, reactions, and wants in your daily life, and understand them; out of that comes the reality of fulfillment. For this deep comprehension there cannot be any system.[27]

Mindless awareness is not a withdrawal from life, as in samadhi where the external world vanishes and only the sense of cosmic unity remains. Instead, it is a state in which ego-consciousness dissolves leaving only a vivid awareness of the external world:

> Meditation is not a withdrawal from life. It is not concentration. Meditation is the constant discernment of what is true in the actions, reactions, and provocations of life. To discern the true cause of struggle, cruelty, and misery is true meditation.[28]

As this quotation suggests, Krishnamurti wished to draw a connection between mindless awareness and the ability to love. Krishnamurti equated truth with love, and increased self-knowledge with increased compassion. Indeed, one of the main reasons true knowledge is meaningful is that it creates a loving heart. The ego-centered life is incapable of producing love, only self-interest. By "self," Krishnamurti meant the accumulated memories that produce the idea that the individual stands apart from the web of life, isolated and in competition with other living beings. The self is an evil thing, "because the self is dividing; the self is self-enclosing; its activities, however noble, are separative and isolating."[29] In contrast, the mind emptied of the idea of self identifies its essence with the energy that runs through all of life. Identity brings empathy and the ability to truly love: "Only when the brain has cleansed itself of its conditioning, greed, envy, ambition, then only can it comprehend that which is complete. Love is this completeness."[30] The *that,* the *it* that Krishnamurti hinted at—the unifying sacred thread running through all things that can be seen when the self is cleansed of intellectualism and ego—is the source of love itself:

> There was, this morning that peculiar sacredness, filling the room. It had great penetrating power, entering into every corner of one's being, filling, cleansing, making everything itself. The other [person there] felt it too. It's the thing that every human craves for and because they crave for it, it eludes them.

The monk, the priest, the sanyasi torture their bodies and their character in their longing for this but it evades them. For it cannot be bought; neither sacrifice, virtue nor prayer can bring this love.[31]

In order to be filled with this love, this sacred power, it is first necessary to overcome the sense that the world is divided into a duality, the "I" and the "not-I." According to Krishnamurti, "When the mind and heart are free of all sense of duality, in that completeness there is immortality."[32] Unless one overcomes duality, the mind remains deluded by false dichotomies and cannot grasp the truth. Not only is the distinction between self and other false, but the sense of distinction between mind and heart as well: "True search can begin only when we do not separate mind from emotion."[33] Krishnamurti's objection to all dichotomies cannot be overstated:

The conflict in which we exist is not a struggle between good and evil, between the self and the not-self. The struggle is in our own self-created duality, between our various self-protective desires. There cannot be a conflict between light and darkness; where light is, darkness is not.[34]

When one learns to meditate effectively, however, the false sense of duality evaporates and the person is able to grasp reality as it is, whole and undivided. Sorrow, confusion, and ignorance are replaced with clarity and compassion, and the mind is freed.

Krishnamurti believed that he had realized this freedom and therefore represented the epitome of human spiritual evolution. He held himself up as an example of the perfected man and was accepted as such by his followers. His public career was based on the assumption that he had discovered a reliable and universal technology for inducing spiritual evolution that could be put into practice by anyone. In this, he shared many assumptions concerning the science of religion and universality of religious truth with Paramananda and Yogananda. All three teachers believed that a spiritual practice had to prove itself by delivering the goods. A religious teaching was considered true if and only if it worked by helping those who put their faith in it to advance perceptibly toward their spiritual goals.

KRISHNAMURTI: MASTER OR MORTAL?

This is why I have dwelt at length on Krishnamurti's personal life. If, as he claimed, he had perfected the technique of mindless awareness and mindless awareness leads without fail to perfect love, then we could expect his personal life to be a blameless example of ethical compassion. This does not appear to be the case. Sadly, Krishnamurti's biography paints a portrait of a man who dealt poorly with personal relationships. While advocating fierce honesty, he lied; while cultivating the impression of a celibate renunciant, he secretly slept with Rosalind, the wife of his devoted and loyal business manager; he routinely fled from intimate, complex relationships to the comfort of the infatuated new devotee, leaving behind a trail of broken promises and disappointments. His failures are detailed in a biography by Rosalind and Rajagopal's daughter,[35] but even Pupul Jayakar, whose memoirs of Krishnamurti are unabashedly hagiographic, suggests that Krishnamurti was prone to cutting off devoted friends with no explanation or warning, sometimes after years of service and sacrifice on the part of the disciple.[36]

Some loyalists, like his official biographer, Mary Lutyens, explained these discrepancies by understanding Krishnamurti to be two persons in one body: the enlightened Master and the frail mortal. Critics maintain that his sins make him a charlatan who took advantage of his reputation as a religious teacher in order to gain power and money. Debates concerning the imputed purity of a religious figure tend to polarize around extremes; this tells us more about our own expectations of sainthood than the intentions of the teacher in question. In East and West, the spiritual seeker longs for perfection; the desire is so great that the inspiring teacher is interpreted by his or her followers to be perfect and, therefore, saintly, holy. But humans are never perfect. Saintliness is not perfection, but an ongoing struggle to become so. The perfected saint is not a person who actually exists but, rather, an idea produced by believers. This is why a prophet is not honored in his hometown. It is easier to idealize a person who is only partly known, rather than intimately understood in all her imperfections. This is also why the past will always hold more saints than the present; hagiography is the process by which mortals become gods. It is possible that the advance of modern scholarship, which (when done well) produces biography rather than hagiography, will lead to a new understanding of what it means to be saintly by refusing to allow the reader to ignore the whole personality of the revered figure in favor of an idealized icon. Krishnamurti was neither the perfected vehicle of Maitreya nor was he a contemptible man. He was a troubled but well-meaning man whose mistakes should not negate the extent to which he triumphed over a painful past and devoted his life to teaching and helping others.

This being said, Krishnamurti's hurtful actions say something about the effectiveness of his teachings. Since his program for achieving enlightenment did not even work for him, one might reasonably question how useful his advice might be. Krishnamurti believed that his method of mindless awareness, freedom from intellect, and abandonment of the self in favor of union with the infinite had allowed him to achieve perfection. Yet the facts of his life contradict his belief. Ironically, it appears to the detached reader of his biographies that Krishnamurti's Achilles heel was a dogmatic clutching at certain ideas he had developed in his youth —such as the idea that he was a special and superior person— even though the most vital strands of his thought concern giving up dogma in favor of the real. Krishnamurti himself said that "a good mind must be related to action, to relationship. It must be related to depth. Great scientists sometimes lead the most shoddy lives. They are ambitious, greedy, they fight each other for position and acclaim. Would you say they have good minds?"[37] Yet it was precisely in the realms of action and relationship that Krishnamurti was most ineffective. Good intentions and good words came easier for him. "Only when talking and writing does 'this' come into play,"[38] he told friends, referring to his spiritual power.

To Krishnamurti's credit, this analysis is possible only because he really did value honesty and encouraged it in his followers. As a result, we know more about the gritty details of his life than, say, Yogananda's. Unlike the Krishnamurti Foundation, the Self-Realization Fellowship does not make its historical archives open to the public and does not encourage the objective study of the movement's history. It is therefore impossible to say whether or not Krishnamurti was a more fallible man than Yogananda. On the other hand, Yogananda's followers have created a body of literature praising his interpersonal skills that does not exist among Krishnamurti's supporters. Krishnamurti made people think; Yogananda and Paramananda made them feel loved and loving.

At issue here is the correct relationship between self and other in the spiritually driven life. By uncoupling the religious path from tradition, the seekers discussed in this book were forced to re-examine their goals and values; old strategies for balancing freedom and intimacy could no longer be taken for granted. Krishnamurti valued individual freedom over loving union; for Yogananda, it was the reverse. Perhaps one of the ongoing attractions of religious worldviews is their tendency to promise that the tensions between these two contradictory human needs can be gracefully transcended, whereas secularism asks us to accept their necessary incompatibility.

NOTES

1. Krishnamurti, *Commentaries on Living, First Series,* 97.
2. Campbell, *Ancient Wisdom Revisited,* 102.
3. Washington, *Madame Blavatsky's Baboon,* 98.
4. Campbell, *Ancient Wisdom Revisited,* 54.
5. Washington, *Madame Blavatsky's Baboon,* 122.
6. Blau, *Krishnamurti: 100 Years,* 21.
7. Lutyens, *Krishnamurti: The Years of Awakening,* 151.
8. Ibid.
9. Ibid., 156.
10. Ibid., 158.
11. Ibid., 162.
12. Ibid., 170.
13. Ibid., 170–171.
14. Ibid., 184.
15. Blau, *Krishnamurti: 100 Years,* 38.
16. Ibid., 39. This passage, incidentally, suggests that K. had acquaintance with, and appreciation for, classical Hindu bhakti poetry.

17. Lutyens, *Krishnamurti: The Years of Awakening,* 242.

18. Ibid., 293–294.

19. Sloss, *Lives in the Shadow with J. Krishnamurti.* Sloss, the daughter of Rajagopal and Rosalind, is my only source for Krishnamurti's romantic history with Rosalind. The book is controversial within Krishnamurti circles.

20. Ibid.

21. Jayakar, *Krishnamurti: A Biography,* 105.

22. Blau, *Krishnamurti: 100 Years,* 42.

23. Ibid.

24. Lutyens, *The Life and Death of Krishnamurti,* 162.

25. Blau, *Krishnamurti: 100 Years,* 92.

26. Lutyens, *Krishnamurti: The Years of Fulfillment,* 58.

27. Krishnamurti, *The Collected Works,* Vol. 3, 19.

28. Ibid., 55.

29. Lutyens, *The Penguin Krishnamurti Reader,* 51.

30. Krishnamurti, *Krishnamurti's Notebook,* 9. This is, incidentally, perhaps his most powerful and lucid book, and a good starting place for the reader who is interested in his writings (which are repetitive and obtuse).

31. Lutyens, *The Life and Death of Krishnamurti,* 118.

32. Krishnamurti, *Collected Works,* Vol. 1, 62.

33. Krishnamurti, *Collected Works,* Vol. 3, 3.

34. Ibid., 121.

35. Sloss, *Lives in the Shadow with J. Krishnamurti.*

36. Jayakar, *Krishnamurti: A Biography.*

37. Ibid., 460.

38. Lutyens, *Krishnamurti: The Years of Fulfillment,* 226.

CHAPTER 7

Authority and Freedom

Since Paramananda, Yogananda, and Krishnamurti navigated the same social context, it is not surprising that they struggled with some of the same themes. In the next two chapters, I take a closer look at two of these shared themes and discuss the similarities and differences in how the three teachers dealt with them. In this chapter, I discuss the tension between external authority and personal freedom in religious life, with special reference to how the idea of the guru was modified to fit into American culture. In the next chapter, I discuss the modern search for a science of religion that would allow humanity to construct a universally true religion based on reason, the postmodern demise of this project, and its possible replacement by a worldview in which religion is understood as an art rather than a science.

Religion is an arena in which we express our deepest values and desires through symbolic drama and play. When one embraces democratic and egalitarian values, then the perfect relationship—whether with parent, child, friend, guru, or even God— must be reinterpreted in terms of those new values. This pattern is illustrated in the ways in which Paramananda, Yogananda, and Krishnamurti modified the traditional guru-disciple relationship to reflect the democratic ideals of their modernizing religious movements. The three teachers employed very different patterns of authority, but each of them struggled to redefine the proper balance between authority and freedom in their relationships with their disciples.

THE GURU-DISCIPLE RELATIONSHIP IN INDIA

In India, there are a variety of traditional patterns of religious authority and mentorship. Of these, the guru-disciple relationship is one. In this pattern, the guru is the sole and omnipotent authority in the life of the devotee. Like God, the guru is both parent and master. In fact, the guru *is* God in that he is the fully perfected, fully divine representative of God on earth. The word *guru* simply means teacher or spiritual guide, but among Hindu sects who use the word, *guru* usually means more than a mere mentor. The guru is understood to be enlightened in the strongest sense of the word. He has reached the pinnacle of human development and is perfect in deed and knowledge. He has magical powers, or powers so beyond normal human capacity that they seem magical by comparison. The guru, like an **icon,** is a window through which the disciple can directly see God.

The disciple has an opportunity, through his relationship with his guru, to realize the same perfection in this lifetime, provided he works hard enough and trusts the guru completely in all things. In this sense, the guru functions as a spiritual parent; although he is now the supreme authority, the purpose of the relationship is to train the disciple to spiritual maturity, at which point the disciple himself becomes the enlightened guru to a new generation of seekers. Even when the disciple reaches that level of ultimate attainment, however, he still humbles himself to his own guru. In this way, as well, the guru-disciple relationship parallels the traditional parent-child relationship, in that the adult will never outgrow the sense of being a "baby" in the eyes of the parent.

For some educated, liberal Americans this model of authority is threatening. Giving absolute authority to another person is taboo in the eyes of many Americans and it can be difficult to analyze objectively situations that evoke such a strong emotional response. Sometimes, new religious movements run by charismatic leaders are justifiably feared, for the leader may be an uncaring, power-hungry narcissist.[1] The groups that we have considered here, however, are more complex than that.

On closer examination, the traditional guru-disciple relationship in India is more complex than that, too. It can be more authoritarian and traditional than contemporary Americans are likely to be comfortable with, as are traditional Indian patterns of power between father and child, husband and wife, ruler and subject. However, real relationships between a particular guru and a particular disciple do not necessarily conform to the ideal type described previously. After all, every ideal type is merely a rhetorical device, an abstraction. Actual narratives of the guru-disciple relationship describe a more nuanced, complex relationship that is often based on affection and sculpted to individual needs.[2]

Rhetorical description may shape a relationship but will not absolutely determine it. Consider, for example, American narratives concerning father-son relations. If you talk to a man who was an adolescent in the 1930s, he will probably describe his relationship with his father as one of respect and obedience. If you talk to a man who was an adolescent in the 1970s, he will probably describe a relationship fraught with tension and rebellion. Yet it is quite possible that, in reality, both men combined deference and disobedience toward their fathers in roughly the same proportions. Only their narrative frameworks differ. In a similar manner, the official story of the traditional guru-disciple relationship can mask the room that it left for compromise on the part of the guru and independent action on the part of the disciple.

For example, consider how Vivekananda rebelled against many of Ramakrishna's teachings, even while continuing to speak of his absolute fidelity to Ramakrishna's authority. As a Westernized skeptic and monist, Vivekananda was not comfortable with the ecstatic, devotional aspects of Ramakrishna's religious life. While Ramakrishna was alive, he not only tolerated but encouraged Vivekananda's skepticism and independent thought; this is one of the traits that makes Ramakrishna such an appealing historical figure to many Americans. Vivekananda was won over by Ramakrishna's sincerity and charisma, but after Ramakrishna died he distanced himself from the more magical and emotional dimensions of Ramakrishna's worldview. When speaking to American audiences, he tended to edit out those dimensions, presenting Ramakrishna as an advaitin and Kali as a sanitized and abstract Holy Mother. It is unclear whether he was entirely conscious of this dichotomy; perhaps he just swept it under his mental rug as an issue too uncomfortable to deal with. If so, that would explain his conversion experience of 1898, when he abruptly shifted to a devotional lifestyle that more closely resembled that of his Master and all but retired from public life. The relationship between Ramakrishna and Vivekananda, although in many ways an exemplary guru-disciple relationship, was never one of absolute authority imposed on absolute submission. The genuine love between the two softened the power issue, making fluid and malleable what might otherwise have been cold and formal.

The dichotomy between the traditional rhetoric and traditional behavior patterns in the guru-disciple relationship in India points toward how difficult it can be to transplant a social role from one culture to another. In a traditional Indian setting, the guru is not an omnipotent figure with absolute authority, although his disciples may pretend that this is the case. In fact, the guru is constrained by a web of social factors. Normally, in order to become a guru, a holy person must be sanctioned by a religious institution that is respected by the community; a group of accepted religious specialists inspects the holy person and gives official sanction for his or her teaching career. Even in the case of ecstatic mystics who are unaffiliated with established lines of authority, the community as a whole carefully and skeptically examines the guru's claims of spiritual mastery and holds traditional expectations that the guru must meet in order to be considered a guru by the community. For example, he or she will be expected to be chaste (if not celibate, at least sedately monogamous), to disdain money and worldly pursuits, to be honest, and to live up to his or her own teachings. Cultural expectations for the guru's behavior are prescribed, and the guru's authority rests on his or her ability to conform to the expected role.

THE GURU-DISCIPLE RELATIONSHIP IN THE WEST

The Western disciple often forgets to pick up a copy of this script and as a result gets only half of the plot. For the Indian, the guru is an everyday figure; the idea that some gurus are scoundrels is not surprising. Everyone understands that care must be used in selecting a guru. For the American, the Hindu guru is an exotic and mysterious figure, whose power stems in part from the fact that normal patterns of skeptical inquiry need not be employed. Instead, the seeker feels suddenly and inexplicably freed from the normal straight jacket of critical thinking, suddenly plunged into a mode of decision making that is more creative, intuitive, and daring.

This model has much in common with the Western tradition of romantic love. In the popular imagination of American Indiophiles, the guru-disciple relationship is often portrayed as unique and preordained; the initial meeting is one of "love at first sight," the immediate intuitive knowledge on the part of the disciple (usually a woman) that she has found "The One" (usually a man). "Just as Western romantics feel that marriages are made in heaven, so Eastern mystics declare that the relationship between guru and disciple is so sacred that it is not wrought by chance. Rather, it is ordained by an inner bond that re-establishes itself in life after life," explains Levinsky.[3] Gurus in India are ordinarily chosen with reference to many practical factors that more resemble an arranged marriage than romantic love. In June McDaniel's words,

> The Western mythos of meeting the guru is much like love at
> first sight—there is a spark when their eyes meet, there is a sense
> of the lost parent or beloved, there is an atmosphere of mystery

and romance, full of bells and incense and exotic yogic disciplines. In contrast, the model devotee for most Śāktas was Vivekānanda, who was much more hesitant when he came to visit Rāmakṛṣṇa, and did not recognize him as guru for a long while. For Vaiṣṇavas, the guru is a representative of a lineage and tradition—he is not expected to have the Śākta charisma and is respected for his entrance into the *līlā* of Kṛṣṇa and Rādhā. The Bengali guru-disciple relationship is not based on romantic love, but more on the model of an Indian marriage—not passion, but growing compatibility.[4]

The absolute freedom of the disciple to choose his or her own guru, and the absolute primacy of intuitive emotional experience in making that choice, is a Western interpretation of the guru tradition. McDaniel's comparison of initiation to marriage is perceptive. In India, both marriage and religion have traditionally been embedded in cultural expectations. In the United States, where such structures have been eroded, the personal and emotional elements have grown more prominent as viable bases for decision making in order to compensate for the vacuum created by the lack of tradition and certainty.

It is worthwhile to reflect on the fact that the Western model of romantic courtship is often unsuccessful and may lead to as many unhappy outcomes as arranged marriages do (but at least unhappy modern American marriages tend to be temporary). Gut instinct, it would seem, may lead to the occasional happy ending, but in itself is far from being a foolproof method for making important decisions. Just as many marriages based on "love at first sight" fail, many guru-disciple relationships eventually end in bitter estrangement and a denouncement of prior commitments that resemble a divorce. In all cultures, the wise know that emotional instinct must be tested against reason and objectively gathered information, whether one is choosing a spouse or a guru.

CHARISMA AND RELIGIOUS LEADERSHIP

In the American setting, then, the success of the guru depends on his ability to arouse desire—not by his physical appearance, or at least not overtly or completely, but by the force of his personality.

In a departure from the social scientific norm, I wish to call this ability *charisma,* using the colloquial rather than the sociological sense of the word. The *American Heritage College Dictionary* defines *charisma* as "a rare personal quality of leaders who arouse fervent popular devotion and enthusiasm" or "personal magnetism and charm." The reference to magnetism is interesting here; it suggests physician Franz Mesmer's theories on animal magnetism, a paranormal theory in which an individual could influence the thoughts, actions, or health of others through the willful manipulation of invisible mental forces. The third definition given is the theological one: "an extraordinary power, such as the ability to work miracles, granted by the Holy Spirit." As the allusion to mesmerism suggests, distinctions between popular and theological definitions are not always clear. The ability to move people emotionally, and to inspire fervent devotion, has sometimes been seen as miraculous. Given the potential power of the placebo effect, it is not surprising that charismatics are often perceived as faith healers by their devotees.

The *Penguin Dictionary of Sociology,* in contrast to standard dictionaries, defines *charisma* more technically as "the authority vested in a leader by disciples and followers in the belief that the leader's claim to power flows from extraordinary personal gifts." This definition comes from Max Weber's analysis of domination, and it is contrasted in his work with other forms of authority, such as legal-rational authority (obedience to formal rules that have been established by regular, public authority). In this context, the sociological definition of charisma is unsatisfactory for two reasons. First, I wish to point out that charisma is a trait of personality, rather than a kind of relationship. The sociological definition of charisma emphasizes the relationship between leader and followers, and locates charisma in that matrix. In contrast, many religious believers, including many of the individuals discussed in this book, believe that spiritual progress produces a form of personal power that is very real and very tangible. In the academic study of religion, it is often appropriate to withhold judgment when the interpretations of insiders and outsiders clash on a given subject. I remain open to the possibility that charisma is, just as the believers claim, a force radiating outward from the charismatic rather than merely a mechanical by-product of the right person being in the right place at the right time.

Second, it is not clear to me that charisma is *necessarily* a type of authority. The charismatic usually does exercise authority over his or her devotees, but the charisma itself may be prior to, and separate from, issues of power and politics. Charismatic power is the power of one person to affect another's mood, emotion, or frame of mind; it is not always experienced by the charismatic as the pragmatic, political power *over* others that the word *authority* suggests. Experiencing the charisma of another excites, absorbs, energizes. It does not necessarily command or dominate—although perhaps the opportunity for domination is always latent in the exchange.

I am defining charisma, then, as an unusual ability to capture the interest and imagination of another person through the power of one's integrated personality, rather than instrumentally through a certain trait. After an initial meeting, an ordinary person may leave behind a lasting impression of being physically beautiful, witty, or kind. A charismatic person will leave behind an impression of being unforgettable and desirable, but for no particular reason; the charisma itself will be the prominently remembered feature. Paramanda, Yogananda, and Krishnamurti were all strongly charismatic, and this was crucial to their success.

LIMITS TO THE GURU'S AUTHORITY AND BEHAVIOR

In India the idea of the guru included a traditional set of social constraints that gave limits to his authority and behavior. When Hindu religious teachers exported the word *guru* to the United States, these constraints were not taken along. Once in the States, the guru found a new set of social limitations, also based on the values of the authority-granting audience. Yogananda, Paramananda, and Krishnamurti—as well as all the other Hindu-style gurus who worked the lecture circuit in the 1920s and 1930s—needed to conform not only to the needs of their inner circle of devotees in order to succeed, but also to the expectations of the religious counterculture (e.g., the freemason who allows the swami to book the Freemasonry Society's hall) and, to some extent, the American mainstream (e.g., the café owner who allows a poster advertising the swami's lecture to be hung in her Kansas City establishment).

In some ways, the need to allay fears and prejudices concerning foreign religions imposed strict limits on the behavior of the successful guru. The traditionalists in Calcutta may have sniggered at Paramananda's dapper wardrobe, but his attention to fashion can also be seen as a canny political move that ensured the success of his mission. It would have been more difficult to gain recognition as a viable religious option in Edwardian America dressed in a loincloth. His modifications of dress, furniture, and hygiene paved the way for philosophical eccentricity; his disciples were willing and able to give up Christianity, but not indoor plumbing. Regardless of the rhetorical script in which the disciple gave full authority to the guru, the underlying truth was that the disciple could leave at any time, taking her endowment with her. This provided a counterbalance in the arrangement of power.

Of the three religious authorities that we have examined, Yogananda was the most authoritarian. Unlike Paramananda and Krishnamurti, he did not value individuation, preferring his disciples to work hard at transcending their personal idiosyncrasies in the service of the One True Person. This Person was God, but also Yogananda, who as a perfected soul had realized his full identity with God. This is what he meant by Self-Realization—and what all of his disciples were struggling toward. "Self-scrutiny," he writes, "pulverizes the stoutest ego. But true self-analysis mathematically operates to produce seers. The way of 'self-expression,' individual acknowledgments, results in egotists, sure of the right to their private interpretations of God and the universe." Self-expression breeds delusion; truth "humbly retires before such arrogant originality."[5]

Yet even Yogananda left room for individual taste and freedom, in practice if not in theory. Most disciples, remember, were mail-order customers who had little social contact with other kriyabans, let alone Yogananda himself. Yogananda was able to maintain a high degree of control over his inner circle of monastics, but not over the lay members. Lay members, then as now, used as a "guru" an interiorized, imaginative representation of Yogananda, not Yogananda himself as an external human being. In a way, this mechanism allows the "disciple" to use their own unconscious mind, symbolized by the "guru as imaginary friend," as the source of authority. Anxieties concerning one's own power are quelled while the self is underhandedly still recognized as the authority. This process can be used as a halfway house between the other-directed and inner-directed lives. "I would not have been able to get my Ph.D.," one kriyaban wrote to me, "without the inner mystical guidance of Yogananda." It can be argued that this person cannot consciously trust himself as an authority in life, but can fall back on a symbolic "inner director" who authorizes action in the world and provides faith in one's chosen course.

In SRF, the guru functions as the internalized Perfect Mother. Consider this exchange between Lahiri Mahasaya and his guru, Babaji, reported by Yogananda in *Autobiography of a Yogi*. Lahiri has just met Babaji for the first time in his current human life, and Babaji is explaining how he has been Lahiri's guru for innumerable lifetimes before, always there to watch over Lahiri. With his voice "ringing with celestial love," Babaji says,

> You slipped away and disappeared into the tumultuous waves of the life beyond death. The magic wand of your karma touched you, and you were gone! Though you lost sight of me, never did I lose sight of you! I pursued you over the luminescent astral sea where the glorious angels sail. Through gloom, storm, upheaval, and light I followed you, like a mother bird guarding her young. As you lived out your human term of womb life, and emerged as a babe, my eye was ever on you.[6]

Who among us has not secretly longed to be loved so perfectly? To never be the one left behind during the family expedition to the shopping mall? To never excitedly bring home a finger-painting of a dinosaur only to have Mommy evilly ignore it while talking on the phone? Babaji's monologue reproduces exactly the perennially beloved children's book, *The Runaway Bunny,* in which the baby bunny pretends to hide from Mommy bunny in order to create the satisfying denouement of being tracked down, found, and adored, regardless of the circumstances. For some people, the creation of an internalized, ever-present, all-loving Mommy may be an extremely helpful psychological strategy.

A danger inherent to this strategy, however, is that when one embraces an infantilized view of oneself, one remains dependent on the parentalized authority figure and therefore vulnerable to abuses of power. There is a direct correlation between being a child and being vulnerable; to grow up means to have the strength and savvy to defend oneself successfully. Individuals who choose to manage anxiety by turning their lives over to an authoritarian parent figure cash out on their chances of becoming self-sufficient. Sometimes, this seems like the only viable option, especially when one is very tired and very frightened.

Of course, this set of interpretations is both skeptical and psychological. It makes sense only if one accepts current psychological views concerning the value of personal autonomy. There are other possible ways of understanding the effects of Yogananda's leadership style. In the end, each reader's own worldview will determine which interpretation makes most sense in such matters.

If the guru really was perfect, then there would be no risk in putting absolute faith in his absolute power. Yogananda taught that the guru could never hurt or fail the disciple and that apparent failures were misunderstandings on the part of the disciple. For example, in the *Autobiography,* Yogananda tells a story in which Babaji and his disciples are sitting around a fire, when all of a sudden the guru seizes a burning coal and strikes the bare shoulder of a young student with it. Lahiri Mahasaya, who was present, recoils at the seeming cruelty of the act, but Babaji explains, "Would you rather have seen him burned to ashes before your eyes, according to the decree of his past karma? . . . I have freed [the boy] tonight from painful death. The karmic law has been satisfied through [his] slight suffering by fire."[7] Yogananda's own disciples used this form of reasoning to justify to themselves apparent imperfections in their guru's behavior; an act might seem cruel because they are not yet self-realized, but if they were omniscient like Yogananda they would see how the act was really for the best.

In Yogananda's case, it seems that no great harm was done by suspending critical reasoning in this manner, for he was generally a kindhearted man. In other cases, the results have been much more harmful.[8] Even when the guru means well, overindulgence in narcissistic fantasy at the expense of reason and humility can have disastrous effects. Consider, for example, the pain that Krishnamurti was subjected to when, trusting the omniscience of his theosophical elders, he left his brother's side during Nitya's final illness rather than staying with him until his death. Krishnamurti did not want to be absent from Nitya's final days and would not have gone, except that his gurus assured him that Nitya would be fine while Krishnamurti was away. Besant and Leadbetter did not mean to hurt Krishnamurti; I imagine that they were careless and delusional rather than malicious. The result, however, was the same.

Krishnamurti's rage against all forms of outside authority was, in its own way, just as dangerous and unbalanced as Yogananda's infantilizing dependence on imaginary parents. Given Krishnamurti's traumatic experiences as a theosophical pawn, his unresolved grief is understandable and easy to empathize with, but it hardly makes him a paragon of spiritual perfection. One follower noted

> One often had the impression of such [strong residual] reactions in Krishnamurti, as if in his old age he was still fighting the battles of his youth, trying to free himself from the shrinking walls of the prison he had felt himself to be in. It is particularly noteworthy that in his conversations and talks he constantly— and often without any relevance to the topic at hand—returned to harangues against the Brahmins and the Christians, the only two religious groups with whom he had any prolonged contact during his Theosophical phase. It was quite difficult indeed to

discover any compassion, charity or love in him when he happened to mention either of these two groups. A similar and very deep reaction, with the same sort of emotional vehemence, existed in him against teachers, gurus, hierarchies, and spiritual paths—in fact, against any sort of discipline or process.[9]

Like Yogananda's disciples, Krishnamurti's followers tried to explain away apparent imperfections rather than directly confront the failings of their role model. But while kriyabans were able to maintain absolute certainty that all of Yogananda's actions were ultimately for the best, Krishnamurti's circle employed a different strategy:

> It was as if he had two distinct parts. His deep spiritual essence could soar without effort like an angel in the clear skies of Truth. When he spoke from that part, it was as if the heavenly choir were singing. The listener felt blessed and in total accord. Then there was the relatively superficial personality, formed by his personal history and his struggles to be free of spiritual tyranny. This part was born of conditioning and not of insight. When it took over, it was like the discordant note introduced by the uninvited thirteenth fairy in the tale of Sleeping Beauty.[10]

Lutyens, too, spoke of two Krishnamurtis, the perfected spiritual teacher and the frail human. Krishnamurti seems to have experienced himself as a battlefield of dissociated personalities rather than as an integrated whole. It is possible that he began to use dissociation as a survival strategy after his mother's death. Perhaps ghosts exist and Krishnamurti saw the spirit of his dead mother; perhaps he misinterpreted his overwrought fantasies of her as the perception of an external spirit. If Leadbetter was sexually inappropriate with Krishna and Nitya, this would only have exacerbated an existing pattern. By the time of Nitya's death, Krishna was so dexterous at dissociative strategies that he was able to console himself with the belief that Nitya's spirit had moved into his body so that the death had made his life richer rather than impoverished him.

Krishnamurti also internalized the Theosophical myth that a supreme spiritual being made use of his body for its own purposes. Ten days before his death in 1986, he recorded this statement:

> I was telling them this morning—for seventy years that super-energy—no—that immense energy, immense intelligence, has been using this body. I don't think people realize what tremendous energy and intelligence went through this body—there's a twelve-cylinder engine. And for seventy years—was a pretty long time—and now the body can't stand any more. Nobody, unless the body has been prepared, very carefully, protected and so on —nobody, can understand what went through this body. Nobody. Don't anybody pretend.[11]

In a sense, Krishnamurti employed the same strategy for managing authority that the kriyaban uses: Rather than trusting in an integrated, fallible self, or trusting in an external source of authority, the individual turns to an internalized guru, dissociating the authoritative self and enshrining it as an idealized, perfected spirit within the physical body, but apart from the ordinary functioning ego of daily life. Both Krishnamurti and Yogananda were unable to develop a deeply loving mentor-student relationship with a human teacher. Instead, they jousted internally with imaginary gurus, Babaji and Maitreya.

Yogananda's leadership style, in the hands of the right storyteller, could be transformed into a mythic reaffirmation of the dangers of authoritarian religious leadership. I have tried to show, however, that Krishnamurti represents the flip side of that coin: the danger in total rejection of external reality checking and role modeling. "The most dangerous man in the world," said Thomas Merton, "is the contemplative who is guided by nobody. He trusts his own visions. He obeys the attractions of an inner voice, but will not listen to other men."[12] The trance-visions we induce in ourselves are no more reliable than those induced in us by the authoritarian charismatic. In either case, in order to forge a mature and authentic spiritual path, we must cross-check intuition against reason and compassion. The most reliable method for doing so is to take seriously the advice and example of trustworthy individuals.

PARAMANANDA'S INTERPERSONAL RELATIONSHIPS

From the perspective of contemporary clinical psychology, Paramananda stands out for his mature interpersonal relationships. He was nine when his mother died (Yogananda was eleven and Krishnamurti, ten); the roots of his ability to love authentically may lie in his relationship with his father, who seems to have been more loving and interactive than Yogananda's and Krishnamurti's fathers were. Being closer to his father, Paramananda may have weathered his mother's passing with less internal damage.

A more satisfying explanation, however, for Paramananda's skill at maintaining relationships lies in his healthy relationship with his mentor, Swami Ramakrishnananda. Paramananda had been initiated by Vivekananda, who was therefore formally his guru, but Vivekananda entrusted the bulk of Paramananda's training to Ramakrishnananda. It was a good choice, since Ramakrishnananda's combination of old-fashioned devotion with humble self-discipline suited Paramananda's temperament. He was strict, but Paramananda was undergoing an adolescent rebellion against his doting family and reveled in the challenge. Ramakrishnananda believed in Paramananda entirely, and loved him dearly, but pushed him as far as he could in order to develop his internal discipline; in other words, he functioned as an ideal parent figure for Paramananda. It is common for young adults in late adolescence to need an adult mentor other than their parents to provide a bridge between the family and independent living. Ramakrishnananda was able to provide this sort of apprenticeship period for Paramananda.

Personality, of course, is partly shaped by environment and partly innate. Paramananda was blessed with an unusual capacity to love and be loved. He loved individuals authentically, for themselves, shortcomings and all. He did not try to pass himself off as perfect, nor did he expect the people around him to be perfect. He loved real human beings in their entirety, not just an idealized shard of their personality. This may be why he appeals to some as a role model for living a spiritual life in the modern world.

One of the reasons Paramananda's leadership system worked as well as it did is that he shared authority rather than consolidating it. As a young renunciant in Dakshineswar and Madras, Paramananda had not consolidated his devotion to an authoritarian figure; instead, he revered a variety of elders. His guru, Vivekananda, and his direct superior, Ramakrishnananda, were particularly influential, but he also looked up to and learned from the other monks. In the United States as a young man, he continued to learn from and revere elders, especially Sister Devamata. As a religious leader, he assumed that his charges would also benefit from this strategy, and he shared leadership roles with Devamata, Daya, and Gayatri Devi.

Some human beings come closer to perfection than others do, and blessed are those who have a supportive relationship with a saintly role model. "And who are great men?" asked Paramananda, "Those who are unselfish, all-loving and who remain unmoved under praise or blame; who live in this world not to gain anything for themselves, but to serve and help mankind for love's sake. When we come in contact with such lofty souls, a deep impression is made on our mind and this gradually changes the whole character."[13] At its best, a life devoted to religious heroism is meant to transform one's soul from an ordinary, chaotic mess of conflicting desires and base instincts into a luminous tribute to the inherent possibilities of the human spirit. Enlightenment means to make one's own character the medium with which one strives to create beauty out of disorder, art out of found objects. If this project is successful, said the Apostle Paul, then it will bear fruit: love, joy, peace, patience, kindness, goodness, faithfulness, gentleness, self-control. When students achieve this level of integration and sanctity, then they are drawn to an awakened one. "When the flower opens," said Ramakrishna, "the bees come of their own accord."

This is what the guru-disciple relationship is supposed to be about; the fact that it is sometimes twisted into something less than that should not mask the beauty and heroism of the ideal itself. Those who seek a source of spiritual authority in their life should proceed cautiously, for the world is full of charlatans preying on the needy and naive. Perhaps the best strategy is to seek the goodness itself, rather than the claim to goodness. It might be that one's true guru, the person capable of providing a living role model for how to live a life filled with light rather than darkness, is the kindhearted old woman next door rather than the charismatic prophet at the ashram across town.

NOTES

1. For a discussion of this kind of group, I recommend Oakes' *Prophetic Charisma.*
2. Narayan, *Storytellers, Saints and Scoundrels.*
3. Levinsky, *A Bridge of Dreams,* 105.
4. McDaniel, *The Madness of the Saints,* 242.
5. Yogananda, *Autobiography of a Yogi,* 51.
6. Ibid., 358.
7. Ibid., 349.
8. See, for example, Storr's discussions of the mad guru in *Feet of Clay.*
9. Ravindra, "J. Krishnamurti: Traveler in a Pathless Land," 326.
10. Ibid.
11. Ibid., 334.
12. Kornfield, *A Path With Heart,* 268. This book has a wise discussion of the pros and cons of religious leadership.
13. Paramananda, *Vedanta in Practice,* 51.

CHAPTER 8

Science and Art

Paramananda, Yogananda, and Krishnamurti thought they could advance human understanding of universal spiritual truth by pooling all the relevant insights on the matter from Eastern religion, Western religion, and modern science. Paramananda worked for the Vedanta Society, but he dreamed of building a Temple of the Universal Spirit. Yogananda was trained as a Kriya Yogi but founded the Self-Realization Fellowship. Krishnamurti was groomed as the next Maitreya, then denounced all organized religions, East and West, urging listeners toward the unexplored landscapes of their secret selves. Each believed that Truth was one and that it used to go by various names, but the time was nigh when modern advances in reason and knowledge would establish a global spiritual language.

These men accomplished many things, but this was not one of them. There is no universal religion today; religion is more likely to be wiped out altogether than universally standardized. Consider, for example, the logistical problems simply of establishing religious union between the gurus we have examined in this book. Most of the variables in their individual lives that might be expected to predict religious beliefs overlapped; even so, they could not agree on what universal religion should look like.

SHARED AND CONFLICTING
RELIGIOUS BELIEFS

Yogananda, Paramananda, and Krishnamurti did share some fundamental convictions. They all believed in a spiritual power that could be perceived as personal but was at root impersonal. This power, though not anthropomorphic, has something to do with love, truth, consciousness, and creation. They believed that the individual human being could rise above his inborn tendency to see the world as profane and actually know this divine power. This experience would be transformative, providing the seer with the ability and desire to orient his life toward this power, seeking union and cooperation with it. This would transform the interior life of the seer, but also do more: Divine power would then flow through the realized person out into the world in a tangible, beneficial way. These three men believed that the path to union with the Divine was primarily individual and internal, based on meditation and perception, and could only indirectly be aided by tradition and dogma. The best aid to such an inner transformation was a guide and teacher who had discovered this source of power and subsequently become a fountain through which it flowed into the world.

This is not an exhaustive list of their shared religious beliefs, but it comes close. But that is all it is: a list of shared beliefs. It is not a shared religion because the word *religion* makes sense only when it is applied to a coherent system of belief and action, rather than an isolated part of an integrated whole. Santeria is a religion; killing goats is not. Without splitting hairs concerning the exact dividing line between a part of a system and a whole one, at minimum an attempt should be made, when describing a particular religion, to include the elements that strike the participants themselves as absolutely crucial. The shared beliefs of Yogananda, Paramananda, and Krishnamurti do not do so.

While Paramananda, Yogananda, and Krishnamurti agreed on some very vague basics, their visions of religious truth conflicted as often as not. Yogananda taught kriya yoga. Paramananda taught vedanta. Krishnamurti taught the pursuit of a selfless awareness leading away from labels and toward direct perception of the lack of real boundaries between self and other and of the numinous and sacred quality of that totality. Paramananda and Yogananda called the focus of their religious life God; Krishnamurti did not. Krishnamurti and Yogananda sought the annihilation of the personal ego; Paramananda sought its enhancement, believing that God created unique individuals for a reason and that to exercise personal freedom was to worship God. Yogananda believed that the key to spiritual advancement was manipulation of the physical body. Krishnamurti believed the key was mindless awareness. Paramananda believed that it was loving devotion to a Higher Power. Yogananda and Paramananda believed that long-term, emotionally intimate relationships with others furthered spiritual advancement, whereas Krishnamurti did not. These are substantial disagreements concerning the nature and purpose of the spiritual quest.

It is easy to imagine how the unlikelihood of success in establishing a universal faith could have been overlooked by each guru. Like countless other sincere believers, each was certain that he possessed absolute truth. Yogananda and Krishnamurti went so far as to imply that they were infallible; Paramananda was more modest but still believed he had all the basics down. They also believed that spiritual realization was not a fluke but, rather, an orderly process toward a certain goal that many individuals completed. If this were true, one would expect that all enlightened souls would be in agreement on the relevant facts of the matter. Apparent disagreements must be due to (a) miscommunication or (b) the other person getting it wrong.

They respected science's success at authoritatively establishing universally acknowledged truths concerning the physical world. It was hard not to be impressed; the triumph of science seemed to have been proved again with every new technological marvel. If a theory could be proved by its successful technological application, then perhaps religious beliefs could be proved if they successfully and uniformly produced the predicted results—if, for example, vigilant kriya practice produced the ability to communicate with the dead as flawlessly as an assembly line produced Model T's.

SCIENCE AND RELIGION

It would be misleading to suggest that Paramananda, Yogananda, and Krishnamurti believed in a "science" of religion, if one defined science as the employment of contemporary scientific method (or even state-of-the-art scientific method circa 1920). Their platform was "scientific" in the popular sense of the word, meaning that they pursued the discovery of universally effective technologies and irrefutable knowledge through the use of rational inquiry and experimentation. Like many religious intellectuals of their time, these gurus believed that their knowledge of the spiritual life was based on rational deductions drawn from careful observation, rather than on received wisdom, sloppy thinking, or self-delusion. They believed that divine power was as real as electricity, that it followed its own natural laws, and that its effects could be observed. Paramananda, Yogananda, and Krishnamurti may have been naive or self-deluding concerning their actual scientific rigor, but they were no more so than many other venerable religious (and social scientific) leaders of the time.

There are plenty of premodern precedents for this strategy for determining religious truth. Modernization has led to an absolutely unprecedented set of material conditions for human life. It has also led to a unique constellation of beliefs and subjective experiences, but no single belief in this constellation is unprecedented in the way that computers or reliable birth control are unprecedented. While modernity may have coincided with more widespread preoccupation with reason and personal experience, and a (marginally) wider overall likelihood that actions will be primarily motivated by them, it did not invent these attitudes. Nor has it destroyed other motivations for action; the most scientific person alive still acts out of habit and instinct more often than out of reasoned deduction from justifiable facts.

Science need not conflict with religion. You will remember, from my introduction, that in this book I have defined religion as "a system of beliefs and actions that renders life meaningful and understandable to its adherents, and includes (a) descriptions of supernatural or spiritual forces and (b) an ethical hierarchy of human goals." Science can disprove specific religious dogmas when the dogma makes a truth claim about the physical world that conflicts with scientific evidence. However, it cannot adjudicate between competing values. In fact, science tells us nothing about values at all; in order to find meaning in our lives, we must turn to other ways of knowing and thinking.

Scientific knowledge has, in some cases, undermined the authority of traditional religions that claim to have infallible knowledge about the physical world when those claims turned out to be untrue. Scientific education may make individuals less likely to trust arguments from authority, especially if the authority has been known to be wrong in the past. Unbelievers may be less inclined to convert to the discredited religious institution than would otherwise be the case. However, the believer whose credibility has been challenged has two options other than religious disaffiliation: She can ignore the scientific evidence; or she can deem the debunked article of faith to be of trivial importance, excise it from her religious worldview, and ignore the breach of faith on the part of her religious authorities. People routinely exercise these options.

Scientific progress, then, is only problematic for certain kinds of religious worldviews. A more pervasive challenge to religious faith in the modern age has been religious pluralism, meaning knowledge about religions that seem internally coherent, or even admirable in certain respects, yet in conflict with one's own understanding of truth. As long as competing religions are unknown, disliked, or slandered, they pose no cognitive challenge. Sometimes, however, an individual's faith in his own tradition can be shaken by positive contact with other religions. If one's own religious leaders have provided misinformation about other religions and the behavior of their members—as they have been known to do—and personal experience later disproves the authoritative teaching, skepticism may creep in concerning the leader's reliability. To give a different example, it is not uncommon for religious believers to justify their doctrines by asserting that the doctrines produce greater virtue. Evangelical Christians sometimes assume that a person who has accepted Jesus as Personal Lord will sin less often than unbelievers; Buddhists sometimes expect that regular meditation will produce individuals who are more compassionate than nonpractitioners. On close examination, there is no strict correlation between doctrinal belief and virtuous action. Too much reflection on this fact may weaken an individual's enthusiasm about the doctrine's necessity.

A person who is skeptical of blind faith in received wisdom is not necessarily uninterested in religious questions. To the extent that the scientific debunking of certain Christian doctrines had provoked doubt in their American audiences, Hindu lecturers had much to gain by purging their teachings of any inessential beliefs about the physical world, organizing their message around scientifically inscrutable beliefs like the meaning of life and pursuit of spiritual enlightenment, and capitalizing on their appeal to disenchanted seekers. Krishnamurti did just that. Paramananda played down the Vedanta Society's bolder claims concerning the material world (e.g., yogic theories of physiology, which many of the swamis accepted but Paramananda rarely referred to). It would be rash to assume that they were insincere just because these changes were fortuitous to their careers. Paramananda joined a modernizing religious order by choice because it fit with his inclinations. Krishnamurti had an abundance of personal reasons to despise institutional religion and any additional demands on his abused credulity.

Whether from divine inspiration, dumb luck, or a genius for marketing, Yogananda's work was successful even though he was considerably less cautious about invading science's turf. He rhetorically assured his audiences of his commitments to reason and science, then turned around and delivered an intoxicating cocktail of magic, traditional wisdom, and popular psychology. Yogananda also attracted more devoted disciples than Krishnamurti, more money than Paramananda, and bigger American crowds than either (plus, he got to go to the White House).

THE NEEDS OF THE DISCIPLES

A natural inclination toward religion, and the social freedom to follow one's own intuitions in crafting one's own spiritual trajectory, might account for why these people left one religion to join another. What, if anything, can we say about why each individual chose as they did? What, if anything, might that suggest about their religious needs as a group?

For one, the disciples did not appear to care much about how much proof their new religion could muster; they trusted their own experience and intuitions when they chose a guru, rather than carefully investigating conflicting claims to truth. For example, Paramananda and Yogananda promised their audiences that they were reliable, knowledgeable, and truthful guides toward spiritual realization. They asked their audience to trust their accounts because (a) they had personally experienced proof that their statements were true, and (b) audience members would be able to do the same if they tried the recommended approach for themselves. The lifestyles and values that the two men recommended nonetheless conflicted. Each did say that there were different "right" ways for different people, but, like most relativists, they acted as if some right ways were better than others. Each had fundamental convictions that were incompatible with the other's. Despite their proximity to one another and their many shared values (e.g., functioning as cultural ambassadors from India, dispelling bigotry), they were rivals rather than collaborators. This, remember, from fellow Bengalis preaching universal religious tolerance. They preached their different versions of self-evident truth at separate ashrams within thirty miles of each other for years. Each had a devoted following who believed that their guru beheld the truth, but that the other guru was mistaken—even though both gurus had identical arguments for why they deserved to be believed. A careful religious seeker might well have noted that, at the least, both men were less than entirely truthful concerning either their universalism or their infallibility.

An even more careful seeker might be led to reflect on the reliability of arguments for religious truth based solely on internal, personal experience. In the absence of faith in an external authority, faith in widespread social consensus on the matter, or justifications from reason or science, the *only possible* criterion for adjudicating between competing religious truths is personal experience: "Does this claim match my understanding of the world? Does it help me to make sense out of my life? To implement my ideals more fully?" The future disciples were aware of this and were almost certainly drawn to their respective gurus because they emphasized this point, repeatedly arguing from experience rather than institutionalized authority. The basis of their universalizing dreams, remember, was that since the spiritual life was based on the accurate, direct perception of real things, there was no reason why humanity should not be able to investigate this domain of reality as carefully and successfully as science investigated the physical world.

From a turn-of-the-century perspective, this premise is reasonable and understandable. From a contemporary, postmodern perspective, this idea appears naive. It rests on the assumption that experience can be trusted and has a reliable relationship with reality. The postmodern intellectual does not make this assumption, for the very good reason that individual perceptions of a given object can conflict wildly. We know that this is true for observations of physical facts about the world, as in conflicting eyewitness testimonies of the same event. Experiences that cannot be intersubjectively verified, like religious visions, vary even more extremely.

Consider, for example, the possibility that Yogananda used hypnosis to induce positive hallucinations in his disciples. I bring this up to illustrate how it is possible to have different interpretations of the same event, given one's point of view. While Yogananda's devotees interpreted certain phenomena as proof of his divine status, it is also possible to interpret the same phenomena as the results of hypnosis. You may recall from Chapter 5 that Yogananda's brother alleged that Yogananda had studied hypnosis as a young man in India. He was also familiar with Western texts on the subject, at one point referring to noted psychologists of his time in order to argue that "autosuggestion" was more effective on an emotional person than an intellectual person.[1] Yogananda's devotees often had vivid experiences of magical and miraculous events. It is possible that Yogananda used hypnosis to modify the cognitive patterns of his disciples. In general, his aim was probably well-meaning and therapeutic. However, evidence suggests that he used his skills to induce positive hallucinations (seeing things that are not really there) and that he encouraged his devotees to take those hallucinations literally rather than metaphorically. This brings up some ethical issues concerning manipulation. It also illustrates how problematic trusting personal experience can be when altered states of consciousness are involved.

YOGANANDA'S USE OF HYPNOSIS

First, it is necessary to define hypnosis, since many readers will be unfamiliar with all but sensationalized accounts of this practice. Over the past twenty years, there has been a paradigm shift within psychology and psychiatry concerning hypnosis. It used to be considered a flaky pseudoscience; now the theories behind it are debated, but the phenomenon itself is generally accepted as a legitimate field of research.[2] Debates center around whether the trance state induced by hypnosis is biologically distinct from normal states of consciousness, or whether the hypnotic state is a result of social psychology with no underlying physiological distinctions. Nevertheless, it is surprisingly easy for one person, given enough technical skill and a willing and suggestible subject, to induce an altered state of consciousness that closely resembles the experiences of Yogananda's disciples.

The American Psychiatric Press' *Textbook of Psychiatry* defines *hypnosis* as "a state of attentive, receptive concentration with a relative suspension of peripheral awareness."[3] Hypnosis is a kind of trance. It can be induced in a variety of ways: One person can lead another into the trance; one can provoke the trance in oneself; or the trance can occur naturally without any conscious provocation, as when a person becomes deeply engrossed in a movie or experiences an altered state of consciousness after twenty minutes of drumming or chanting. Psychological characteristics of the hypnotic trance state include selective attention (focusing on one sensation at the expense of another, which does not enter awareness), dissociation (the ability to break global experience into its component parts, amplifying awareness for one part while diminishing awareness for the others), increased response to suggestion, literal interpretation, trance logic (the hypnotized person's tendency to disengage from objectivity during the trance), hallucinations, and relaxation.[4]

Hypnosis is not innately therapeutic; it is a skilled form of social interaction that utilizes trance states to increase one person's ability to deeply influence another person. It can be used as a therapeutic tool and is becoming increasingly popular among psychotherapists as a possible strategic option in the course of therapy. For example, hypnotherapy has good success in quickly modifying habitual behavior patterns and can be used to help a client stop smoking, control panic attacks, control compulsive behavior, or control eating disorders. It can also be useful when a client wishes to change habituated "loop tapes" of thought that interfere with psychological well-being; for example, the person who thinks over and over "I am no good and deserve to die" can use hypnosis to replace that internal dialogue with a more positive message like "I am strong and capable." Hypnosis is also used for pain management and the alleviation of psychosomatic symptoms.

Some individuals are easier to hypnotize than others. Many different factors go into whether or not person X will be able to hypnotize person Y at a given time. Success will be more likely if the following criteria are met: the hypnotist adapts his or her technique to the particular psychological style of the client; the client trusts the hypnotist; the client wants to enter a trance state; the client is highly motivated to change the behavior that the hypnotist is attempting to modify; and, even in an ordinary state of consciousness, the client is highly suggestible with a low level of skepticism concerning new information.

Once the hypnotist has induced the hypnotic trance in the client, the hypnotist then has an opportunity to influence the habits of the client. Because the hypnotized person is in a highly suggestible state, he or she is unusually easy to manipulate at this time. It is not true that a hypnotized person can be induced to do something against his will; rather, the subject will do things that he is willing to do but would not allow himself to do under normal circumstances. Client suggestibility seems to be tied to hypnotism's dissociative effects. It is common for the hypnotized person to dissociate the conscious and unconscious minds and for the unconscious mind to come to the fore and interact with the hypnotherapist in an unusually forceful manner. The hypnotist can then make suggestions directly to the unconscious mind of the client, bypassing the conscious mind altogether. This mechanism makes it possible for the client to experience amnesia for the hypnotherapy session, yet still benefit from the hypnotist's manipulations. For example, a smoker might not remember her hypnotherapy session at all, yet feel less desire for a cigarette. If the hypnotist has implanted a posthypnotic suggestion in the client's subconscious, an external cue may automatically trigger a desired response in the client, even though the client is not consciously aware of this planned consequence. For example, when the smoker lights a cigarette, she may suddenly feel uncomfortable, even nauseous.

The hypnotic trance can be used to produce hallucinations, both positive (seeing what is not there) and negative (not seeing what is there). Sometimes, hallucinations are purposely provoked by the hypnotist; sometimes they occur spontaneously as the hypnotized client creates vivid, symbolic imagery from unconscious material. It is important to understand that images that present themselves during the hypnotic trance do not necessarily have any real-world correlates. They are not necessarily factual. Misunderstanding of the hallucinatory properties of trance have recently led to some terrible real-world consequences, as when victims of *false memory syndrome* assume without any external validation that their trance visions are literally true. Mental images that occur during trance are not necessarily metaphorical; sometimes they do reflect what's happening in the real world. However, there is no foolproof way of sorting out the factual from the fantastical material. Trance images function like dream images, with real memories and fantasy woven together in order to symbolically express unconscious perceptions.

The most popular method of hypnotherapy at present is based on the work of Milton H. Erickson. According to the Ericksonian school, it is not necessary for the hypnotist to use formal rituals to induce a hypnotic trance. Rather, the skilled hypnotist can induce trance in a naturalistic manner, building off the client's preexisting psychological dispositions. Given enough skill on the part of the hypnotist and cooperation on the part of the subject, it is not necessary for the subject to be aware of the fact that hypnosis is taking place.

When one compares Yogananda's interpersonal techniques for inducing religious ecstasy with the Ericksonian hypnotist's techniques for inducing trance, the parallels are striking. The kriya practitioner begins a meditation session by sitting in a comfortable and upright posture and relaxing the body, closing or half-closing the eyes, and taking deep, slow, and relaxing breaths. By concentrating on slow breathing, the practitioner enters a state of focused attention, which is accompanied by "peaceful and soothing sensations."[5] The life force is then "mentally guided to the inner cosmos."[6] In short, the meditator experiences a trance state structurally similar to the trance induced by the clinical hypnotherapist in a secular setting.

Yogananda's trance-inducing techniques would have produced vivid results on only a small subset of the population. However, Yogananda was touring the country giving lectures to thousands of people at a time. He spoke on neutral, populist topics like "How to Be a Smile Millionaire" and led the audience in chants and guided visualizations. The consequences would have excited the small number of audience members who were already adept at manipulating trance states to produce desired emotional effect and who had rich, imaginative inner lives. That targeted subgroup was then encouraged to sign up for Yogananda's seminars, which would have given him a chance to work with them directly in a smaller, personalized environment. If he was successfully employing hypnosis techniques, the effect over the course of the next few weeks must have truly seemed miraculous to the participants: Bad habits abruptly faded away, psychosomatic illnesses vanished, ecstatic visions of saints materialized, depressions lifted.

The kriya yogi is taught how to induce the trance state himself when alone (autohypnosis). Yogananda's basic instructions for meditation are available in his book *Metaphysical Meditations,* first published in 1932:

> Sit on a straight chair, or in a cross-legged position on a firm surface. Keep the spine straight and the chin parallel to the floor. With eyes closed, gently focus your gaze and concentrate your attention at the point between the eyebrows. This is the seat of concentration, and the spiritual eye, or divine perception, in man. With the attention fixed at this center of calmness and concentration, practice the meditation you have chosen. Audibly or mentally repeat the words slowly, concentrating on them intently until you become absorbed in the inner meaning. Meditate until you feel that the concept on which you are meditating has become a part of your own consciousness.[7]

Assuming that the practitioner was prone to the naturalistic manipulation of trance states, Yogananda's style of meditation would be very likely to result in self-hypnosis, in which one provokes a hypnotic trance in oneself and then uses it to manipulate the unconscious through use of suggestive scripts. *Metaphysical Meditations* is a compendium of such scripts, and a glance through it reveals that they were probably beneficial. Yogananda recommends that practitioners begin their sessions with this guided visualization:

> Lock the eyelid-doors and shut out the wild dance of tempting scenes. Drop your mind into the bottomless well of your heart. Hold the mind on your heart that is bubbling with life-giving blood. Keep your attention tied to the heart, until you feel its rhythmic beat. With every heartbeat feel the pulse of almighty Life. Picture the same all-pervading Life knocking at the heart-door of millions of human beings and of billions of other creatures. The heart-throb constantly, meekly announces the presence of Infinite Power behind the doors of your awareness. The gentle beat of all-pervading Life says to you silently, "Do not receive only a little flow of My life, but expand the opening of thy feeling-powers. Let Me flood thy blood, body, mind, feelings, and soul with My throbs of universal life.[8]

If one posits that Yogananda was a skilled hypnotist, then many of the miracle narratives recounted by his devotees make sense in a whole new way. For example, Donald Walters' description of kriya initiation sounds matter-of-fact rather than magical. Initiation was an important ritual in SRF during Yogananda's life; disciples could participate over and over, and it was normally performed ceremonially and in groups, not unlike Catholic communion. Here is Walters' description of his first initiation:

> Master told us all to sit upright in meditative posture. "I am sending the divine light through your brain, baptizing you," he said from where he sat across the room. I felt immediately blessed; a divine current radiated through my brain from the Christ Center. He went on to guide me in the practice of the technique.[9]

In this narrative, Yogananda first induces a trance in his audience, guiding them into a meditative state of relaxation, dissociation, concentrated focus, and enhanced suggestibility. He then uses guided imagery to provoke a mystical experience. In SRF, the "Christ Center" refers to the center of the forehead, which is understood to be a locus of spiritual power.

On another occasion, a disciple describes an experience that sounds very much like the result of a posthypnotic suggestion:

> After the evening lecture by the Swami, I returned home, and as I walked in the door, before turning on the light, the rooms were raining golden light. It was golden rain everywhere, from ceiling to floor. The raindrops were very long and golden in the darkened house. It kept raining gold after the lights were on. I turned them off, again on, but it was the same. . . . Shortly there was the sound of a car coming around the hill, and it all ceased instantly. A serene feeling was with me during this unusual vision —a peacefulness that seemed part of it.[10]

Often, the academic student of religion automatically assumes that stories like this one are fictional or symbolic because the idea that an apartment could actually, in a physical sense, fill with cascades of light from a spiritual source is too foreign to the scientific worldview. If hypnotism works the way contemporary Ericksonian hypnotherapists claim, and if Yogananda was adept in similar techniques, then Kamala's experience has a straightforward, causal explanation.

Although I have used Yogananda as an example of how hypnosis might be used to create the perception of magical experiences in a religious settings, it is not my intention to single him out. If one accepts this theory as valid in Yogananda's case, it is only fair to extend the analysis to similar situations in other religious traditions. It is possible that the same psychological mechanisms that make hypnotherapy possible are also deployed in a wide range of religious settings around the world. What is at issue here, however, is an awareness of how complicated the relationship between perception and reality can be in religious life.

Neither am I suggesting that Yogananda's use of hypnotic techniques, if he did in fact use them, made him a charlatan. It is possible, even likely, that Yogananda tried to use hypnosis therapeutically, genuinely intending to improve the lives of his disciples. However, one might legitimately question the manner in which Yogananda encouraged his disciples to uncritically accept the mental images that arose in the course of trance work as empirical facts with real-world correlates. He insisted that the visual images that arose during meditation were the direct perception of spiritual reality. Perhaps it is more reasonable to theorize that the images were symbolic productions of the unconscious mind. Scientific research into hypnosis defends this theory. If one values reality testing and the ideal of objectivity, it is difficult to believe that Yogananda was acting in the best interests of his disciples in this matter. Of course, he may have been wrong but not known any better; in this case, his ethics would not be at fault, but his status as a fully enlightened and infallible avatar of God would come into question.

An argument can be made that Yogananda would not have had the power over others that he did without recourse to magical thinking, and that he used this power for good, and that his deceptions were therefore ethical. As the saying goes, a spoonful of sugar helps the medicine go down. Perhaps a spoonful of magic can be used to coax a little selflessness into the human ego. Without the magical element in *Autobiography of a Yogi,* Donald Walters never would have dropped everything, gotten on the first bus West, and dedicated his life to the service of his guru. The human mind craves illusion, and the magician fills that need. Yogananda, to his credit, used his ability to control others through the production of yearned-for illusions to promote peace, compassion, and service. A lesser person would have had more dangerous uses for such power.

Ironically, Yogananda's "science of religion" may be scientifically explainable. Yogananda's techniques seem to have functioned as a reliable method for producing hypnotic trance that could then be manipulated by the guru to produce both hallucinations and positive behavior modification. In other words, Yogananda had a sophisticated technology for inducing altered states of consciousness. From a social scientific perspective, Yogananda's mistake was in assuming that the experiences human beings have while in a trance state are a reliable and literal source of knowledge about the world. Scientific evidence suggests that this is not the case.

POSTMODERN SKEPTICISM

On close examination, the results of Krishnamurti's, Paramananda's, and Yogananda's experiments with the science of religion support postmodern skepticism. In science, one must be able to duplicate the outcome of an experiment exactly before the findings are considered valid. These men, embarking on basically the same experiment, produced three different and conflicting results. If, as they all claimed, the source of their power and knowledge was the same source—the one divine reality that permeates the universe—and if their perceptions of it were as true and undeniable as they believed them to be, then we could expect them to be in closer agreement concerning its nature and message. Yet among them, only Yogananda delivered reports on the astral consumption of luminous raylike vegetables; no amount of scientific zeal would have been able to reveal said vegetables to Paramananda or to shake Yogananda's faith in them.

This sort of reflection might have dampened some enthusiasm, but it did not deter the disciples. This does not imply that they were unconcerned with truth. These individuals had many options open concerning a choice that they cared deeply about; there is no reason to think they were unintelligent or unthoughtful. What, then, were their criteria for choosing a guru?

It is likely that the disciples were unconcerned about the guru's grounds for making truth claims because they already had their own that they trusted. Before disciples met their future gurus, these two desires must have propelled their religious search:

1. The desire to have their own intuitive sense of the world made articulate and intersubjectively shared.

2. The desire for an exemplar in the art of life who could demonstrate how to employ their unrealized ideals in everyday behavior.

The centrality of these desires is demonstrated over and over again in the literature in the form of "the first time I met my guru" stories. Devamata had already seen Paramananda in a dream. Daya recalled "how my whole being was stirred when I met him."[11] Kriyananda got on a bus and moved to Mount Washington immediately after reading *Autobiography of a Yogi*. It was love at first sight; the guru fulfilled an ancient longing. This is a different kind of conversion experience than the popular Christian model that goes "I grew up in the church, but I did not believe/I turned away. It was not until I reached the bottom that I saw the light; what I needed had been right in front of me all along." This "girl next door" scenario works across religions too, as in Paul's conversion on the road to Damascus. In some ways, the "love at first sight" model is not even a conversion experience; it is the "eureka" of inchoate sensation met and illustrated in the external world.

The initial meeting, remembered after the fact, becomes a symbol for the long-term fit of the relationship; for every disciple who stayed, there would have been many who also experienced an initial rush of identification but whose expectations were not met later on. That Paramananda and Yogananda were able to attract lifetime devotees says a lot about the power of their religious alternatives—and their substance as individuals.

The disciples, then, tended to come to the movement with a strong sense of their own religious needs and were looking for a religious environment that would fit comfortably with their highly individualized sense of self. They were willing to make changes, but only if the changes could be internally justified as changes toward intuitively acceptable ideals and goals. They were rugged individualists.

UNIVERSAL RELIGION
VERSUS PERSONAL RELIGION

To recap, the gurus wanted universal religion, but *the disciples wanted personal religion*. To a certain extent, these are mutually exclusive desires. I do not want to reduce religion to a psychological phenomenon, yet it appears that the religious impulse is inextricably bound to the need for the unconscious mind to express itself symbolically. If there were to be a universal religion, then it would need to be based on reason, not on intuition. It is through reason alone that different groups of people can find a consensus on the nature of reality. Intuition, on the other hand, is always localized, always rooted in a particular individual's reaction to a particular social location.

Religion is best understood as an art rather than a science. There is no such thing as universal art; attempts to produce it have given us Soviet realism and 1970s concrete-block architecture. No great work of art can speak to all individuals at all times. To the extent that great works of art speak to a large cross section of the population, they do so because they are complex and multivalent enough to show different faces to different people, each according to their need.

To say that religion is a kind of art says nothing about its correspondence with empirical reality. Art can be realistic or not, according to personal taste and circumstance. I do mean, however, that the power of a religious formulation does not hinge on its realism but, rather, on its finesse in giving voice to human passion.

Many religious seekers in modern society prefer the realist genre in religious life. They seek to create a religious worldview that not only accords with science, but also holds objectivity and truth-seeking as high ideals. Keenly aware of humanity's capacity for self-deception, they believe that a life of spiritual heroism entails setting aside self-serving delusion in the search for external truth. Without reason, it is impossible to be ethical. Wishing to be compassionate is not in itself sufficient; one must pay close attention to the experiences of other individuals, and understand them as sentient beings with needs and desires separate from one's own, in order to act in a compassionate manner.

Yet reason alone is insufficient. Facts alone are not enough to get one out of bed in the morning. So in comes art, the art of living, which is what religion, at its best, is all about. What is deepest in a person cannot be expressed analytically; it must be hinted at with story, song, and dance. Sometimes people worry that modernization necessarily entails secularization, a loss of faith. They worry that by taking over on the traditional turf of institutionalized religious authorities, science will strip culture of something precious, necessary, mysterious. This is not necessarily the case. Perhaps the modern, scientific worldview has done the religious virtuoso a great service by stripping the spiritual impulse down to its original essence and perhaps it has provoked individuals to start over again from the root of things. The result can be glorious.

Krishnamurti thought so too. Conversing with Mary Lutyens, he also tied the spiritual quest to the artistic impulse:

> ML: What if one could understand it but not be able to put it into words?
>
> K: You could. You would find a way. The moment you discover something you have words for it. Like a poem. If you are open to inquire, put your brain in condition, someone could find out. But the moment you find it, it will be right. No mystery.
>
> ML: Will the mystery mind being found?
>
> K: No, the mystery will be gone.
>
> MARY ZIMBALIST: But the mystery is something sacred.
>
> K: The sacredness will remain.[12]

In an age of science, mystery must yield to new information. Human life will never be free from mystery, but in a world where mysteries keep yielding to science, it may be a mistake to equate the mysterious with the sacred. The sacredness will remain. A scientific understanding of reproduction does not reduce the holiness of a newborn child. What can, however, reduce the child to a meaningless hunk of meat in the eyes of the beholder is the rejection of nonscientific ways of thinking, the rejection of art.

The task of religion today is to cultivate those fields of human experience that science falls back from. Released from the unnecessary burden of mapping physical reality, delegating that task to science, the religious virtuoso is free to pursue her true calling: the transubstantiation of the mundane into the sacred.

NOTES

1. Yogananda, *Scientific Healing Affirmations,* 20.
2. An indication of this change is that books on hypnosis written prior to 1970 are usually filed in the "B" section under the Library of Congress call numbers, whereas newer research has been promoted to the "RC" section of modern science.
3. Spiegel and Maldonado, "Hypnosis," 1244.
4. Yapko, *Trancework.*
5. Ibid., 280.
6. Ibid., 281.
7. Yogananda, *Metaphysical Meditations,* viii.
8. Ibid., 3.
9. Kriyananda, *The Path,* 240.
10. Kamala, *The Flawless Mirror,* 96.
11. Daya, *The Guru and the Disciple,* 2.
12. Lutyens, *Krishnamurti: The Years of Fulfillment,* 229.

CHAPTER 9

Conclusion

Today, contemporary Americans playing at the fringes of the religious counterculture are more likely to dabble with Buddhism than Hinduism. In part, this is due to a series of scandals that occurred during the 1970s and 1980s in which Hindu gurus were viewed as abusing their authority. Guru Maharaji, Bhagwan Shri Rajneesh, and the International Society for Krishna Consciousness became associated in the public imagination with corruption, guns, and brainwashing. While yogis and swamis continue to circulate, they do not have the prestige they enjoyed in the 1920s. Most contemporary Hindu organizations cater to Hindu-Indian immigrants rather than non-Indian converts and sympathizers.

Likewise, the dream of having a universal religion has been largely abandoned as modernist hopes for unity have become replaced among intellectuals with postmodern celebration of diversity. Paramananda and Yogananda hoped to build their churches of all religions on the rock of devotional monotheism; Krishnamurti could have told them that this was an insufficient basis for a coalition of all spiritual seekers, and the rise of American Buddhism has sharply illustrated the market for nontheistic spiritual paths.

217

The gurus of the 1920s, then, were not wildly successful in either of their goals—to bring the "wisdom of India" into the Western mainstream and to transcend culture altogether by forging a science of religion. However, it is not the case that they were entirely unsuccessful in either of these projects. In odd and unexpected ways, their ministries have left traces on American culture. I do not want to overemphasize the influence of Paramananda, Yogananda, and Krishnamurti. I have used them here as examples of a wider movement, one in which many Indians and Americans participated. Furthermore, it is impossible to sort out the extent to which these men and their disciples influenced American culture from the extent to which American culture influenced them. Nevertheless, there are themes in their life stories and philosophies that have continued to haunt the radical religious counterculture. In some cases, parts of their messages that would have appeared highly eccentric for their time have spread toward mainstream American culture.

HINDU LEGACIES IN THE AMERICAN RELIGIOUS COUNTERCULTURE

Five examples of such snowballing themes that can be found in the preceding pages and have subsequently spread outward in the American imagination are (1) thinking of the body as a gateway to the spirit; (2) the primacy of experience over text-based dogma; (3) divinity as Higher Power; (4) the Divine as feminine; (5) tolerant acceptance of religious pluralism.

Thinking of the Body as a Gateway to the Spirit

One of the most visible legacies of Hindu influence on American religion has been yoga, defined here in the contemporary American sense of a system of precise control of the physical body leading to emotional, psychological, or spiritual enrichment. Paramananda, Yogananda, and Krishnamurti all practiced and recommended yoga (though Krishnamurti did not teach it).

While yoga remains popular in the United States, it has been joined by other Asian systems designed to harmonize the physical and spiritual selves, such as martial arts, Tai Chi, Qi Gong, and acupuncture. Newly invented techniques pursuing the same end have entered the mix, for example, Rolfing, Feldenkreis, and the Aleksander Technique; altogether, the movement goes by the name of "bodywork."

All bodywork shares a common assumption that the body stands between the individual soul/spirit/self and the universal spirit and that, by manipulating the body, what was once a metaphysical barrier can be transformed into a gate. In addition to matter and spirit, reality is understood to include "subtle energies" or "subtle bodies" that bridge the gap. The Western dichotomy between the physical and spiritual worlds is rejected in favor of a model of reality in which "matter shades off into spirit."[1]

It is likely that the availability of yoga instruction in the United States in the first half of the twentieth century helped change American attitudes about the relationship between the body and spirit. Traditionally, Christianity has viewed the body as an impediment to spiritual growth. Many Americans (including many Christians) view the body as a vehicle for spiritual growth, provided it is correctly cared for. Yoga has been one of many factors contributing to this trend.

The Primacy of Experience over Text-Based Dogma

Paramananda, Yogananda, and Krishnamurti all stressed that true religion is something that is lived, not something that one accepts on faith from an external authority. Their optimism concerning the coming science of religion was based on this premise. By insisting on the infallibility of personal experience, the gurus helped popularize an idea that later became a core tenet of the religious counterculture.

As discussed in Chapter 8, reliance on internal states of consciousness for religious realization does not lead to a unified field of experience for all believers. This lack has not stopped the religious counterculture from embracing the "therapeutic turn."[2] In a society that values individualism, adaptability, and popularized scientific methods, individuals often reject the dogmatic, traditional platforms of their religious heritage. For the builders of the American spirituality movement, the future of religion lies in our ability to mine religious traditions for metaphors that will help us understand and name our own reality, while jettisoning the pieces of tradition that no longer speak to contemporary experience.

Divinity as Higher Power

Although Paramananda and Yogananda were devotional theists, they were not Christians. They characterized the Supreme Being as infinite, compassionate, formless, creative, and beyond gender. They recommended a religious worldview in which traditional Christian constrictions about the nature of God are rejected in favor of a more amorphous conception of a "Higher Power" that is beyond human comprehension (though not beyond human apprehension). This worldview is increasingly common among Americans today.

In Christianity, the Supreme Being is traditionally understood as a trinity of the Father, the Son, and the Holy Spirit. In India, conceptions of the nature of the Divine are much more diverse. Hinduism also contains a long philosophical tradition of intentional vagueness concerning the nature of the Divine, indicating the belief that such matters are beyond the powers of human comprehension. Many Americans who use the phrase "Higher Power" to refer to the Divine do so in order to give voice to their sense that although there is a Divine presence animating the universe, their understanding of who it is and how it works is limited and sketchy. These people may not be comfortable with the specificity of Christian claims concerning the nature of God. The Hindu gurus studied here, then, contributed to the increasing tendency among Americans to affirm belief in a spiritual dimension to reality while shying away from a concrete representation of that reality. This attitude is particularly understandable in a pluralistic society in which many plausible religious worldviews are available.

The Divine as Feminine

For both Paramananda and Yogananda, that Higher Power was also Mother. While ultimately beyond gender, God chose to take on forms in order to interact with the universe and devotees and, in doing so, chose female as well as male personalities. This is an ancient belief in India and historically has also been found in other parts of the world. In affirming the divine nature of the feminine, they were ahead of their time for the Western world; not until the women's movement of the 1970s would feminist theology make such bold assertions. Even then, old habits died hard. Contrast, for example, Paramananda's 1912 essay "God as Mother," with Carol P. Christ's 1979 essay "Why Women Need the Goddess." Unlike Christ, Paramananda asserts that both men and women need the Goddess: "Of all the relations we know in the world . . . the relation of the mother with her child is the holiest and highest, as well as the most universal. . . . our Mother is the Mother of the Whole Universe."[3] Christ, on the other hand, more modestly asserts that women need a symbol of female power. She does not argue that this would also be good for men, nor does she strongly state, as Paramananda did, that such power actually exists, eternally, outside of human power struggles and symbolism, "the Mother of the Whole Universe." She fumbles apologetically with the issue of what, exactly, having a Goddess means:

> When asked what the symbol of the Goddess means, feminist priestess Starhawk replied, "It all depends on how I feel. When I feel weak, she is someone who can help and protect me. When I feel strong, she is the symbol of my own power. At other times I feel her as the natural energy in my body and the world." How are we to evaluate such a statement? Theologians might call these the words of a sloppy thinker. But my deepest

intuition tells me they contain a wisdom that Western theological thought has lost.[4]

Starhawk's reply might have seemed sloppy to Christ in 1979, but
it would not have seemed so to either Paramananda or Yogananda, steeped in Vedantic philosophy and the Goddess traditions
of Bengal. Within their worldview, the Supreme Being was simultaneously Self and Other, the One behind the myriad appearances
of the world, including our own selves.

Goddess worship does not necessarily lead to greater social
equality for women; it did not in India. It can, however, contribute
to the self-empowerment of individual women in the right social
context. It appears to have done so for Paramananda's and
Yogananda's congregations, as it does today for participants in
feminist spirituality movements. By imagining the feminine aspect
of the divine other, individual women were simultaneously affirming the divine aspect of their female bodies and selves. "Think
what you can do!" urged Yogananda in 1941. "From an ordinary
woman to Divine Mother! And why not? The Universal Mother
made you in Her image and you should manifest that image by
bestowing on all beings Her illimitable love."[5]

Tolerant Acceptance of Religious Pluralism

I have argued that the dream of a universal, scientific, modern
religion, as it was conceived by Paramananda and Yogananda, is a
failed and impossible dream. For individuals steeped in the postmodern tradition, this conclusion might seem foregone. For
many Americans, however, the universalist legacy is alive and well.
Universalism has been absorbed into popular culture, and its rhetoric infuses the worldview that many young, liberal Americans
take for granted.

Consider, for example, my students at San Diego State University. Roughly one half of these students are committed to a traditional form of religion (such as Evangelical Protestantism, Roman
Catholicism, or Judaism). A smattering are atheist. Of the remainder, however, a majority seem to accept universalist ideals. They

believe that there is a single, benevolent Higher Power that controls and guides the universe. They believe that "truth is one, though the wise call it by various names." They believe that there is more than one way to salvation and that there is something to be learned from each of the world's religious traditions. They crinkle their noses at the word *missionary,* which simultaneously connotes a rude assumption that one person can impose values on another and dull sex. During their college careers, some of these students may be convinced by some brilliant deconstructionist to put aside such naive modernism. As a teacher, one is left with the suspicion that many of them will be at the beach for that lecture.

"Attention to Asian religions in America," writes Thomas Tweed, a scholar of American religion, "not only reminds us that combination is common and significant, it also calls attention to another type of religious identity." This new identity is what Tweed calls that of the "sympathizer," people who "have fallen between traditions," either sequentially moving from one group to another or combining influences from a variety of groups into a personalized worldview. Tweed defines a sympathizer as those whose "framework of meaning has been shaped in part by elements of a tradition but who blend those elements with beliefs and practices from another tradition. Most important, they fail to affiliate exclusively with the institutions of the religion with which they have some sympathy."[6]

An independent religious identity was also remarked on by an earlier scholar of Asian religion in America, Wendell Thomas: "Many of these teachers of wisdom from abroad are more than lecturers, and yet can hardly be called founders of new cults. . . . A fairly new religious form seems to be developing in America: something between a sacred community and a secular audience . . . a religious class that appeals chiefly to chronic 'seekers.'"[7]

Throughout this book, I have referred to this community of seekers as the American religious counterculture. With every passing decade, however, the "counterculture" edges a little closer to the mainstream. Perhaps, by the time this year's freshmen have become middle-aged, it will have become commonplace for presidential candidates to appeal to a Higher Power while trolling for votes among a pluralistic, tolerant, and universalist American public.

NOTES

1. Albanese, "The Subtle Energies of Spirit," 318.
2. Rieff, *The Triumph of the Therapeutic.*
3. Paramananda, "God as Mother," 156.
4. Christ, "Why Women Need the Goddess," 279.
5. Yogananda, *Man's Eternal Quest*, 248.
6. Tweed, "Asian Religions in the United States," 205.
7. Thomas, *Hinduism Invades America,* 185.

Glossary

advaita One of three schools of philosophy within vedanta, advaita teaches that the Self and God are identical and that the apparent differences between things are merely an illusion masking their fundamental unity.

ashram A small spiritual community headed by a guru. Also spelled "ashrama."

atman The individual soul, or true self.

babu Originally meaning an educated person, in Anglo-Indian slang the word is used as a denigrating term for educated Bengalis who prefer British culture to their own. In American slang, the word means a mixture of an Uncle Tom and a nerd.

bhadralok A member of Bengal's native knowledge class during the colonial period.

Bhagavad-Gita A chapter within the Mahabharata and one of India's most beloved pieces of religious literature.

bhakta A person who follows the path of bhakti.

bhakti A path toward spiritual liberation that focuses on the cultivation of loving devotion toward God. Also used to refer to the branches of Hinduism that regard God as separate from human beings, rather than identical to them.

bhedabheda A branch of Indian philosophy that teaches that individual souls and God are both the one and separate, depending on how you define your terms. The gist is similar to vishishtadvaita vedanta, differing mainly in historical development and philosophical technicalities.

Brahman God. Whether Brahman is understood as an impersonal Absolute or as a Supreme Person (or both, or neither) depends on one's philosophical orientation and varies within Hinduism. Brahman is also defined as pure being, pure consciousness, and pure bliss.

brahmin A member of the highest rung of the caste hierarchy. Traditionally, Brahmin men functioned as priests for Orthodox Hindus.

caste system A complicated, hereditary, and pyramid-shaped social hierarchy that was accepted as part of the natural order of things by Orthodox Hindus. Groups near the top of the hierarchy have more power and privilege; groups toward the bottom have less. Social groups at the very bottom were traditionally considered unclean and lowly, and they were subject to severe restrictions and taboos. Today, the caste system is outlawed in India, but Orthodox Hindus continue to accept it.

dharma Natural law, or the divinely ordained order of the universe. Also, proper conduct for human beings. In Orthodox Hinduism, this includes following the traditions of the ancestors, including the social regulations associated with the caste system.

dvaita One of three schools of philosophy within vedanta, dvaita teaches that God is unique, that he created the world and souls out of nothing, and that human beings should worship God rather than identify with him, as advaita teaches.

God Used in this text as shorthand for the Absolute or Supreme Being, whether that ultimate reality is understood as personal or impersonal.

guru An authoritative spiritual teacher with Asian Indian philosophical leanings.

hagiography A biography of a saintly person written by someone who admires the subject greatly. Scholars sometimes assume that a hagiography is not as "objective" as a biography because the writer's uncritical love for the subject leads to a skewed perspective.

hatha yoga The parts of raja yoga that focus on increasing physical health through breathing, stretching, and posture techniques.

icon A physical representation of a spiritual person or divine being. In many religions, icons help a worshipper focus his or her attention on the spirit represented. In the past, Westerners have sometimes called these representations "idols"; the word *icon* is considered by contemporary scholars to be more respectful.

jnana A path toward spiritual liberation that focuses on the cultivation of the intellectual understanding of truth.

jnani A person who follows the path of jnana.

Kali A persona, or representation, of the Great Goddess, sometimes worshipped as the Supreme Being and sometimes worshipped as the feminine half of the Supreme Being.

karma (1) Action in the world. (2) The law of cause and effect; the belief that good actions bring good rewards and bad actions bring bad retribution. (3) In the context of "karma yoga," a path toward spiritual liberation that focuses on taking care of your responsibilities in the world with diligence and doing good works.

kirtan A Hindu worship service in which God is praised through song and dance; popular among bhakti groups.

Krishna The most popular of the incarnations of Vishnu and the focus of religious devotion for many Hindus.

kriya yoga The kind of raja yoga taught by Yogananda and his school.

kriyaban A person who has mastered kriya yoga.

kundalini A kind of yoga based on the belief that a person's life force moves up from the base of the spine through a series of stages to the crown of the head, that this progression leads to spiritual liberation, and that there is a series of rituals that can cause this progression.

laws of Manu A classic Orthodox Hindu text that describes correct behavior for humans based on their position in society and stage of life.

lila The creative play of God. Some Hindus believe that God created the universe for the same reasons that an artist creates art and that reality therefore has intrinsic worth for the same reasons a work of art is its own justification.

Mahabharata An epic poem and classic religious text in the Hindu tradition.

mantra A formulaic prayer or slogan on which one focuses during meditation.

maya "Illusion." Used to refer to the philosophical idea that the world as it appears is an illusion masking reality, an idea that is associated with advaita vedanta.

mleccha A foreigner, who by definition is outside the traditional caste system and therefore unclean and lowly.

nirguna "Without form." Used to refer to the idea that God is a formless spirit, beyond human comprehension or imagination.

Om Also spelled "Aum," this verbalization symbolically represents the underlying unity of all reality and is used as a centering mantra in some forms of meditation.

Orthodox Hinduism A branch of Hinduism that reveres the Vedas as sacred scripture, accepts the caste system as right and natural, and expects only Brahmin men to act as priests. Orthodox Hindus follow a complicated set of traditions and rituals that have been passed down unchanged through countless generations, although they do vary slightly from region to region. These rituals regulate all aspects of life, including eating, bathing, socializing, working, and marrying. In this book, the word *orthodox* is also used more broadly to mean "loyal to the traditions of one's ancestors." Orthodox Hinduism is sometimes called Brahmanism or Brahminism.

Paramahansa An honorific title used to refer to a person who is believed to have attained spiritual perfection.

puja Worshipping the divine or a particular deity through the symbolic use of icons.

Puranic Having to do with the Puranas, a body of classical religious texts in Hinduism traditionally used to teach Hinduism to the masses through story and myth. Associated with Hinduism's bhakti movements.

purdah The practice of secluding women in the home so that only close relatives see them. Upper-caste Hindus borrowed this practice from the Muslims during the medieval period.

raja yoga A path toward spiritual liberation that focuses on the manipulation of the body in order to attain altered states of consciousness. Classical raja yoga uses breathing, posture, and stretching exercises with meditation techniques. Kriya yoga is a modernized version of raja yoga. Hatha yoga focuses on the physical aspects of this tradition to promote physical health.

sadhu A person who has renounced the world in order to attain spiritual liberation.

saguna "With form." Used to refer to the idea that God can be pictured and imagined by the worshipper.

samadhi A state of consciousness in which the ego is transcended and only Brahman—pure being, consciousness, and bliss—is experienced. A person experiencing samadhi appears to fall into a trance and does not perceive surrounding events.

sannyas Renunciation of worldly pursuits in order to reach spiritual liberation.

satchitananda Pure being, pure consciousness, and pure bliss. Used to describe and define Brahman.

Shaivism The branch of Hinduism that holds Shiva to be the Supreme Being.

Shaktism The branch of Hinduism that worships the Supreme Being in the feminine form as Mother.

Shiva A divine person, sometimes believed to be the Supreme Being and sometimes understood as a lesser deity, depending on the branch of Hinduism. Hindus who believe in the trimurti—the trinity of Brahma the Creator, Vishnu the Preserver, and Shiva the Destroyer —portray Shiva as the god of death and destruction. Shaivites, however, believe Shiva to be the Supreme Being, the creator of the world as well as the preserver and destroyer. In some branches of Hinduism, Shiva is understood to be the male half of the Supreme, with Shakti as the female half, and creation is believed to be a result of their union.

sudra A member of the fourth, lowest, and most populous social class in the orthodox caste system.

Swami An honorific title used to refer to a member of a monastic order.

Tantra A branch of Hinduism teaching that spiritual liberation can be reached quickly through a process of psychotherapy designed to radically confront a person with his or her social conditioning, with the aim of moving beyond the artificial assumptions instilled by society and experiencing reality as it is. Tantra sometimes uses sexual rituals to further these goals; in America, "tantra" is sometimes used as a euphemism for spiritualized sexuality.

universalism The belief that one can and should separate cultural conditioning from universal truth.

Upanishads A subset of the Vedas containing philosophical dialogues.

Vaishnavism The belief that Vishnu is the Supreme Being.

vedanta A school of philosophy within Hinduism that starts with the belief that the Vedas contain divinely inspired truth and works from there. Traditionally, vedanta is subdivided into three schools: advaita, dvaita, and vishishtadvaita. In Modern Hinduism, however, vedanta is sometimes used to refer to a popularized synthesis of these philosophical traditions (e.g., the Vedanta Society). This modern reinterpretation is sometimes called neo-vedanta.

Vedas Ancient, sacred scriptures of Hinduism.

vishishtadvaita One of three schools of philosophy within vedanta, vishishtadvaita teaches that individual souls have an analogous relationship to God as our cells have to us—each is a tiny piece within the whole, but the whole is greater than the sum of its parts. In other words, reality is both unified and diversified, depending on how you look at it.

Vishnu A divine person. Vaishnavas are Hindus who worship Vishnu as the Supreme Being. Other branches of Hinduism portray Vishnu as a lesser deity. Vaishnavas believe that Vishnu periodically clothes himself in a physical form in order to come to earth and teach religious truth to humans. These divine appearances in human history are called avatars, or incarnations. Krishna is the most popular avatar.

yoga A path toward spiritual liberation. In modern Hinduism, it is often said that there are four yogas: jnana, bhakti, karma, and raja. Also used in the United States as slang for a system of breathing and stretching exercises, borrowed or adapted from Indian traditions, that are designed to promote physical and/or spiritual health. The physical exercises associated with yoga are sometimes used on their own and sometimes combined with meditation techniques.

yogic Having to do with yoga.

Bibliography

All of the books in the bibliography were useful to me, but some are more fun to read than others. I recommend the following for the interested lay reader:

For information on the Hindu Renaissance, see David Kopf's *The Brahmo Samaj and the Shaping of the Modern Indian Mind* and *British Orientalism and the Bengal Renaissance*. Also very good is *India's Agony over Religion* by Gerald J. Larson. For a lovely portrait of the traditional guru-disciple relationship in a contemporary context, see Kirin Narayan's *Storytellers, Saints and Scoundrels: Folk Narrative in Hindu Religious Teaching*.

For an overview of Hinduism in America, read Carl T. Jackson's two books, *The Oriental Religions and American Thought* and *Vedanta for the West: The Ramakrishna Movement in the United States*. For alternative religions in the United States, I recommend Peter Washington's unscholarly but highly entertaining *Madame Blavatsky's Baboon: A History of the Mystics, Mediums, and Misfits Who Brought Spiritualism to America*.

On Yogananda, the classic is still his own *Autobiography of a Yogi*. On Paramananda, you must read *A Bridge of Dreams: The Story of Paramananda, A Modern Mystic, and His Ideal of All-Conquering Love* by Sara Ann Levinsky. On Krishnamurti, Mary Lutyen's hagiographic works should be seasoned with Radha Rajagopal Sloss' *Lives in the Shadow with J. Krishnamurti*.

Abercrombie, Nicholas, et al. *The Penguin Dictionary of Sociology*. London: Penguin Books, 1988.

Ahlstrom, Sydney E. The *American Protestant Encounter with World Religions*. Beloit, WI: Beloit College, 1962.

———. *A Religious History of the American People*. New Haven and London: Yale University Press, 1972.

Albanese, Catherine L. *Nature Religion in America: From the Algonkian Indians to the New Age*. Chicago: University of Chicago Press, 1990.

———. *America: Religions and Religion*. Belmont, CA: Wadsworth, 1992.

———. "The Subtle Energies of Spirit: Explorations in Metaphysical and New Age Spirituality." *Journal of the American Academy of Religion* 67, no. 2 (1999).

American Heritage Dictionary. 3rd ed. New York: Houghton Mifflin, 1993.

Babb, Lawrence. Redemptive Encounters: *Three Modern Styles in the Hindu Tradition*. Berkeley: University of California Press, 1986.

Baird, Robert, ed. *Religion in Modern India*. New Delhi: Manohar, 1981.

Belenky, Mary F., Blythe M. Clinchy, Nancy R. Goldberger, and Jill M. Tarule. *Women's Ways of Knowing: The Development of Self, Voice and Mind*. New York: Basic Books, 1986.

Berger, Peter. *A Rumor of Angels: Modern Society and the Rediscovery of the Supernatural.* New York: Anchor Books, 1990.

Berger, Peter, and Thomas Luckmann. *Modernity, Pluralism and the Crisis of Meaning: The Orientation of Modern Man.* Guetersloh, Germany: Bertelsmann Foundation Publishers, 1995.

Berman, Marshall. *All That Is Solid Melts into Air.* New York: Simon and Schuster, 1982.

Blau, Evelyn. *Krishnamurti: 100 Years.* New York: Stewart, Tabori & Chang, 1995.

Bloom, Harold. *The American Religion: The Emergence of the Post-Christian Nation.* New York: Touchstone, 1992.

Borthwick, Meredith. *Keshub Chunder Sen: A Search for Cultural Synthesis.* Columbia, MO: South Asia Books, 1978.

Bourdillon, J. A. *Report on the Census of Bengal, 1881.* Calcutta: Bengal Secretariat Press, 1883.

Braude, Ann. *Radical Spirits: Spiritualism and Women's Rights in Nineteenth-Century America.* Boston: Beacon Press, 1989.

Broomfield, J. H. *Elite Conflict in a Plural Society: Twentieth-Century Bengal.* Bombay: Oxford University Press, 1968.

Brown, Judith M. *Men and Gods in a Changing World: Some Themes in the Religious Experience of Twentieth-Century Hindus and Christians.* London: SCM Press, 1980.

Brown, Michael F. *The Channeling Zone: American Spirituality in an Anxious Age.* Cambridge and London: Harvard University Press, 1997.

Burke, Marie Louise. *Swami Vivekananda in America: New Discoveries.* Calcutta: Advaita Ashrama, 1958.

———. *Swami Vivekananda, His Second Visit to the West: New Discoveries.* Calcutta: Advaita Ashrama, 1973.

Campbell, Bruce F. *Ancient Wisdom Revisited: A History of the Theosophical Movement.* Berkeley: University of California Press, 1980.

Chakravarty, Ramakanta. *Vaisnavism in Bengal.* Calcutta: Sanskrit Pustak Bhandar, 1985.

Christ, Carol P. "Why Women Need the Goddess: Phenomenological, Psychological, and Political Reflections." In *Womanspirit Rising: A Feminist Reader in Religion,* edited by Carol P. Christ and Judith Plaskow, 273–287. New York: Harper & Row, 1979.

Christy, Arthur E., ed. *The Asian Legacy and American Life.* New York: John Day, 1942.

Conser, Walter H., Jr., and Sumner B. Twiss, eds. *Religious Diversity and American Religious History: Studies in Traditions and Cultures.* Athens and London: University of Georgia Press, 1997.

Coward, Harold, ed. *Modern Indian Responses to Religious Pluralism.* Albany: State University of New York Press, 1987.

Crooke, W. "Bengal." In *Encyclopedia of Religion and Ethics,* edited by James Hastings. New York: Scribner's, 1917.

Danielou, Alain. *Hindu Polytheism*. Princeton: Princeton University Press, 1964.

Das, Sisir Kumar. *The Shadow of the Cross: Christianity and Hinduism in a Colonial Situation*. New Delhi: Munshiram Manoharlal, 1974.

Das, Veena. *Structure and Cognition: Aspects of Hindu Caste and Ritual*. Delhi: Oxford University Press, 1982.

Das Gupta, Shashibushan. *Obscure Religious Cults*. Calcutta: Firma K. L. Mukhopadhyay, 1969.

Dawson, Lorne. "Self-Affirmation, Freedom and Rationality: Theoretically Elaborating 'Active' Conversions." *Journal for the Scientific Study of Religion* 29 (June 1990): 141–163.

Daya, Sister. *The Guru and the Disciple*. Cohasset, MA: Vedanta Centre Publishers, 1976.

Dean, Thomas, ed. *Religious Pluralism and Truth: Essays in Cross-Cultural Philosophy of Religion*. Albany: State University of New York Press, 1995.

Devamata, Sister. *Swami Paramananda and His Work*. 2 vols. La Crescenta, CA: Ananda Ashrama, 1926.

———. *The Open Portal*. La Crescenta, CA: Ananda Ashrama, 1929.

———. *The Companionship of Pain*. La Crescenta, CA: Ananda Ashrama, 1934.

———. *Days in an Indian Monastery*. Cohasset, MA: Vedanta Centre Publishers, 1975.

Devi, Srimata Gayatri. *One Life's Pilgrimage*. Cohasset, MA: Vedanta Centre, 1977.

Dhar, Niranjan. *Vedanta and the Bengal Renaissance*. Calcutta: Minerva Association, 1977.

Dhar, Sailendra Nath. *A Comprehensive Biography of Swami Vivekananda*. Madras: Vivekananda Prakashan Kendra, 1975.

Diem, Andrea Grace, and James R. Lewis. "Imagining India: The Influence of Hinduism on the New Age Movement." In *Perspectives on the New Age*, edited by James R. Lewis and J. Gordon Melton. Albany: State University of New York Press, 1992.

Dillon, Jane. "The Social Significance of a Western Belief in Reincarnation: A Qualitative Study of the Self-Realization Fellowship." Ph.D. dissertation, University of California at San Diego, 1997.

Dimock, Edward C. *The Place of the Hidden Moon: Erotic Mysticism in the Vaisnava-Sahajiya Cult of Bengal*. Chicago: University of Chicago Press, 1966.

Dr. M. W. Lewis: The Life Story of One of the Earliest American Disciples of Paramahansa Yogananda. Los Angeles: Self-Realization Fellowship, 1960.

Dumenil, Lynn. *Freemasonry and American Culture: 1880–1930*. Princeton: Princeton University Press, 1984.

Dumont, Louis. *Homo Hierarchicus*. Chicago: University of Chicago Press, 1970.

Dutta, Krishna, and Andrew Robinson. *Rabindranath Tagore: The Myriad-Minded Man*. London: Bloomsbury, 1995.

East-West, vols. 1–6 (1925–1934). Los Angeles: Yogoda and Sat-Sanga Headquarters.

Eastern and Western Disciples. *The Life of Swami Vivekananda*. Calcutta: Advaita Ashrama, 1965.

Edgette, John H., and Janet Sasson Edgette. *The Handbook of Hypnotic Phenomena in Psychotherapy*. New York: Brunner/Mazel, 1995.

Ellwood, Robert. *Alternative Altars: Unconventional and Eastern Spirituality in America*. Chicago: University of Chicago Press, 1979.

Evans, Warren F. *Esoteric Christianity and Mental Therapeutics*. Boston: H. H. Carter and Kerrick, 1886.

Farquhar, J. N. *Modern Religious Movements in India*. New York: Macmillan, 1915.

Fenton, John Y. *South Asian Religions in the Americas: An Annotated Bibliography of Immigrant Religious Traditions*. Westport, CN: Greenwood, 1995.

Field, Sidney, and Peter Hay. *Krishnamurti: The Reluctant Messiah*. New York: Paragon, 1989.

Fox, Richard W. "The Culture of Liberal Protestant Progressivism, 1875–1925." *Journal of Interdisciplinary History* 23, no. 3 (Winter 1993): 639–660.

French, Harold W. *The Swan's Wide Waters: Ramakrishna and Western Culture*. Port Washington, NY: Kennikat Press, 1974.

Fuchs, Stephen. "The Cultural and Religious Dimensions of Neo-Hinduism." *Update* 8, no. 1 (1984): 9–15.

Gambhirananda, Swami. *History of the Ramakrishna Math and Mission*. Calcutta: Advaita Ashrama, 1957.

———. *The Apostles of Sri Ramakrishna*. Calcutta: Advaita Ashrama, 1967.

Gaustad, Edwin Scott. *Dissent in American Religion*. Chicago: University of Chicago Press, 1973.

———. *A Documentary History of Religion in America to the Civil War*. Grand Rapids, MI: William B. Eerdmans, 1993.

———. *A Documentary History of Religion in America Since 1865*. Grand Rapids, MI: William B. Eerdmans, 1993.

Ghosh, Sananda Lal. *Mejda: The Family and Early Life of Paramahamsa Yogananda*. Los Angeles: Self-Realization Fellowship, 1980.

Grohe, Friedrich. *The Beauty of the Mountains: Memories of Krishnamurti*. Ojai, CA: Krishnamurti Foundation of America, 1991.

Gupta, Giri Raj, ed. *Religion in Modern India*. New Delhi: Vikas, 1983.

Gupta, Mahendranath. *The Gospel of Sri Ramakrishna*. Translated by Swami Nikhilananda. Mylapore: Sri Ramakrishna Math, 1942.

Gyanamata, Sri. *God Alone: The Life and Letters of a Saint*. Los Angeles: Self-Realization Fellowship, 1984.

Handy, Robert T. *A Christian America: Protestant Hopes and Historical Realities*. New York: Oxford University Press, 1984.

————, ed. *Religion in the American Experience: The Pluralistic Style.* New York: Harper & Row, 1972.

Hatch, Nathan O. *The Democratization of American Christianity.* New Haven, CT: Yale University Press, 1989.

Hay, Stephen. *Western and Indigenous Elements in Modern Indian Thought: The Case of Rammohun Roy.* Princeton: Princeton University Press, 1965.

————, ed. *Sources of Indian Tradition.* New York: Columbia University Press, 1988.

Higham, John. *Strangers in the Land: Patterns of American Nativism.* New York: Atheneum, 1955.

————. "The Reorientation of American Culture in the 1890's." In *Writing American History,* edited by John Higham, 73–102. Bloomington: Indiana University Press, 1970.

Hinduism Comes to America. Chicago: The Vedanta Society, 1933.

Holroyd, Stuart. *Krishnamurti: The Man, the Mystery, and the Message.* Rockport, MA: Element, 1991.

Hume, Robert Ernest. *The Thirteen Principal Upanishads.* Delhi: Oxford University Press, 1993.

Hutchinson, William R. *The Modernist Impulse in American Protestantism.* New York: Oxford University Press, 1976.

————. *Errand to the World: American Protestant Thought and Foreign Missions.* Chicago: University of Chicago Press, 1987.

Hutchison, Brian. "Guru, Godman and Individuation." *Journal for the Study of Religion* 4 (March 1991): 35–50.

Isherwood, Christopher, ed. *Vedanta for the Western World.* New York: Viking Press, 1960.

————. *My Guru and His Disciple.* New York: Farrar, Straus & Giroux, 1980.

Jackson, Carl T. "The Meeting of East and West: The Case of Paul Carus." *Journal of the History of Ideas* 29 (January–March 1968): 73–92.

————. "The New Thought Movement and the Nineteenth-Century Discovery of Oriental Philosophy." *Journal of Popular Culture* 9 (Winter 1975): 523–548.

————. *The Oriental Religions and American Thought.* Westport, CT: Greenwood, 1981.

————. "The Influence of Asia upon American Thought: A Bibliographical Essay." *American Studies International* 22 (April 1984): 3–31.

————. *Vedanta for the West: The Ramakrishna Movement in the United States.* Bloomington: Indiana University Press, 1994.

Jayakar, Pupul. *Krishnamurti: A Biography.* San Francisco: Harper & Row, 1986.

Judah, J. Stillson. *The History and Philosophy of the Metaphysical Movements in America.* Philadelphia: Westminster, 1967.

Kamala. *The Flawless Mirror.* Nevada City, CA: Crystal Clarity, 1992.

Kerr, Howard. *Mediums, Spirit-Rappers and Roaring Radicals.* Urbana: University of Illinois Press, 1972.

Kerr, Howard, and Charles L. Crow, eds. *The Occult in America: New Historical Perspectives.* Urbana: University of Illinois Press, 1983.

Kinsley, David R. *The Sword and The Flute: Kali and Krsna, Dark Visions of the Terrible and Sublime in Hindu Mythology.* Delhi: Vikas Publishing House Pvt. Ltd., 1975.

Kopf, David. *British Orientalism and the Bengal Renaissance: The Dynamics of Indian Modernization 1773–1835.* Berkeley: University of California Press, 1969.

———. *The Brahmo Samaj and the Shaping of the Modern Indian Mind.* Princeton: Princeton University Press, 1979.

Kornfield, Jack. *A Path with Heart: A Guide through the Perils and Promises of Spiritual Life.* New York: Bantam Books, 1993.

Kripal, Jeffrey J. *Kali's Child: The Mystical and Erotic in the Life and Teachings of Ramakrishna.* Chicago: University of Chicago Press, 1995.

Krishnamurti, J. *Commentaries on Living, First Series.* Wheaton, IL: The Theosophical Publishing House, 1956.

———. *The Urgency of Change.* London: Gollancz, 1971.

———. *The Awakening of Intelligence.* New York: Avon Books, 1973.

———. *Krishnamurti's Journal.* New York: Harper & Row, 1982.

———. *Freedom from the Unknown.* London: Gollancz, 1983.

———. *Krishnamurti's Notebook.* San Francisco: Harper & Row, 1984.

———. *Krishnamurti to Himself: His Last Journal.* London: Gollancz, 1987.

———. *The Krishnamurti Reader.* London: Gollancz, 1990.

———. *The Collected Works of J. Krishnamurti.* 17 vols. Dubuque, IA: Kendall/Hunt, 1991–1994.

Kriyananda, Swami (Donald Walters). *The Path: Autobiography of a Western Yogi.* Nevada City, CA: Ananda Publications, 1979.

Kuhn, Alvin Boyd. *Theosophy: A Modern Revival of Ancient Wisdom.* New York: Henry Holt & Co., 1930.

Kyle, Richard. *The Religious Fringe: A History of Alternative Religions in America.* Downers Grove, IL: Intervarsity Press, 1993.

Larson, Gerald J. *India's Agony over Religion.* Ithaca: State University of New York Press, 1995.

Lavan, Spencer. *Unitarians in India: A Study in Encounter and Response.* Boston: Beacon Press, 1977.

Lears, Jackson. *No Place of Grace: Antimodernism and the Transformation of American Culture, 1880–1920.* New York: Pantheon, 1981.

Levinsky, Sara Ann. *A Bridge of Dreams: The Story of Paramananda, A Modern Mystic, and His Ideal of All-Conquering Love.* West Stockbridge, MA: Lindisfarne Press, 1984.

Lindholm, Charles. *Charisma.* Cambridge: B. Blackwell, 1990.

Lippy, Charles H., and Peter W. Williams, eds. *Encyclopedia of the American Religious Experience.* New York: Charles Scribner's Sons, 1988.

Lutyens, Mary. *To Be Young: An Autobiography.* London: R. Hart-Davis, 1959.

————. *Krishnamurti: The Years of Awakening.* New York: Farrar, Straus and Giroux, 1975.

————. *Krishnamurti: The Years of Fulfillment.* London: John Murray, 1983.

————. *Krishnamurti: The Open Door.* London: John Murray, 1988.

————. *The Life and Death of Krishnamurti.* London: John Murray, 1990.

————, ed. *The Penguin Krishnamurti Reader.* London: Penguin Books, 1954.

Madan, T. N. *Non-renunciation: Themes and Interpretations of Hindu Culture.* Delhi: Oxford University Press, 1987.

Marriott, McKim, ed. *India through Hindu Categories.* New Delhi: Sage Publications, 1990.

Marty, Martin E. "The Occult Establishment." *Social Research* 37 (Summer 1970): 212–230.

Mata, Durga. *A Paramahansa Yogananda Trilogy of Divine Love.* Beverly Hills, CA: J. Wight Publications, 1992.

Mata, Sri Daya. *Only Love.* Los Angeles: Self-Realization Fellowship, 1976.

Mathew, C. V. *Neo-Hinduism, a Missionary Religion.* Madras: Church Growth Research Centre, 1987.

Maxwell, Patrick. "The Enigma of Krishnamurti." *Journal for the Study of Religion* 7 (1994): 57–81.

Mayo, Katherine. *Mother India.* New York: Harcourt, Brace & Co., 1927.

McDaniel, June. *The Madness of the Saints: Ecstatic Religion in Bengal.* Chicago and London: University of Chicago Press, 1989.

————. "The Embodiment of God among the Bauls of Bengal." *Journal of Feminist Studies in Religion* (Fall 1992): 27–39.

McDermott, Robert A., and V. S. Naravane, eds. *The Spirit of Modern India.* New York: Thomas Y. Crowell, 1974.

McLane, John R., ed. *Bengal in the 19th and 20th Centuries.* East Lansing: Asian Studies Center, Michigan State University, 1975.

Melton, J. Gordon. "How New Is New? The Flowering of the "New" Religious Consciousness since 1965." In *The Future of New Religious Movements,* edited by David G. Bromley and Phillip E. Hammond. Macon, GA: Mercer University Press, 1987.

————. *Encyclopedia of American Religion.* 5th ed. Detroit: Gale Research, 1996.

Message of the East, vols. 1–52 (1912–1964). Cohasset, MA: Vedanta Centre.

Miller, Timothy, ed. *When Prophets Die: The Postcharismatic Fate of New Religious Movements.* Albany: State University of New York Press, 1991.

————. *America's Alternative Religions.* Albany: State University of New York Press, 1995.

Moore, R. Laurence. *In Search of White Crows: Spiritualism, Parapsychology, and American Culture.* New York: Oxford University Press, 1977.

————. *Religious Outsiders and the Making of Americans.* New York: Oxford University Press, 1986.

————. *Selling God: American Religion in the Marketplace of Culture.* New York: Oxford University Press, 1994.

Mukerji, Swami. *The Doctrine and Practice of Yoga.* Chicago: Yogi Publication Society, 1922.

Naravane, V. S. *Modern Indian Thought.* Bombay: Asia Publishing House, 1964.

Narayan, Kirin. *Storytellers, Saints and Scoundrels: Folk Narrative in Hindu Religious Teaching.* Philadelphia: University of Pennsylvania Press, 1989.

Nash, Roderick. *The Nervous Generation: American Thought, 1917–1930.* Chicago: Elephant Paperbacks, 1990.

Neevel, Walter G., Jr. "The Transformation of Sri Ramakrishna." In *Hinduism: New Essays in the History of Religions,* edited by Bardwell L. Smith. Leiden: E. J. Brill, 1976.

Niebuhr, H. Richard. *Social Sources of Denominationalism,* 1929.

Nikhilananda, Swami. *Vivekananda: A Biography.* New York: Ramakrishna-Vedanta Center, 1953.

Nivedita, Sister. *The Complete Works of Sister Nivedita.* Calcutta: Sister Nivedita Girls' School, 1967.

Oakes, Len. *Prophetic Charisma: The Psychology of Revolutionary Religious Personalities.* Syracuse, NY: Syracuse University Press, 1997.

Organ, Troy. "Humanness in Neo-Vedantism." In *Being Human in a Technological Age,* edited by Donald M. Borchert and David Stewart. Athens: Ohio University Press, 1979.

Pangborn, Cyrus R. "The Ramakrishna Math and Mission." In *Hinduism: New Essays in the History of Religions,* edited by Bardwell L. Smith. Leiden: E. J. Brill, 1976.

Paramananda, Swami. *The Path of Devotion.* New York: The Vedanta Society, 1907.

———. *The True Spirit of Religion Is Universal.* New York: The Vedanta Society, 1908.

———. *Vedanta in Practice.* Boston: Vedanta Centre Publishers, 1908.

———. *Principles and Purpose of Vedanta.* Washington, DC: The Carnahan Press, 1910.

———. "God as Mother." *Message of the East* (October 1912).

———. *Plato and Vedic Idealism.* Boston: Vedanta Centre, 1913.

———. *Power of Thought.* Boston: Vedanta Centre, 1913.

———. *Science and Practice of Yoga.* Boston: Vedanta Centre, 1918.

———. *The Upanishads.* Boston: Vedanta Centre, 1919.

———. *Soul's Secret Door.* Boston: Vedanta Centre Publishers, 1922.

———. *Reincarnation and Immortality.* Boston: Vedanta Centre, 1923.

———. *Self-Mastery.* Boston: Vedanta Centre, 1923.

———. *Spiritual Healing.* Boston: Vedanta Centre, 1923.

———. *The Vigil.* Boston: Vedanta Centre Publishers, 1923.

———. *Civilization and Spiritualization.* Boston: Vedanta Centre, 1925.

———. *Rhythm of Life.* Boston: Vedanta Centre Publishers, 1925.

———. *Book of Daily Thoughts and Prayers.* Boston: Vedanta Centre Publishers, 1926.

————. *My Creed.* Boston: Vedanta Centre Publishers, 1929.

————. *Christ and Oriental Ideals.* 4th ed. Boston: Vedanta Centre Publishers, 1968.

Potter, Karl H., ed. *Advaita Vedanta up to Samkara and His Pupils.* Vol. 3, *Encyclopedia of Indian Philosophies.* Princeton: Princeton University Press, 1981.

Prebish, Charles S. *American Buddhism.* North Scituate, MA: Duxbury Press, 1979.

Prothero, Stephen. "From Spiritualism to Theosophy: 'Uplifting' a Democratic Tradition." *Religion and American Culture* 3 (Summer 1993): 197–215.

————. *The White Buddhist: The Asian Odyssey of Henry Steel Olcott.* Bloomington: Indiana University Press, 1996.

Rajarsi Janakananda (James J. Lynn): A Great Western Yogi. Los Angeles: Self-Realization Fellowship, 1959.

Rambachan, Anantanand. *The Limits of Scripture: Vivekananda's Reinterpretation of the Vedas.* Honolulu: University of Hawaii Press, 1994.

Ravindra, Ravi. "J. Krishnamurti: Traveler in a Pathless Land." In *Hindu Spirituality: Postclassical and Modern,* edited by K. R. Sundararajan and Bithika Mukerji. New York: Crossroad, 1997, 321–340.

Rawlinson, Andrew. *The Book of Enlightened Masters: Western Teachers in Eastern Traditions.* Chicago and La Salle, IL: Open Court, 1997.

Reed, Elizabeth A. *Hinduism in Europe and America.* New York and London: G. P. Putnam's Sons, 1914.

Reynolds, Frank E., and Donald Capps, eds. *The Biographical Process: Studies in the History and Psychology of Religion.* The Hague: Mouton, 1976.

Richards, Glyn, ed. *A Source-Book of Modern Hinduism.* London: Curzon Press, 1985.

Richardson, E. Allen. *East Comes West: Asian Religions and Cultures in North America.* New York: Pilgrim Press, 1985.

Rieff, Philip. *The Triumph of the Therapeutic.* Chicago: University of Chicago Press, 1987.

Riepe, Dale. *The Philosophy of India and Its Impact on American Thought.* Springfield, IL: Charles C. Thomas, 1970.

Rivera, Joseph de, and Theodore R. Sarbin, eds. *Believed-In Imaginings: The Narrative Construction of Reality.* Washington, DC: American Psychological Association, 1998.

Rodriques, Hillary. *Insight and Religious Mind: An Analysis of Krishnamurti's Thought.* New York: P. Lang, 1990.

Rosser, Brenda Lewis. *Treasures Against Time: Paramahansa Yogananda with Doctor and Mrs. Lewis.* Borrego Springs, CA: Borrego Publications, 1991.

Roy, Asim. *The Islamic Syncretistic Tradition in Bengal.* Princeton: Princeton University Press, 1983.

Roy, Rammohun. *The English Works of Raja Rammohun Roy.* Edited by J. C. Ghose. New Delhi: Cosmo, 1982.

Schumaker, John F. *The Corruption of Reality: A Unified Theory of Religion, Hypnosis and Psychopathology.* Amherst, NY: Prometheus Books, 1995.
————, ed. *Human Suggestibility: Advances in Theory, Research and Application.* New York and London: Routledge, 1991.
Seager, Richard H., ed. *The Dawn of Religious Pluralism: Voices from the World's Parliament of Religions, 1893.* La Salle, IL: Open Court, 1993.
————. *The World's Parliament of Religions: The East-West Encounter, Chicago, 1893.* Bloomington: Indiana University Press, 1995.
Self-Realization Fellowship. *Paramahansa Yogananda: In Memoriam.* Los Angeles: Self-Realization Fellowship, 1986.
Self-Realization Magazine, vols. 20–42 (1948–1971). Los Angeles: Self-Realization Fellowship.
Sharma, Arvind, ed. *Neo-Hindu Views of Christianity.* Leiden and New York: E. J. Brill, 1988.
————. *Ramakrishna and Vivekananda: New Perspectives.* New Delhi: Sterling Publishers, 1989.
Shridharani, Krishnalal. *My India, My America.* New York: Duell, Sloan and Pearce, 1941.
Siegel, Lee. *Net of Magic: Wonders and Deceptions in India.* Chicago: University of Chicago Press, 1991.
Sil, Narasingha Prosad. "Vivekananda's Ramakrishna: An Untold Story of Mythmaking and Propaganda." *Numen* 40 (January 1993): 38–62.
Singer, Milton B. *When a Great Tradition Modernizes: An Anthropological Approach to Indian Civilization.* New York: Praeger, 1972.
Sloss, Radha Rajagopal. *Lives in the Shadow with J. Krishnamurti.* Reading, MA: Addison-Wesley, 1991.
Smith, W. C. "Vedanta and the Modern Age." *Religious Studies and Theology* 13 (April 1995): 12–20.
Spiegel, David, and Jose R. Maldonad. "Hypnosis." In *Textbook of Psychiatry,* 3rd ed., edited by R. E. Hales. Washington, DC: American Psychiatric Press, 1999, 1243–1275.
Star Bulletin (1927–1933). Ommen, Holland: Star Publishing Trust.
Storr, Anthony. *Feet of Clay: Saints, Sinners and Madmen: A Study of Gurus.* New York: Free Press, 1996.
Straus, R. "Changing Oneself: Seekers and the Creative Transformation of Life Experience." In *Doing Social Life,* edited by John Lofland. New York: John Wiley, 1976, 252–272.
Tagore, Debendranath. *Autobiography of Maharshi Debendranath Tagore.* Translated by S. N. Tagore and I. Devi. London: Macmillan, 1914.
Tagore, Rabindranath. *Personality: Lectures Delivered in America.* New York: Macmillan, 1921.
————. *The Religion of Man.* New Delhi: Indus, 1981.
Taylor, Charles. *Sources of the Self: The Making of Modern Identity.* Cambridge, MA: Harvard University Press, 1989.
Taylor, Eugene. "Swedenborgianism," in *America's Alternative Religions,* edited by Timothy Miller. Albany: State University of New York Press, 1995, 77–86.

Thomas, Wendell. *Hinduism Invades America.* New York: Beacon Press, 1930.

Tweed, Thomas A. *The American Encounter with Buddhism, 1844–1912: Victorian Culture and the Limits of Descent. Religion in North America Series.* Bloomington: Indiana University Press, 1992.

———. "Inclusivism and the Spiritual Journey of Marie de Souza Canavarro." *Religion* 24 (1994): 43–58.

———. "Asian Religions in the United States: Reflections on an Emerging Subfield." In *Religious Diversity and American Religious History: Studies in Traditions and Cultures,* edited by Walter H. Conser, Jr., and Sumner B. Twiss. Athens and London: University of Georgia Press, 1997.

———, ed. *Retelling U.S. Religious History.* Berkeley: University of California Press, 1997.

Varenne, Jean. *Yoga and the Hindu Tradition.* Chicago and London: University of Chicago Press, 1976.

Versluis, Arthur. *American Transcendentalism and Asian Religions.* New York: Oxford University Press, 1993.

Vivekananda. *The Complete Works of Swami Vivekananda.* 8 vols. Calcutta: Advaita Ashrama, 1989.

Washington, Peter. *Madame Blavatsky's Baboon: A History of the Mystics, Mediums, and Misfits Who Brought Spiritualism to America.* New York: Schocken Books, 1993.

Watson, Lawrence C., and Maria Barbara Watson-Franke. *Interpreting Life Histories.* New Brunswick, NJ: Rutgers University Press, 1985.

Weber, Max. *The Sociology of Religion.* Boston: Beacon Press, 1993. (Originally published 1920)

Wessinger, Catherine Lowman. "Annie Besant's Millenial Movement: Its History, Impact, and Implications Concerning Authority." *Syzygy* 2 (Winter–Spring 1993): 55–70.

———. "Woman Guru, Woman Roshi: The Legitimation of Female Religious Leadership in Hindu and Buddhist Groups in America." In *Women's Leadership in Marginal Religions,* edited by C. Wessinger. Urbana: University of Illinois Press, 1993.

———. "Hinduism Arrives in America: The Vedanta Movement and the Self-Realization Fellowship." In *America's Alternative Religions,* edited by Timothy Miller. Albany: State University of New York Press, 1995.

Western Disciple, A. *With the Swamis in America.* Mayavati, India: Advaita Ashrama, 1946.

Williams, George M. *The Quest for Meaning of Swami Vivekananda.* Chico, CA: New Horizons Press, 1974.

———. "Swami Vivekananda's Conception of Karma and Rebirth." In *Karma and Rebirth: Post Classical Developments,* edited by Ronald W. Neufeldt. Albany: State University of New York Press, 1986.

Williams, Raymond Brady. *Religions of Immigrants from India and Pakistan: New Threads in the American Tapestry.* Cambridge: Cambridge University Press, 1988.

————, ed. *A Sacred Thread: Modern Transmission of Hindu Traditions in India and Abroad.* Chambersbury, PA: Anima, 1992.

Winterhalter, Robert. "New Thought and Vedanta." *Journal of Religion and Psychical Research* 16 (January 1993): 14–20.

Yapko, Michael D. *Trancework: An Introduction to the Practice of Clinical Hypnosis.* New York: Brunner/Mazel, 1990.

Yogananda, Paramahansa. *Songs of the Soul.* Los Angeles: Self-Realization Fellowship, 1923.

————. *Yogoda.* Boston: Satsanga, 1923.

————. *The Science of Religion.* Boston: Satsanga, 1924.

————. *Scientific Healing Affirmations.* Boston: Satsanga, 1924.

————. *Psychological Chart.* Los Angeles: Yogoda and Satsanga Headquarters, 1925.

————. *Metaphysical Meditations.* Los Angeles: Self-Realization Fellowship, 1932.

————. *Whispers from Eternity.* Los Angeles: Self-Realization Fellowship, 1935.

————. *The Master Said: A Collection of Paramhansa Yogananda's Sayings and Wise Counsel to Various Disciples.* Los Angeles: Self-Realization Fellowship, 1952.

————. *Cosmic Chants.* Los Angeles: Self-Realization Fellowship, 1963.

————. *Sayings of Yogananda; Inspired Counsel to Disciples.* Los Angeles: Self-Realization Fellowship, 1968.

————. *Man's Eternal Quest.* Los Angeles: Self-Realization Fellowship, 1976.

————. *The Second Coming of Christ: From the Original Unchanged Writings of Paramahansa Yogananda's Interpretations of the Sayings of Jesus Christ.* Dallas, TX: Amrita Foundation, 1979.

————. *The Law of Success.* Los Angeles: Self-Realization Fellowship, 1980.

————. *The Sermon on the Mount.* Dallas, TX: Amrita Foundation, 1980.

————. *How You Can Talk with God.* Los Angeles: Self-Realization Fellowship, 1985.

————. *The Divine Romance.* Los Angeles: Self-Realization Fellowship, 1986.

————. *Autobiography of a Yogi.* Los Angeles: Self-Realization Fellowship, 1988. (Originally published 1946)

————. *Where There Is Light: Insight and Inspiration for Meeting Life's Challenges.* Los Angeles: Self-Realization Fellowship, 1988.

————. *The Bhagavad Gita: God Talks with Arjuna: Royal Science of God Realization.* Los Angeles: Self-Realization Fellowship, 1995.

Yukteswar, Swami Sri. *The Holy Science.* Los Angeles: Self-Realization Fellowship, 1949.

Zablocki, Benjamin. *Alienation and Charisma.* New York: Free Press, 1980.

Ziolkowski, Eric J., ed. *A Museum of Faiths: Histories and Legacies of the 1893 World's Parliament of Religions.* Atlanta: Scholar's Press, 1993.

Credits

TEXT

Chapter 4, p. 74, Sister Devamata, *Paramananda and His Work*. La Crescenta, CA: Ananda Ashrama, 1926. Reprinted with permission of the Vedanta Centre; pp. 76, 77, 81, 85, 86, 87, 89, 90, 92, 94, 95, 97, 103, 105, 106, 107, 111, 122, Sara Ann Levinsky, *A Bridge of Dreams: The Story of Paramananda, A Modern Mystic, and His Ideal of All-Conquering Love*. West Stockbridge, MA: Lindisfarne Press, 1984. Reprinted with permission of Lindisfarne Press.

Chapter 5, pp. 120–121, 122, 126, 135–136, 138, 150–151, Swami Kryananda (Donald Walters), *The Path: Autobiography of a Western Yogi*. Nevada City, CA: Ananda Publications, 1979. Reprinted with permission of Crystal Clarity Publishers.

Chapter 6, p. 161, 168, 169, 177, 179, Evelyn Blau, *Krishnamurti: 100 Years*. New York: Stewart, Tabori & Chang, 1995. Reprinted with permission of Stewart, Tabori & Chang; pp. 163, 164, 165, 166, 167–168, 169, 171–172, excerpts from *Krishnamurti: The Years of Awakening* by Mary Lutyens. Copyright © 1975 by Mary Lutyens. Reprinted by permission of Farrar, Straus and Giroux, LLC.

Chapter 7, p. 200, Ravi Ravindra, "J. Krishnamurti: Traveler in a Pathless Land." *Hindu Spirituality: Postclassical and Modern,* K. R. Sundarajan and Bithika Mukerji, eds. New York: Crossroad Publishing Company. Reprinted by permission of Crossroad Publishing Company; p. 192, Sara Ann Levinsky, *A Bridge of Dreams: The Story of Paramananda, A Modern Mystic, and His Ideal of All-Conquering Love*. West Stockbridge, MA: Lindisfarne Press, 1984. Reprinted by permission of Lindisfarne Press.

Chapter 8, p. 221, Swami Kryananda (Donald Walters), *The Path: Autobiography of a Western Yogi*. Nevada City, CA: Ananda Publications, 1979. Reprinted with permission of Crystal Clarity Publishers.

PHOTOS

Page 73, Courtesy of the Vedanta Centre, Inc.; page 111, Courtesy of Crystal Clarity Design; page 149, used with permission of Archive Photos.

Index

Entries in **bold** type also appear in the glossary.